TRESEDER
MAN OF ADVENTURE

This book is dedicated to our long-suffering families.
With their support, all is possible.

Martin Long & Peter Treseder

TRESEDER
MAN OF ADVENTURE

Martin Long

First published in Australia in 1999 by
New Holland Publishers (Australia) Pty Ltd
Sydney • Auckland • London • Cape Town

14 Aquatic Drive Frenchs Forest NSW 2086 Australia
218 Lake Road Northcote Auckland New Zealand
24 Nutford Place London W1H 6DQ United Kingdom
80 McKenzie Street Cape Town 8001 South Africa

Copyright © 1999: Martin Long and Peter Treseder
Copyright © 1999 in photographs: Peter Treseder and Operation Chillout with the exception of those credited individually.

All rights reserved. No part of this publication may be reproduced, stored in a retrieval system or transmitted, in any form or by any means, electronic, mechanical, photocopying, recording or otherwise, without the prior written permission of the publishers and copyright holders.

National Library of Australia Cataloguing-in-Publication Data:

Long, Martin.
 Treseder : man of adventure

ISBN 1 86436 570 6

1. Treseder, Peter. 2. Marathon running - New South Wales - Biography. 3. Bank employees - New South Wales - Biography. 4. Search and rescue operations - New South Wales - Biography. 5. Runners (Sports) - New South Wales - Biography. I. Title.

920.71

Publishing Manager: Anouska Good
Project Co-ordinator: Jennifer Lane
Editor: Jan Hutchinson
Designer: Nanette Backhouse
Typesetter: Midland Typesetters
Printer: Australian Print Group

Cover photograph (background) © New Holland Image Library

Foreword

It is a privilege to know Peter Treseder, an Australian whose impressive achievements are an inspiration to many.

Peter's unyielding spirit is in the tradition of great Australians who strive to reach seemingly impossible goals. His courage is distinguished, not by an absence of fear or despair, but by the strength to conquer them.

I have followed Peter's achievements over recent years and have come to understand that he is a person with extraordinary drive and focus.

As patron of Peter's successful first expedition to the South Pole and of his second expedition planned for later this year, what continues to impress me is Peter's optimism and belief in the innate worth and quality of individuals.

His efforts have taken him on speaking tours across the nation to share his experiences as well as his dreams with typical Australians. These public presentations are full of hope and the message that all individuals can reach their full potential.

When Peter's team returned from the South Pole, I asked him to give the first of these presentations to my colleagues in the Federal Government. It was a moving and motivating occasion for us all.

As you read Peter's story be inspired by his example. Enjoy his successes and struggle with him as he relives some of his great challenges. Above all, understand that every one of us has the potential to achieve beyond our highest expectations.

The Right Hon. John Howard
Prime Minister of Australia, 1999

Acknowledgments

The process of researching and writing this book was made so much easier through the willing cooperation of the Treseder family. I am indebted to Dorothy and John Treseder, Neil Treseder and Wendy Cunliffe. Peter's own cooperation was invaluable. I have drawn on many written and oral sources for my research and many friends and colleagues of Peter's over the years have added useful information and insight. To them I offer my thanks. In particular I would like to thank Lincoln Madden and Mark Foster for information about Peter's earlier years, and Peter's fellow expeditioners, including Ian Brown, Keith Wiliams, Neil Cocks and Ron Moon whose descriptions of some of Peter's expeditions have been very useful. Thankyou also to John Leece who kindly gave me full access to his copious notes on the South Pole expedition. I am grateful to *Wild* and *Australian Geographic* magazines, two publications that have regularly reported Peter's outdoor achievements. Where possible, I have acknowledged the source of material throughout the text. My thanks to the publishing team at New Holland, in particular to Anouska Good for taking on the project and to Jennifer Lane for her constant encouragement in the art of biography.

Contents

Page			
1	Chapter 1		Claustral Canyon Rescue
10	Chapter 2		Growing up in Ashfield and Canterbury
23	Chapter 3		Out in Front
43	Chapter 4		Mount Cook in a Hurry
52	Chapter 5		Mickey Mouse Ran up the Clock
70	Chapter 6		Tiger Walker
86	Chapter 7		From Record Breaker to Silly Walks
98	Chapter 8		Finding the Bunker
107	Chapter 9		Unsung Hero
119	Chapter 10		Near Death in Murdering Gully
128	Chapter 11		Crocodile Country
141	Chapter 12		Solo on Cape York
147	Chapter 13		Sprirt of Adventure I—Hinchinbrook
159	Chapter 14		Conquering Bass Strait
170	Chapter 15		Spirit of Adventure II
187	Chapter 16		Pirates in the Timor Sea
201	Chapter 17		Walking the Simpson Desert
211	Chapter 18		Operation Chillout
225	Chapter 19		Traversing Silence
243	Chapter 20		Desert Runner
256	Chapter 21		Beyond the South Pole 1999–2000
263	Appendix		Highlights and Milestones of an Adventure Career
278	Index		

Chapter 1

Claustral Canyon Rescue

'On every day, the miracle of another dawn; adventure that startles wonder, imagination and excitement; opportunities for everyone to draw together in the joy of life and understanding. All of us have the essence and the spirit to achieve our wildest dreams. Dream them first, with truth, into positive visions for the future. Stand out from the rest to challenge the risk of failure, for in all mistakes there lurk important learnings. Know also that your ruler is in your thoughts. Free them into the light and soar forward into the decades of all that awaits for you to win.'

As told to Tim Lamble by Peter Treseder

Sometime after 9.30pm on Friday 4 April, 1997 Peter Treseder was asleep in the back of his station wagon, exhausted from his latest record-breaking 500 kilometres expedition—across the Gibson Desert on foot.

Peter had pulled into the Claustral Canyon car park to catch up on some much needed sleep before completing the drive home to Sydney. He had been driving for nearly two days after his four-day, eleven-hour crossing of the desert and was obviously near the end of his own physical endurance.

'I presumed that no-one would be canyoning because it was extremely cold at the time,' he recalls. 'I put my head down at about 9pm but within 30 minutes I was awoken by a man.'

The rain pelted down on the car, drowning out almost all other noise. Except the banging and then the screaming, panic-stricken voice.

'Help me! Help!'

Still heavily asleep, Peter stirred into consciousness, his brain trying to separate and understand the sounds. As he opened his eyes he became aware of a man outside the car. He was hitting the window with his hand and shouting. Peter caught the words 'girlfriend ... dying ... canyon ... help'.

Suddenly wide awake despite his extreme tiredness, Peter sat up and warily rolled down the rear window a bit, telling the man to slow down. 'Tell me what's happened. What's wrong?'

'My girlfriend's trapped in the canyon!' shouted the man. 'She's going to die. You have to help!'

Quickly, Peter scrambled out of his sleeping bag, opened the door, pulling on his Gore-Tex shell and stretching. 'Calm down. Tell me exactly what's happened,' he said to the distressed man.

Beside himself with fear and suffering from the cold and rain, the man explained the situation.

Claustral Canyon is a deep gorge in the Blue Mountains west of Sydney. The most popular of the Blue Mountains canyons for the sport of canyoning, it is usually attempted in summer months during the day. The river follows the course of the canyon, forming deep pools and waterfalls through the sandstone. Canyoners negotiate the obstacles by abseiling, jumping, swimming and sliding down the gorge which can sometimes be hundreds of metres deep and only shoulder wide. The more rain there is the more water rushes down the canyon, making some parts completely impassable as passageways become blocked by rising water levels. Even at the best of times the water is extremely cold and hypothermia is always a real risk.

When Peter had parked in the Claustral Canyon car park, which he expected to be empty, he had noticed another car and assumed its occupants were already asleep. He certainly never dreamed that anyone would even attempt the canyon in this cold and dangerous weather. But this man and his girlfriend had—and now she was trapped somewhere and in grave danger.

The man explained that they had completed the first part of the canyon without difficulty. The first abseil, a drop of about 10 metres, had been successful and the couple moved down the canyon to the second abseil. The man abseiled down this pitch and waited in the gloom in thigh deep water for his companion to descend. That's when disaster struck. As the woman started her descent her long hair became jammed in her abseil device, which forced her body into a bent position with her head pushed hard against the device. Yelling for help, she couldn't move up or down and very quickly ran out of strength to struggle further.

The man was unable to climb up to help her and finally was forced to abandon her to seek help. Luckily the rope was just long enough to reach the bottom for the third abseil. The man took almost eight hours to get out of the canyon and back to the car park and was desperately worried his companion might already be dead.

Peter knew the canyon extremely well, and was concerned that the woman was in the most inaccessible part of the canyon called the Black Hole of Calcutta. A rescue attempt without a rope for the first abseil, in the extreme cold and dark, was risky and potentially very dangerous. The man had abandoned his own harness and gear and there was no time to go back to get it if the woman was to have any chance of survival.

Peter decided he had no alternative but to make the rescue attempt immediately. Borrowing the man's wetsuit and taking some dry clothes for the woman, a small fuel stove and an air mattress, he proceeded into the canyon with his headtorch the only light. He instructed the man to take his car and go for help immediately.

Despite his tiredness, the task spurred Peter on and he felt 'like a low flying jet' as he negotiated the steep country that led into the canyon, over slippery rocks and through shallow pools. After what seemed like ages, but was probably about 25 minutes, Peter stood at the top of the first abseil and peered into the blackness below. The 10 metre drop looked menacing and Peter remembered there were rocks in the bottom of the pool. Without a rope he could only jump. Would he miss the rocks? Would his headtorch survive the fall? Questions raced through Peter's head then, without hesitation, he leapt.

Down and down he went until he struck the water, gashing his left arm badly on a rock. His arm felt broken, but the light still worked, so there was a chance. Swimming to the edge of the waterfall above the second abseil, Peter strained to see down into the hole. The woman was about 2 metres down, unconscious and in the waterfall. Numbingly cold water flowed over her continuously.

Still without a rope, Peter had no alternative but to take the risky option of climbing hand over hand down the taut rope to the woman. As soon as he reached her he attached a 'cow's tail'—a length of rope already fixed around his waist—to her abseil device. This would enable Peter to use the woman's gear to secure and lower both of them together.

The woman's hair was still stuck and Peter needed to cut it to release her. Taking a pocket knife from a cord around his neck, Peter cut at her long wet hair, grimly thinking this was a small price to pay for her life. It was difficult because of the position of her head and the tonnes of water by now cascading over both of them.

Peter had learnt the technique of 'assist abseil', which enables two people to abseil on the same equipment, on a Vertical Rescue training course. But the woman was still unconscious and not able to cooperate. Slowly, Peter descended with the woman to the base of the abseil.

Here his difficulties increased as the third abseil starts with a relatively small keyhole through which the water plunges to the base of the third waterfall some 10 metres below. Positioning the woman just below him, and with both still attached to the same device, Peter eased their bodies through the keyhole and slowly down the remaining rope to a long narrow pool requiring a swim of about 50 metres before emerging at some large boulders.

Releasing the dead weight of the unconscious woman from the rope without losing her proved difficult as they were still being buffeted by the roaring torrent. During the 50 metre swim Peter had to keep the woman afloat and her head out of the water until the widening canyon gave him an opportunity to get her out of the water for the first time in over 10 hours. Moving quickly, Peter removed her wetsuit and wet clothes, replacing them with the dry ones and replacing her wetsuit. While out of the water this would help warm her up. Lighting the stove, he heated some water and slowly fed this to the woman as she gradually regained consciousness.

Explaining to her the need to keep moving, Peter remembered that three people had died at this exact spot several years previously when rising waters prevented their escape. The rain continued to fall heavily. Inflating the air mattress, Peter helped the woman onto it and assisted her through the rest of the canyon, keeping her torso out of the water as much as possible to help keep her warm. There were still several cold swims, boulder fields to negotiate, slippery rocks, climbs and jumps before safety was reached. At one point the pair reached a high point where Peter could have started a fire, but they both decided to continue rather than wait to see if a major rescue attempt had been instigated.

Progress was slow as both the woman and Peter were very tired and cold. It took another three hours to reach the entrance to Rainbow Ravine, the canyon exit point, where Peter was shocked to find the woman's companion sitting on a rock waiting for them. There was no sign of any other help as he had decided, knowing Peter's reputation, that he would leave the rescue to him. An incredibly risky decision!

Peter was too tired to argue the point and the three started the steep climb back to the car park. The short climbs proved extremely difficult as the woman was, by now, very weak. Once back at the car the couple drove to hospital. Unable to sleep and not wanting to get involved with a group of young men who had arrived, apparently to challenge themselves in the canyon, Peter drove home where he cleaned the pool, mowed the lawns and played with his children like any other suburban Dad!

'I'm certain,' says Peter looking back, 'that the woman would have died without immediate help. A further delay of even 20–30 minutes would probably have proved fatal. The incredible thing is the coincidence of me pulling into that exact car park after driving halfway across Australia.' What Peter doesn't talk about is the amazing effort that would have been necessary for him to complete the rescue successfully.

In the previous week Peter had completed the first unsupported crossing of the 500-kilometre Gibson Desert in just four and a half days. This meant walking across rolling dunes of sand and clay for up to 20 hours non-stop each day, carrying only the essentials of 20 litres of drinking water and two family blocks of Cadbury chocolate. After completing the desert crossing and wanting to get home quickly, Peter had then driven almost non-stop for two days across Australia. Fatigue had finally caught up with him in the Blue Mountains and he looked for a place to stop. That he chose Claustral Canyon car park was perhaps fate, but Peter's swift and decisive actions definitely saved a life.

The Gibson Desert expedition marked a new chapter in Peter's life, as he began to realise his dream of crossing all thirteen Australian deserts, solo and unsupported, on foot. This extraordinary achievement would be a daunting enough goal for most people on its own. But for Peter Treseder, explorer and adventurer, it is only one small part of his impressive catalogue of outdoor achievements.

From tiger walking in the Blue Mountains to ocean kayaking in the Timor Sea, from technical mountaineering to snowshoe traverses of the Australian Alps, Peter has always set his sights high. His ultimate challenge, realised on January 1, 1998 was to lead the first Australian expedition on foot from the edge of the Antarctic ice shelf to the South Pole—a 1400 kilometre journey which he completed in just 59 days.

What motivates a man like Peter Treseder to these almost super-human achievements? In his business suit he looks every centimetre the bank employee, but his appearance belies his physical strength and endurance and masks a strong and resolute character. An *Australian Geographic* article, 'Man on the Run', by Lincoln Hall in the January—March 1990 issue reported Peter's successful AG sponsored run from Cape York to Wilsons Promontory. The author described Peter as 'a mild-mannered bank employee (who) ... dresses conventionally, wears metal-rimmed glasses, works at a demanding job, is happily married and has a comfortable suburban home'. Hall continued with a rhetorical question: 'How does (Peter) discard the cloak of conventionality and become this sort of superman? Exceptional fitness, determination and thorough training—24 years of weekends and holidays spent on outdoor activities—are only part of the answer.'

'I don't really understand what drives me on,' said Peter. 'There's an incredible satisfaction in forcing yourself to do what you think is your limit, and then pulling the same effort out of the hat again, day after day. Conservation and encouraging the spirit of adventure also mean a lot to me.'

Hall concluded his article by observing that Peter 'performs without the encouragement of an admiring crowd, without hope of medical help, without the certainty that he will survive. Ultimately, he runs for himself, alone in the wilderness'. Peter has an amazing determination and is anything but average in everything he does. That he can be pushy and demanding stems from his impatience with people who can't understand his vision. In

Peter's own words, 'Most people just don't appreciate what's going on.'

'What's going on' is a complex mixture of dreaming and planning, training and survey trips, expeditions and careful self-promotion to aid charities or fund the costs of the next adventure. 'There has been a lot of heartache, many abandoned trips and bad weather,' Peter comments, 'together with numerous planning and survey trips before I got anywhere near breaking records. The public see it as almost an instant fix because the only trip they hear about is the one that breaks the record.'

Peter minimises the risks through meticulous planning. He spends time building his skills and confidence with each trip before attempting record breaking and potentially dangerous trips. There is a massive history of planning and gathered experience behind every record attempt. Such planning goes down to measuring the length of rope required for every abseil to avoid carrying unnecessary weight. Exact amounts of food and, in particular, water requirements are calculated to ensure survival with the least effort expended. To achieve the expeditions themselves Peter has combined the mindset of an outdoors person with that of a professional athlete.

During his solo expeditions, Peter needs to navigate his way through a landscape that at worst is hostile and dangerous, at best confusing and unrelenting. Sometimes he travels in the dark, often in bad weather. Without backup his personal safety is critical so he cannot afford to make a mistake. A competitive marathon or ultra marathon runner on the other hand has regular drink stops, support vehicles, a constant surface to run on and medical aid close by. In comparison Peter's expeditions and tiger walks can be seen in an even more impressive light.

The records are important to Peter in a number of ways. He talks frequently about 'the nobility of the spirit', 'personal pride', a sense of 'making history' and 'the high' he gets from achieving records. At the same time he says that he has always avoided general publicity. 'Recognition sought was always low key, from a small group of people who knew about the records,' he says. Compare this with his mother's memory. Dorothy Treseder says that 'Peter always seemed to make sure that the right people knew what he had achieved, so he received recognition along the way'.

Despite the 'limited knowledge' of his activities, Peter has been recognised and rewarded for his efforts and considerable achievements by several associations and government bodies, culminating in an OAM in 1992. And it is interesting to note that, as if thinking about future possibilities from a very young age, Peter has kept every certificate, every press clipping and every piece of reference material from his adventures since he was a small child, storing them in big red binders. A biographer's dream—but his sense of history seems at odds with his genuine modesty.

So why does Peter Treseder, husband to Beth and father to Marnie and Kimberley, put himself in positions where he risks his life to achieve his driving ambitions in the outdoors? 'I have found,' Peter said in an interview in the Commonwealth Bank's June, 1980 issue of *Bank Notes*, 'that by placing myself voluntarily into dangerous situations I learn to face my own fears and doubts, my innermost feelings.'

Fellow South Pole expeditioner, Ian Brown, remarks on Peter's fitness and ability in his January, 1999 *Australian Geographic* article 'Extreme South'. He describes him as 'a Clark Kent of a character—an outwardly conservative family man and bank employee but with a man of steel in his soul—his legendary fitness and tenacity have produced unparalleled feats of wilderness endurance.'

Both Brown and Keith Williams, the third member of the successful party, recognise that Peter's determination surpasses his own mindblowing physical abilities. He just won't give up!

Peter's normal daily routine is impressive enough. He packs more into a day than most people manage in a week. His normal working weekday involves a run at lunchtime with colleagues—anything from 4–15 kilometres out from the city, with lunch eaten at his desk. He may have spent half an hour on his rowing machine before going to work or leave that until he gets home.

When he is in training for a major event—and that is most of the time—he will then go out training after dinner, or sometimes instead of dinner. For the desert crossings and the South Pole trip Peter devised a body harness to which he has attached a truck tyre. This heavy tyre is then dragged along bush tracks in simulation of the desert cart or polar sled. The tyre has seen so much use that Peter has worn holes in it, and he increases the resistance by adding rocks to increase the weight.

At weekends Peter makes sure that jobs around the house are up to date and may also do a training trip. On one weekend during the research for this book he had returned home by 10am on Sunday morning having completed a Claustral Canyon trip that morning!

A man obviously devoted to his family, Peter still spends a lot of time away from his wife and two young girls. To make up for this he is very conscious of the time he does spend with the children and shows more patience in this direction than any other. However, when an expedition is on, it's on, and family life takes a back seat.

Presentations too take up a lot of Peter's time, with him often travelling within New South Wales or interstate. These illustrated talks to community groups have played a part in Peter's life for many years. Originally he accepted public speaking activities on a totally ad hoc basis and his availability and style was known only by word of mouth. He has received many letters of appreciation for the way his talks have inspired and motivated other people to success. Now, however, most of Peter's speaking engagements are managed by a professional speakers' bureau and his fee goes straight to a charity.

During these presentations Peter finds that the most emotion is generated not so much from his descriptions of the actual trips, but from his record of achievement in charity fundraising and inspiring kids. These are the two triggers that get audiences excited.

This story is about Peter Treseder, explorer, and Peter Treseder, family man. It's about an extraordinary risk taker whose personal self-control leaves nothing to chance. A man who, in the words of his brother Neil, 'has always controlled his own destiny'. A man who pushes himself to the physical and emotional limits while leaving Beth to mow the lawns while he is away.

CHAPTER 2

GROWING UP IN ASHFIELD AND CANTERBURY

'I am on hand
To herald in the day,
And to announce its exit.
I thrive by clockwork and precision.
In my unending quest for perfection
All things will be restored to their rightful place.
I am the exacting taskmaster.
The ever-watchful administrator.
I seek perfect order in my world.
I represent unfailing dedication.
I AM THE ROOSTER.'

Theodora Lau, *The Handbook of Chinese Horoscopes*, Souvenir Press, 1980

The auspicious time and date of Peter Treseder's birth led his sister, Wendy, to compile astrological charts and a Chinese horoscope. She believes that they describe Peter very accurately and maintains that his quiet determination was pre-ordained.

From the Chinese horoscope we learn that Peter is a rooster, the dauntless hero who must look to all the earth to survive. The most misunderstood and eccentric of all the signs, outwardly the rooster is the epitome of self-assurance and aggression, but at heart he could be conservative and old-fashioned.

Peter is a fire rooster and this description is uncannily accurate. With fire as his element this type of rooster is vigorous, highly motivated and authoritative. He is able to operate independently and with great precision and skill. Strongly principled and single-minded in his pursuit of success, he displays above average managerial abilities and leadership. Unmoved and unswayed by the feelings or personal opinions of others, he will nevertheless be professional and ethical in his dealings. The fire rooster always has the noblest intentions behind his actions—and the capacity to project a stimulating and dynamic personal image.

Peter John Treseder was born at 11am on Monday 11 November, 1957 to Dorothy and John Treseder at the Braeside Hospital in Stanmore, an inner city suburb of Sydney. The newborn Peter became very sick with gastroenteritis and needed six visits from Dr Barry White before he was considered well enough to go home. The young family was living in Hillcrest Avenue, Ashfield at the time. Purchased with a staff loan from the Commonwealth Bank, where John was working his way up the management ladder, the house was the family's first home. John and Dot had spent six months renovating it before moving in and starting their family. A typical Victorian style blue brick house, it had three bedrooms and an ornately decorated hallway, complete with wooden fretwork features around the doorways.

Always exploring, even as an infant, one day Peter repeatedly crawled to a power point in the wall where a new fridge had just been plugged in. Each time he crawled over John would bring him back and lightly slap his hand, telling him 'No'. But Peter continued to go back time after time until finally he had to be taken from the room.

When he reached school age Peter was sent to Yeo Park Infants School but he didn't do well. Eventually, the deafness in his left ear was picked up. The auditory nerve was dead, almost certainly the doctor felt the result of either mumps or measles. A hearing aid would be no use and Peter would have to learn to adapt. He did so with such typical determination that even to this day few people are aware of the disability.

This small handicap didn't stunt Peter's imagination however, which worked in overdrive in the school yard. A star picket lay buried under a tree in the school grounds. It was called 'the Devil's Spike'. A rusty steel fence post with three points, the 1.5 metre picket had been hammered in so just 5 centimetres remained above the surface. The kids at Yeo Park firmly believed that if anyone touched it they would go straight to hell. Led by Peter, they held meetings around it planning and scaring each other.

Peter started his primary education at Summer Hill Public School at the bottom of the ladder. He found learning very hard and his hearing problem didn't help. It was time to learn to read and the teacher used a 'reading machine'. Peter absolutely hated it! Mrs Richardson would take the young students to the library where a machine projected words on the wall. A shadow blocked out the words in turn—and the speed of the moving shadow could be controlled by the teacher. It always seemed to go too fast for Peter who couldn't keep up, which made the following comprehension test pretty difficult. Not surprisingly, it was a long time before Peter could read well.

In class 3B, however, he had a sympathetic teacher and Peter was able to work his way up to the top of the class. John was so pleased he took Peter out—a rare treat. 'Dad took me to tea at the Thornleigh Milk Bar and to see a movie—*Chitty Chitty Bang Bang*—at the old Thornleigh picture theatre,' Peter recalls.

When he went into class 4A he hung on, even though he still found things difficult. Always choosing to sit at the front of the class and to one side so he could hear what the teacher said, Peter made every effort to learn everything, although his favourite subjects were drawing and history.

By the time he reached 6th class he was achieving a high standard, both academically and as a member of the school. He won several achievement awards including 'Outstanding School Spirit & Citizenship', 'Outstanding Effort in Organising Teams for Athletic Carnival', 'Continued Efficiency in Milk Distribution', 'Neat Work in Geometry' and 'Outstanding Reliability'. Clearly Peter was an invaluable member of the school, always helping the teachers, ringing the bell and helping with chores. During a fund raising program he sold more lamingtons than anyone else. All this combined to earn him the coveted Award for Citizenship in 1969, presented to him by the headmaster at the time, Rodney Hoare.

Such efforts were the first indications that Peter was prepared to put his energies and drive into helping other people. In the years since he has raised considerable amounts of money for charities through his activities. Indeed the grand total is now well over a million dollars.

Around this time Dot and John decided to send Peter to Sunday school. Brought up as Anglicans, they still attended church themselves and John was in the choir. It was natural that their children would learn about Christianity and attend Sunday school. Barbara Gordon, Peter's Sunday school teacher, says he didn't respond to teaching. She just couldn't get through to him. She still finds it difficult to reconcile the child of five who she knew with Peter and his later achievements.

Peter's memory is of hating Sunday school. Being dressed in his Sunday best clothes with Brylcremed hair and a little bow tie was not his idea of what Sundays were for. Nor was having his photograph taken in his Sunday best in the neat, ordered garden next door. The Treseder's neighbour at the time was Gilbert Rawson, head of the Signals Department on the railways. An imposing character in young Peter's eyes, Mr Rawson was collected daily for work in a big black car.

Eventually, Peter decided he had had enough of Sunday school. Sunny Sunday mornings were for playing. In fact his first memory of rebellion was the time he decided to skip Sunday school.

'I walked around the streets of Ashfield,' Peter recalls. 'I remember feeling guilty but can't remember the consequences. Whatever they were it was probably worth it!'

Like most children in the 1960s, Peter and Wendy walked to school. With only 17 months between these siblings Wendy's memories of their childhood are an interesting counterpoint to Peter's own. She claims that Peter at first objected to the daily walk.

Walking home from school, Peter and Wendy would often go via a park that had a bandstand in the middle of an ornamental lake stocked with small fish. A sliding drawbridge arrangement was the official way to the middle, but it was kept closed to keep children out! That wasn't going to stop the Treseder children however and Peter and Wendy soon worked out a way with planks and bits of wood to get across. Although appearing large and dangerous to these young children with vivid imaginations, the real distance was probably one an adult could almost step over!

Using a net to catch small fish, which they kept in a glass jar, the children spent many happy hours in the park. One day, playing with friends and with his school shoes and socks removed to keep them dry, Peter badly gashed the inside of his right foot and still bears the scar.

Wendy cheerfully describes herself as the 'sister from hell' in those days. Walking home past the Trinity Grammar School she would shout out 'Trinity Trash' among other unpleasant taunts to the boys. Peter would tell her repeatedly that she would get caught and eventually refused to walk with her anymore. Meanwhile though he'd been enviously watching the Trinity boys on their cross country runs—he wanted to do that, too.

While walking home, Peter would often collect bits of timber from discarded fruit and vegetable boxes. From these scrap bits he built billy carts, spending hours in Dad's garage, becoming proficient with basic hand tools. Sometimes Wendy's dolls' prams were stripped for parts, and large ball bearings were used for wheels. The billy carts provided endless fun as the kids raced them. But later they also became the means for Peter's first commercial enterprise.

In those days, many glass bottles were returnable and had small deposits. Peter organised the neighbourhood kids to help him collect the bottles, using billy carts as transport. Peter took all the bottles back to the shops and claimed the deposits, sharing them out according to a scale related to effort. The neighbourhood kids met in the Club House under the back verandah.

'There was this big area underneath the house and our understanding of wall to wall carpet meant it went up the walls,' Wendy remembers. 'Peter soon had carpet all over the area, sculpted around pillars and up the walls. This became a cubby and the local Club House. Peter of course was leader.'

Around this time too Peter built a tree house in a huge camphor laurel tree at the bottom of the garden, developing his building skills and the strength in his arms, as he continually pulled himself up through the lower branches to the platform.

Peter also loved his toys as much as any other kid. One of his favourites was Astro Boy. A metal toy based on the television character, Astro Boy led to many hours of fun in the back garden. Peter would tie him onto the Hills Hoist and spin him around and around. 'You'd play chicken with your head as it whizzed past. Then Peter would make it go faster and faster!' Wendy recalls.

Peter also loved all the adventure characters too, particularly Gigantor. He later discovered 'Superman' with George Reeves and would sit and watch him on the TV, imagining himself in the lead role—not unusual for a young boy however and perhaps no more influential in Peter's life than in many others'.

Nonetheless, to this day Peter often talks about the 'nobility' of his adventures in the bush and remote places. He has a deeply held conviction that humankind should have more to its existence than work and progress. The 'Clark Kent' concept of a very ordinary and somewhat shy and retiring man with an alter ego as superhero is in fact not so far from the mark for Peter, as if he is reliving the exploits of some of his childhood heroes. And, in addition, his genuine concern for others, particularly young people, shines through all his exploits. Perhaps, also, Peter was just born in the wrong century and should have been around when there was more of the world to explore!

Most of the family relationships during Peter's childhood were with Dorothy's family. Not only were they physically close, they were also an emotionally close family which liked to socialise. Peter's strong sense of family is deeply rooted in these early years.

The children were often taken to Dot's sister's house. Dot would leave them there while she shopped. Peter would walk to Auntie Elsie's with Neil in the pram and Wendy sitting on a special seat above Neil. Dot remembers the walks too. 'It was quite a long way for a small boy—3 kilometres or so—but he managed it very well and got used to walking at a young age.'

Elsie says Peter was 'a nice, ordinary little boy'. 'He was a bit shy in those days,' she remembers, 'and often hung back rather than get involved in games. Like most children he was sometimes good and sometimes naughty. Once he tipped a bucket of tadpoles down a sink. My youngest son had collected them and was very put out!'

Elsie is six years older than her sister, Dorothy, and her experience as a mother was to be an important factor in Peter's early childhood. With boys of her own she was used to their antics, remaining patient but firm—a terrific role model for her younger sister.

Other relatives were nearby too. Dorothy's parents, Pardi and Grandma, lived in Myra Road, Dulwich Hill. Steam trains puffed along at the end of the street. Their house backed onto a lane, with a toilet at the back of the house which was emptied by the night soil men who carried the cans on their shoulders. Visits to Grandma and Pardi were always welcomed by the Treseder children. The bread was delivered by horse and cart, with no wrapping paper or bag. In the early days the milk too was delivered—into a billycan left out by Grandma in a box at the side of the house.

Luxuries were few and far between in the Treseder house however as John's income went solely into the house and the costs of raising a family. So Peter and Wendy both loved the cakes and sweet biscuits, the meat pies and lemonade that were often served up at Pardi and Grandma's. In fact the love of meat pies and lemonade has stayed with both Peter and Neil. Even now, Peter still relishes a good meat pie or two!

John's family, on the other hand, was not close and always seemed to be at war. They never really socialised or talked to each other. The exception seemed to be regular Sunday lunches at Nana and Pop's house. Peter remembers the house as dark and formal. Wood panelling and large dark wood furniture including a sideboard dominated the rooms. 'Pop was gruff and stern,' says Peter. 'He had a pianola on which Dad used to play Handel's "Largo". We used to visit for a formal Sunday lunch which was always a big roast dinner with all the trimmings.

'Nana was a small woman who gave us thin little bars of chocolate as a treat. She produced these terrific lunches from a very small kitchen. And there was some sort of secret passage in the house which led to a secret room. I don't know what it was used for. Dad's brother Mervyn lived in the front room to the side of the front door and we were scared of both him and his room. We thought that if we ever went in we would never come out again! Much later I realised that he was slightly retarded but at the time just the fact that he was different was enough to scare us.'

Christmas throughout Peter's childhood was always an important family time. 'I can remember presents under the tree at Auntie Elsie's,' Peter says. 'We would open a few presents at home, nothing very extravagant, and then go down to Auntie Elsie's for lunch and more presents. The tradition of sharing still remains today and we still have big family Christmases, taking turns to play hosts. I also remember that I never seemed to receive as many presents compared with my friend down the road, Steven Salisbury. But it didn't bother me.'

Peter's childhood in Ashfield was very typical of growing up in suburban Sydney in that era. Dad went to work every day at the bank. Mum stayed home and ran the domestic side of things, although before having the children she had been secretary to L.J. Hooker, the building and real estate millionaire. When Dad came home from work, young Peter and Wendy would run down the street to meet him off the 409 bus then wrestle and rough and tumble with him in the hallway of the house.

Peter tended to socialise with and lead other local children. The impetus for games and activities often came from Peter as he overcame his early shyness. And his leadership of small groups developed naturally as other children fell in line with his ideas.

Regular trips to Tony Lucas the dentist however were not welcomed, but Peter put up with fillings without a needle. This may have provided him with a sound basis for emergency self-dentistry many years later on the trip to the South Pole.

Like the rest of the family's lifestyle, holidays for the Treseders were necessarily planned to a budget. John still remembers their first trip to Smiggin Holes when Peter was about eight. It was the first time the children had ever seen snow. With little money and unprepared for the conditions, the family took gumboots. Out on a walk, Peter was way ahead as usual. Always willing to try something new, he decided to walk across the unfenced hotel swimming pool which was iced over. 'Unfortunately for Peter, the ice was too thin. It cracked and Peter fell into the near freezing water and disappeared under the ice. Luckily for us all a man saw the accident from the hotel verandah and rushed down to quickly pull him out.'

But with no spare set of clothes to change into, Peter spent the rest of the day shivering in the car while the rest of the family enjoyed their time in the snow.

Just after his eighth birthday, Peter became a Wolf Cub with the 2nd Summer Hill Pack. Meeting in a now demolished hall attached to St Andrews Church, the pack was run by the late Neil Clancy with Greg Mallin as the Assistant Cub Leader. Peter didn't like Cubs much and left shortly after one of the leaders told him that he didn't have the 'right attitude' to become a Scout.

At Mum's suggestion however, Peter rejoined in April 1967 and took part in many activities, including camps. He became a Sixer just before going up to Scouts. But while achieving badges, Peter always found Wolf Cubs somewhat restrictive. It would be Scouts, he realised, that would give him the opportunity to 'go it alone' without parental and adult restrictions.

Bob Mallin was a close neighbour and the Scouts' District Commissioner for Ashfield. He has a strong memory of Peter's time in Cubs—and of Peter's determination to pass tests and pass along the Cubbing trail.

Mark Clancy, Neil's son, was at primary school and Cubs with Peter. 'He didn't stand out at school in any particular way, except by winning the Citizenship Award,' he recalls. Although he does remember his father saying that Peter had 'leadership potential' that showed up while he was in Cubs. Mark also remembers the Group Leader, the late Jack Robinson, who also spoke highly of Peter.

In 1969 Peter went up to Scouts at 2nd Summer Hill where he stayed until the family moved to Westleigh in mid 1970. Earning a few badges, including his Swimmer's badge and First Aid, Peter went from Tenderfoot to Second Class Scout during the course of that year.

It was around this time that hikes started to feature in Peter's life. Among his first were walks in the Royal National Park south of Sydney. There would usually be three or four in the Patrol—a Scout doing a 1st Class level hike, another doing it for his 2nd Class level and a Tenderfoot. 'This was the learning process,' Peter said. 'You moved up a level each time you tackled a hike.'

One of the Scouts Peter walked with was Peter Blunt. Sometimes they got hopelessly lost. 'Once I had to climb a tree and look out for where the water was,' explains Peter. 'I then led the Patrol in a straight line towards it. We reached Waterfall after walking many extra miles.'

In spite of such incidents Peter thoroughly enjoyed all the outdoor activities, including the traditional Scouting ones of campcraft. He particularly liked being able to go out in the bush without his parents' involvement and control. His Backwoodsman badge was easily, if somewhat irregularly, earned in 1970.

'We went to the Baden-Powell Scout Training Centre at Pennant Hills,' Peter recalls. 'David Allen and myself were told to go down to the Lane Cove Creek and catch a fish which we were to cook for our dinner. Well, that was pretty difficult as the creek was polluted even then and we doubted there would be any fish at all. We walked to the local fish shop and bought our fish, cooking it and showing the examiner who seemed to be satisfied with the taste test. We threw the rest away—we didn't really want to eat fish!'

Next they had to build a shelter for the night from sticks and bush materials. 'We did build one, but it was raining and we didn't feel like sleeping rough,' admits Peter. 'So, finding the camp hospital, we sneaked in and decided to sleep there. Looking around we found a fridge with a very large tub of ice cream. Once we had demolished that we decided to go up to Hornsby to see a movie as it was still early. We walked straight out of the camp and up to Pennant Hills train station, took a train to Hornsby and then disaster struck. A group of about 12 thugs accosted us at knife point and demanded our wallets and tickets which we had to hand over.'

Without tickets they then ran into trouble with the inspector at Hornsby Station. With no money for the cinema either they had no choice but to go back to camp. They slept in the hospital, getting up early to go down to the bush shelter in time for the examiner. And they passed the badge!

'Another time,' Peter confesses further, 'we were being tested for something and had to build a raft and then light a fire on the raft using two sticks rubbed together. Of course, we used a small firelighter—but we were disqualified when the raft sank in front of the examiner, leaving the firelighter bobbing about on the surface of the water.'

Meanwhile John and Dot had long planned to build their own home, wanting to get out of the city. Westleigh in those days was a newly developing bush suburb and their ideal location. But before they were able to move there they needed to sell the house at Ashfield and rent for a while while the new house was being built.

John got sick with hepatitis around the time they were due to move and it was left to Dot to find somewhere to rent and move the family. John recalls they were on holiday at Nelson Bay when he became ill. Once diagnosed, he was taken off for two weeks to the Prince Henry Hospital for infectious diseases which was on the coast just south of the city. When he was discharged just before the move from Ashfield to Canterbury he was still very weak from the illness and was not able to do very much.

Peter at this time was 12 and in 6th class at school. Dot says that he helped with every aspect of the move. 'He was fantastic, organising much of the packing and transport—very helpful in every direction. The other two children were too young to do much, so it was a lot of work for the two of us.'

The Canterbury home, due for demolition once the Treseder family moved out, was rented for about six months while the new house was being built. Weatherboard with timber floors and big rooms with high ceilings, all the children loved the house, none more than Peter, who was able to use his lively imagination for more pranks and adventure.

Every room in the house had a trapdoor in the ceiling to a large loft area. With a friend, Bill Hawkins, and Neil's help, Peter devised a complicated system of ropes and pulleys from their room to Wendy's. They created a ghostlike figure by using a metal sphere, actually a model moon, as the head and attaching ropes and old clothing to make the body.

Neil was sent to Wendy's room to do a number of tests. 'We checked the apparatus several times to make sure it worked,' he remembers. 'Using the ropes and pulleys and operating them from the trapdoor in our bedroom, Peter would half slide the trapdoor open in Wendy's room and the "man" would fall off and hang dangling. The chains in the roof were jangled for sound effects to add to the terror factor.'

One night soon after, Wendy was in her room with a friend who was staying the night. When they were ready for bed Peter opened her trapdoor, lowered the ghostlike figure complete with flashing torches into the bedroom and jangled the chains, thereby frightening the girls into near hysteria.

'The ghost fell in and we had some difficulty getting it back up,' Peter recalls. 'Wendy and her friend ran screaming from the room in a complete state of fear and Neil and I had to quickly hide the evidence to ensure that we weren't caught. We got away with it!'

The Canterbury house also had a big garden, only half of which was mowed. The rest was weeds and tall paspalum. In this part of the yard Peter built a network of tunnels by excavating then covering the tunnels with corrugated iron sheets which he found somewhere in the yard. To begin with, no-one else knew about the tunnels. But one day Neil discovered one and then started to add to them himself. One afternoon after school he showed Peter. They continued to expand the network, building small chambers along the way.

Peter also managed to link the network to his and and Neil's bedroom by cutting a trapdoor in the floorboards. The tunnels eventually came to light when Peter was sent to his room one day for some misdemeanour. Much to his parents' surprise he reappeared by the BBQ in the garden!

Because the house was to be demolished, the children did not have to be quite so careful as they would have to be in the new one. Playing hide and seek one day with Wendy, Peter decided she was in a cupboard which had double doors that opened inwards. Instead of calling out he smashed the doors straight into Wendy's glasses. 'Peter didn't seem to know his own strength in those days, and always played to win,' Wendy says, recalling her broken glasses. 'It wasn't so much a violent streak as a determination that no-one would beat him.'

Of course, Peter and Neil still pursued outdoor activities whenever they could, and this included kite flying. 'We would make kites from bamboo and brown paper and walk up to Canterbury Oval to fly them,' Neil remembers. 'We were both very good with our hands and we couldn't afford the shop variety.'

Eventually the house at Westleigh was finished and ready for occupation by the Treseder family. Dad was still sick and Peter helped him every weekend both before they moved and after to finish off the house and create a garden out of a building site. The Treseder house was one of the first in the street in what was then a new suburb. 'It felt like moving to the sticks for us,' Peter says. 'We were all used to city life, in very built up areas. At Westleigh we were surrounded by bush. But the constant building gave us lots of opportunity for play and we built better and better cubby houses. Our best effort was a three storey affair built from builders' sheds—complete with a dunny as the third storey! At the bottom we had trapdoors. It was great adventure.'

CHAPTER 3

OUT IN FRONT

'Besides war scouts there are also peace scouts, real men in all senses of the word, and thoroughly up in scoutcraft, they understand living out in the jungles and they can find their way anywhere; are able to read meaning from the smallest signs and foot-tracks; they know how to look after their health when far away from any doctor, are strong and plucky and ready to face any danger. Those who succeed best are those who learnt scouting while they were still boys.'

Lieut-General R.S.S. Baden-Powell, *Scouting for Boys*, 1909 edition

In Scouts Peter had quickly earned the name 'The Racing Goanna' for his ability to walk faster than anyone else. Neil Treseder joined the troop not long before Peter went up to Senior Scouts and remembers hiking with Peter to Burning Palms in the Royal National Park. 'Peter called me up to the front and we both walked ahead of the rest of the troop, who were all too slow for him,' Neil recalls.

On an earlier hike from Lithgow to Capertee, following the old Zig Zag railway tracks, Peter was one of the younger members of the party. Overnight camping was in the old fashioned, heavy canvas cottage tents which had to be carried, making the physical effort quite demanding. The party included Senior Scouts and Peter kept up with the Seniors, walking all the time in the lead group and even faster than the Scoutmaster. The party only made it to Newnes, owing to terrible weather, where they were all picked up and taken home.

In organised expeditions, however, Peter had to keep together with his group. The biggest physical challenge in the Scout section is the First Class Hike (now called the Adventurer Hike) and Peter found this the most exciting and fulfilling of all the activities. He started working on his First Class Hike in March 1971. His first trial journey was undertaken with fellow Scouts Mark Husselbee from Thornleigh troop and Robert O'Brien.

Taking the train from Pennant Hills to Springwood, the trio hiked around 13 miles (21 kilometres) through open country, forested areas and along creeks until they ended their journey at Emu Plains Railway Station. 'A good first attempt,' according to Scoutmaster, Skip Butler.

The second trial hike from Engadine to Heathcote attracted further comment from Skip. 'Another fair effort . . . however your map does not show sufficient detail.' Peter's log for the third and final journey makes fascinating reading. Full of spelling mistakes and grammatical errors, the hike was however carefully and extensively described as well as being well illustrated. Peter had obviously taken account of all the advice from Skip and was not going to risk failure this time. Even The Ration and Personal Gear lists are detailed and precise. Among the entries: 'Chicken—two chicken legs, Bread rolls—6 bread rolls, Jam—3 ounces, Ground sheet, change socks, spare pair of laces and first aid necessities.'

Peter Blunt, Jeremy Price and Peter took the train from Thornleigh to Glenbrook early on the first morning, starting their hike before 8am. Their journey took them on a predetermined route into the Blue Mountains National Park to the Red Hand Caves where Peter sketched the aboriginal art. Compass bearings were taken and recorded every few hundred metres with distances and times. Despite the rain, there was a fire ban in force so no fires could be lit to cook food. The log describes the surroundings so precisely a walker today could follow the route with ease from Peter's description and mapping notes. 'It was raining continuous all the time,' Peter wrote. 'The vegetation was scattered near the dam but getting much denser as we proceeded further. The side of the valley was getting steeper as we proceeded. The only wildlife seen were a few giant crayfish in the creek. The creek was polluted in parts. We reached Euroka Clearing at 8.45. From the clearing we went due north until we came across a rough trail. We followed the trail at a bearing of 288 degrees for 2 miles. It was very hilly and hard walking.'

At the end of the log, Peter includes a 'Personal Opinion' which shows how early in life Peter developed his determined attitude towards expeditions. 'When travelling across country the distances can be deceiving. So the main point is that you never give up. This particular hike was a bit of a challenge in that there were tracks everywhere to make it easy but you had to do what the instruction told you.'

Peter reached his fourteenth birthday only a few days after completing this 20 kilometre overnight hike. He was awarded his First Class Scout badge in October 1972 as a member of Curlew Patrol.

As well as the many hikes there were large combined Area Scout camps at Umina. These were run in traditional competition style with the Scouts sleeping in bell tents. 'We kept two sets of billies,' Peter says. 'One for cooking and one for inspection. The billies had to be clean and shiny and we couldn't see the point of all that hard work when there was fun to be had.'

'We set up our tent with properly brailled walls and laid out neatly inside, then slept rough in the bush to keep it that way for the competition. There were also initiation ceremonies in Scouts back then, and these often occurred at camps when parents were not around. Some Scouts were "blackballed" with shoe polish. Others were unlucky enough to receive their treatment in the KYBO.'

Peter does not elaborate but as 'KYBO' stands for 'Keep Your Bowels Open' it is easy to imagine the rest! 'But the wide games at camp were the best,' Peter claims. 'The Senior Scouts would set up and guard a lantern at the top of the hill and we would try to creep up unseen to capture it.'

Peter maintains his only reason for attending Scout meetings was to organise trips. His involvement and planning helped to push the Troop along and increase the number of outdoor activities. And, as with Wolf Cubs earlier, Peter always had his eye on the next level—Senior Scouts. He saw the opportunity for rock climbing and considered Seniors the epitome of Scouting experience. Once he went up to Senior Scouts, which shortly after was renamed Venturers, he pushed others and arranged trips all the time. If no-one else wanted to go he made a point of going on his own. This was against the rules and must have caused his Venturer leader, Linc Madden, some considerable anxiety but he did it anyway. Peter just couldn't be told.

Nana and Pop had a fibro house near the railway line at Lawson in the Blue Mountains. The Treseder family would often visit as John and

Dorothy had a great love of the Mountains which they passed onto their children, especially Peter. In the back garden was a big rock which the kids used to scramble up and over. Peter remembers these times as his first attempts at rock climbing. They would scramble up a rock face at the back of the garden to visit some girls singing 'Go Tell it on the Mountain' on the verandah of the house next door.

The steam trains ran in and out of Lawson Station, which was a favourite place for the children. They collected coal from beside the tracks from trains which had lurched and lost a bit of their load as they went round the corner by the station. They would watch the trains come in, belching smoke and steam, and help by loading the boiler with wood when the engine driver let them. It was like every child's dream. As the train chuffed out of the station they would run alongside along the platform. One day, running alongside the train as it departed, and against strict instructions from Mum and Dad, Peter and Wendy ran straight into blackberries in the smoke, the sharp thorns shredding legs and ripping Wendy's lips. They had been told not to do it and both got into trouble.

Nana and Pop's house had been designed as a holiday home and had few mod cons. The old fashioned 'Thunder Box' toilet was out the back, there was no television and the radio was located high on a shelf in the kitchen.

But the children enjoyed their stays and got into all sorts of mischief. On hot summer days when the sky was dense with rising eucalyptus oil from the mountain forests, Peter would swim in the town water tank up on the top of a hill. 'I climbed up some sort of ladder attached to the side and got in through the inspection trapdoors,' Peter recalls. 'It was pretty dark in there but the water was lovely and cool. I don't know what the people of Lawson would have thought about me swimming in their water supply, but I didn't tell anyone!'

'Sydney Rock', on the main road near Lawson, is a natural rock feature about 10 metres high. You could scramble up it to see Sydney—which Peter would do at every opportunity.

Peter's parents had a strong affinity with the Blue Mountains and loved bushwalking. Day walks were very much part of the family's activities. Peter always ran ahead, even then, up the path and across suspension bridges. Mum and Dad were always calling after him to slow down. 'After a hike us kids would be made to stand on the bonnet of the old green Holden,' says Wendy. 'We had to strip to our underwear to search for leeches. I hated leeches and would have taken everything off to get rid of them. But Peter took it all in his stride, not worrying about the things.'

Around this time, the town of Lawson and the Blue Mountains community were shocked by the disappearance of a young girl. Vicky Barton was apparently kidnapped in Lawson, just down the road from where the Treseder family stayed. The mystery took many years to solve. Eventually it was discovered that an intellectually handicapped postman had taken her and dismembered her body. 'It's a bit scary to think of how we all wandered around without worrying at that time,' Wendy muses.

By now the family were long settled into Westleigh. The move had been an important event for Peter. Not only did it mean a new set of friends, a new school and Scout Group, it gave him the closest access he had ever had to the Sydney bush. This was to be pivotal in the development of his outdoor skills. Westleigh linked directly with the bush which, abounding with native wildlife, was completely different from the inner city suburbs of Ashfield and Summer Hill. Peter's mother, Dorothy, wonders what life would have been like if they hadn't moved to Westleigh. 'Certainly Peter wouldn't have had the opportunity to explore the bush and join a Scout Group which encouraged him to undertake so much outdoor activity,' she says.

The house was new and there was no established garden. John, who has always been very good as a home handyman, embarked on a program of building and landscaping the grounds. 'I helped Dad build a long and tall retaining wall,' Peter recalls, 'between our garden and next door. We moved large sandstone blocks into place by hand, backfilling each level with stones and earth.'

Peter also helped finish off the new home, learning many building skills which he has used to this day. Apart from work on his own family's house, to make extra pocket money he from time to time helped builders in the local area. Peter always had an eye on accumulating money from an early age.

As Dad was always building, renovating or changing something, younger brother Neil also learnt these skills. Wendy remembers the garden being built and the turf—which came from the South Strathfield Bowling Club where they were tearing up the greens—going down. 'With Dad's encouragement, Peter crawled inside a large cement pipe to add his weight and then this pipe was used to roll the turf in the back garden.'

Peter says that he also helped Dad to rotary hoe the ground before the turf went down and helped clean all the spare bricks around the place for later use. Today neatly kept mature gardens surround a suburban house that is equally neat and tidy, both inside and outside. Everything is well ordered and it is easy to see how in this environment Peter acquired and developed his need for order. His own home bears the same trademark tidiness and luckily wife Beth shares the same philosophy. In fact Neil claims that Peter was always tidying up the bedroom they shared throughout their childhood and teenage years at Westleigh. 'He was a neatness freak,' Neil says. 'But one day he went too far and threw all my sports trophies and models of planes and trucks into the rubbish. They had been safely gathering dust on top of the wardrobe. I got home and they were in bits in a box on the floor, ready to be thrown out. We had a huge fight which resulted in Peter punching me in the kidneys. I threw up. Mum and Wendy were horrified.'

'But,' adds Wendy, 'I think it frightened Peter as much as us. I never saw him do anything like that again.'

Peter too remembers the incident. 'It frightened me silly,' he recalls, 'and I never again used my strength against anyone in the family.'

Neil comments further that everything always had to be done Peter's way. 'He was pigheaded and stubborn,' Neil concludes.

Wendy says however that Peter was always very secretive and quiet as a child. He would stand looking stern and serious when arguments were going on. He stuck to himself much of the time. But Peter was quite happy with his own company and liked to be alone. 'If he had a problem he wanted to sort out, he'd just go bush,' says John.

Neil however was much more gregarious and easygoing than Peter and liked to be with people. While he also belonged to Scouts and enjoyed the activities he was rapidly becoming an impressive athlete and hence had a wider circle of friends from school and sports activities. He was especially keen on team sports like soccer, a game he played competitively into his adult years.

Most of Peter's friends on the other hand were made through Scouts and, especially with so many weekend Scout activities, they grew up together. Neil strongly believes that the move to Westleigh provided the opportunities for Peter to develop his scouting skills in the outdoors in a way that would not have been possible at their previous home. There was luck with the Leaders too, especially Linc Madden.

And like most suburban children, Wendy and Peter would sometimes camp in the backyard during the Treseders' early days at Westleigh. 'Peter had a calico Indian tepee which we used to put up to play in and sometimes sleep in overnight,' Wendy remembers.

John and Dorothy supported Peter, and later Neil, through Scouts and sport but didn't make much fuss about birthdays and their children's extra-curricular achievements. It was as if they took it for granted that their children would achieve and do well in some particular area, but that this success didn't need to be shouted from the rooftops. There is perhaps a reflection of this in Peter's own practice of not parading his successes publicly—except when he has an ulterior motive, such as fundraising.

Peter's parents were also very strict. In the Treseder household, kids were meant to be seen and not heard, perhaps not unusual in the sixties in Sydney. Peter, as the oldest and the most likely to transgress, often received the worst of his father's comments and irritation at what he perceived to be rule breaking. All three children became very independent as a result of this pressure and there was a level of defiance in the family towards Dad.

'Each of our parents wanted control in their own way and there were rules about everything,' Wendy remembers. 'For example, as a teenager, you could be grounded for being just five minutes late home.'

Peter says that he was not allowed to use the mower and that Dad would not start the mowing, using a standard Victa petrol mower, unless all the children were indoors. John maintains he was concerned about safety, and interestingly, Peter has developed the same attitude and only mows his family's Wahroonga lawns when Marnie and Kimberley are safely indoors.

On a funnier note both Peter and Wendy remember that there were rules about using the phone. 'The older you were the more you were allowed to use it,' Wendy laughs.

One day John actually removed the telephone handset and put it in the boot of his car, taking it on one of his country trips to prevent anyone from making calls. This was a long time before mobile telephones and John enjoyed something of a joke with his colleagues when he offered one of them the use of his telephone from the boot of his car!

Wendy recalls that, except when travelling to other branches, Dad used to take public transport to work at the bank. After work he would stop off for a drink with his workmates before coming home for dinner at exactly the same time every day. 'Dad would play roughly with the boys when he arrived home and wind them up when they should have been slowing down for bed,' Wendy says. 'I can remember piggy backs and them crashing into things. Neil once went through part of an internal wall. There was often drama before going to bed.'

John travelled a great deal for the bank and knew many country places well. On an undated postcard Peter has kept, there is a picture of an imposing volcanic rock formation called 'The Bread Knife' in the Warrumbungle Ranges, Coonabarabran, New South Wales. John Treseder sent the card during one of his business trips when Peter was about 15 years old. 'Bet you couldn't climb that bit of rock?' said the message. 'Hope you're keeping well and looking after the house while I'm away. See you next Friday. Love Dad.'

Of course, Peter has climbed it—at least three times—the first time being only a few years after receiving the postcard.

Holidays for the children were 'educational', each well planned by Dad and with a specific purpose. It was a long time until they had 'fun' holidays at the beach. A typical holiday would involve driving to a town where they would be taken to see a ginger factory, chocolate factory, banana plantation, sugar cane factory or something similar. They would stay in onsite vans at a caravan park and move on to the next town the following day. 'There was a routine and we certainly learnt things as we went along, but I don't remember not liking it,' Peter recalls.

Once or twice they towed a caravan and finally came to enjoy beach holidays in caravan parks—particularly at The Entrance or Avoca on the New South Wales Central Coast. 'We would go to The Entrance,' Peter says, 'and stay for two or three weeks and have a water-based holiday with barbecues. The ocean was easily accessible on one side and the lake on the other so we got variety.'

He also remembers the Jago family. They would all go away together. The parents would each sleep in a caravan with all the children sleeping in the annexes.

Following a brief stint at Canterbury Boys High School before moving, Peter applied himself to both study and sport at Normanhurst Boys High School. He was always focused and always studying. He achieved through hard work and application whereas others with more natural ability didn't do so well. In 1971 he took out first place in Science in Second Form, and in 1975 first place in Industrial Arts. He was a champion cross country runner too by now and became a School Prefect. Peter remembers representing the school at every cross country, athletics and swimming competition that was held while he was there. In swimming he was best at sprint swims.

These days, during his presentations, Peter often tells a swimming story against himself to help make the connection with his audience through humour.

'When I was at school I used to hold the school 50 metres swimming record,' he starts. 'Not because I was a brilliant swimmer, but because the better swimmers had gone up to the 100 metres and 200 metres races. One year I was lucky enough to win the school, Zone and Area carnivals and represented the State at the Australian championships. It was held at an open air, saltwater pool by the harbour.

'I was very nervous going into the carnival, had my race in the morning and didn't do very well. I got out of the pool with an enormous sense of relief, wondering how I could reward myself. I bought six meat pies and a 2 litre bottle of Coke, took the whole lot to the back stands and ate the pies one after the other, topping them off with the Coke. Then I promptly fell asleep in the sun.

'About 30 minutes later someone was tugging on my shoulder trying to wake me up. I could hear my name: "Treseder, get down there." I stood up with this pot belly full of pie and Coke. 'Our 800 metre swimmer is sick and you're swimming it,' the state coach told me.

'I tried to explain that I wasn't feeling too well myself at that point—besides which I couldn't swim more than 50 metres. He told me to get over to the pool. I remember standing there while one Arnold Schwarzenegger figure after another took to the blocks. These were big blokes, just back from the Commonwealth Games and I was skinny and blue with fright standing among them. A whole lot of timekeepers were brought in and the announcer said that the 800 metre world record holder, who just happened to be standing next to me, was going to try to break his world record. That made me feel fantastic.

'"On your marks . . . Get set . . ." At that moment my stomach, which had been making fearful gurgling sounds, erupted in an enormous burp. I stood and swayed in this fog of pie and coke fumes watching the disgruntled face of the world record holder as he pulled himself out of the pool after the first false start.

'The race started again and we matched each other stroke for stroke down the pool. I went into my tumble turn a fraction of a second behind him. I could see the crowd of 3000 people shouting and cheering as I turned as no-one had ever kept up with this bloke for the first 50 metres before. Little did they know that 50 metres was about all I had in me.

'As I got further up the pool I could see this black thing hovering in my lane. Eventually I arrived at my swimmers. It was not until I was pulled out that I realised that the yelling had been about my bare bum, not my swimming prowess. At the end of the race, the world record holder pulled me aside and gave me a few pointers on swimmers' etiquette during a world record attempt. He had been too distracted to break it but I reassured him I would never be involved in another one.'

This story always gets a lot of laughs as Peter punctuates it with lots of hand and arm movements. How true is it? He's told it so many times now that even he can't remember exactly what is true and what he has embellished for effect!

Peter competed in athletic events too. His favourites were the 1500 metres and the mile. The 800 metre race was too fast for him. In cross country Peter excelled at the 5000 metres but Neil was even better than him. Tall and athletic, he started running with Peter when he was very young and developed into a seriously good sportsman.

While he achieved easy success athletically, Peter found his trial Higher School Certificate exams really difficult. Even so he got straight A's in the actual examinations—a clear instance of application over natural academic ability, particularly at a time when it mattered. This 'just in time' technique is one that Peter has consciously and subconsciously used all his life.

In his final school report for year 12 in 1975, T.H. Penn, Acting Principal, said Peter was to be '. . . recommended as a pleasant, reliable and gentlemanly young man who has always been cooperative and who has achieved well'. Not exactly the report one would expect of someone who would shortly start breaking records and establishing 'firsts' in pursuits that demanded very special skills and dedication.

By this time a typical school day for Peter had included the usual activities plus his self-imposed physical training. His daily routine, from the age of about 13, was to run 5 to 10 kilometres a day, followed by three hours study. He set up a desk downstairs in the garage at Westleigh and worked there every night after his training. Often there would be parental arguments upstairs while he was doing this, but he was single minded enough to ignore them. 'I even remember studying by lamplight during power strikes,' he says.

Maths was always a struggle but Peter was good at industrial arts and drawing. He even started sculpture around year 10 and did some for his Queen's Scout Award. This started a life-long interest in sculpture for Peter, and he continued to sculpt for about 10 years. Many of the pieces are in his own garden.

Just before the HSC Peter was trying to study hard. He knew that he would only achieve good marks if he applied himself more than his school friends. Invited on a Scout trip to the Blue Mountains that final school winter, he spent all his time on the train studying.

The trip itself was memorable. As snow fell at Katoomba, Rick Jamieson led the group into the mountains to the 'Big Black Wall' where twelve people were roped together, edging up the face one step at a time.

Peter was in 6th form by the time Neil was in 1st form and the two brothers didn't see much of each other at High School. There was plenty of contact outside school however and the two boys got on well, despite the five year age gap. Neil remembers their continued love of meat pies, which went back to the Ashfield days and Pardi. 'We went to the West Pennant Hills pie shop one Saturday morning and bought ten pies. The lady who served us thought we must be having a party but she was wrong. Peter and I ate five pies each!'

And through all this Peter was always running. When friends arranged to go surfing, he would run from Westleigh to Whale Beach or back—sometimes even both ways, more than 60 kilometres all up. Ever since, 'training' has always been a part of Peter's life. Use of the word 'training' is relevant—he is always training for something, unlike many people who exercise just to stay fit.

For many years while both her boys attended, Dorothy worked at the High School as a laboratory assistant. As Mum was working, there was a weekly routine to follow which included a shopping trip with which Peter helped. He willingly helped her every week with the shopping. They would take the car to the supermarket, Peter would push the trolley and load and unload and help Dot put the shopping away. 'He was always so helpful with this job and never complained,' says Dorothy.

Some time around 1970 at the age of 12 or 13, Peter organised himself a job with Con and Jim Andis, two Greek brothers who owned the Thornleigh fruit and vegetable shop, which also sold ice cream and milk shakes.

This job would continue for eight years, almost every Sunday from 9am to 6 pm. Peter would bag up potatoes, trim cauliflowers, remove loose onion skins and serve customers. 'Weighing up produce and working out the correct prices was the hardest part,' Peter says. 'I had to work out the exact price from the dollars per pound on the handwritten sign. I would write each price down on a list and add them up when the order was complete. I got pretty good at it but I was never as fast as Con, who could mentally add a list of prices in his head just by looking at it.'

When the shop was not busy, Peter would sweep the footpath and look around for extra jobs without being asked. This attitude impressed these friendly, hardworking brothers and they recognised his effort. 'There was sometimes a bit extra in my pay envelope and once Dad made me go back and ask what it was for,' Peter recalls. 'They told me it was for my extra work, which pleased Dad as much as the extra money pleased me.'

During the same year Peter also secured a job with the local milkman, John Kandelas. This job lasted a full ten years until John's health deteriorated and the run was sold. By this time Peter was working at the bank, having dropped out of university. 'John smoked and it eventually killed him,' explains Peter. 'My last job after the run was sold was to show the new owner where everyone hid their money.'

The milk run would start between 1 and 2am, every Sunday morning. Peter would run with crates of milk, delivering the right amount to each house and collecting the money when it was left out. Sometimes it was very cold and the bottles were icy to hold. Peter had to wear gloves in winter. But he regarded the milk run as training as much as work. 'I was already very fit and the running all night kept my level of fitness, and especially endurance, very high,' he says.

For a youngster of thirteen it would have been a tough enough physical challenge to begin with. What is rather extraordinary is that the job at the fruit and vegetable shop followed on almost immediately the milk run was finished. Peter would finish the run and John would give him two chocolate milks to take home. He would drink these, have some breakfast, get changed and then go up to Con's for the day's work without any sleep.

What did Peter's parents think of this rather unusual behaviour? After all, by this time the family was not poor, and Peter had no need to work to help support the family. John says that they didn't worry. Peter was fit, the work he was doing was within his physical capabilities and it was not on school days. He had used his own initiative to get the jobs. 'We weren't concerned too much because we knew Peter always had to be occupied and this was a productive way to use his time,' John adds.

Indeed throughout his teenage years Peter's weekend pattern was to leave on Friday or Saturday for a trip to the mountains with Scouts, come home by Saturday night, do the milk run and work in the fruit shop. Mostly without any sleep. Once he had left Scouts he would even take in a party or whatever was going on on Saturday night before going off to work! Some Sunday nights—after the milk run and the fruit and vegetable shop—Peter also went with his friend, Andrew Stiff, to the Sydney Morning Herald building to work on the inserting line. Yet another night without sleep before school or work.

Peter was accumulating quite a sum of money from these jobs and, with little time to spend it, was saving well. In fact he claims that he saved almost all of it. This is supported by Neil and Wendy who maintain that Peter was miserly with his money and very secretive although some of it must have gone into outdoor gear for climbing and expeditions and later on cars. Peter says he started saving very early on with the vision of buying a block of land.

Perhaps not surprisingly, Peter didn't seem to have girlfriends around this time. Neil remembers only one girl—who had short blonde hair, freckles and 'a great body'. According to Neil, this relationship didn't last more than a few weeks as 'Peter always put his own interests before the girl who couldn't cope with his selfishness'.

By general acclamation, there were no girls in Peter's Venturer Unit, even though the Scout Association had opened the doors to girls during those years. 'We thought they would change our focus and get in the way of our rock climbing and expeditions,' Peter says, 'and they would not be able to keep up with us physically.'

For Peter, the most exciting part of Venturers was rock climbing in the Blue Mountains. 'It was a great adventure,' Peter says. 'I would be petrified and excited at the same time. We used to go to the St George Area rock climbing hall at Mount Victoria. The legendary Rick Jamieson was the instructor and his teaching method encouraged all of us to keep trying more and more difficult climbs.'

Rob Tickell used to bring his guitar and song book and the group would have a campfire on the Saturday night which produced a great atmosphere. During the 'Scouts Own' on Sunday morning, Rick used to draw parallels between the struggles on the rock, climbing and the struggles in life—lessons which have stayed with Peter all his life. And he also credits Rick Jamieson with his ongoing desire to be modest about his own achievements.

Indeed Jamieson seems to have been something of a role model. Peter's favourite book in those days was *Outdoor Senior Scouting* written by Rick Jamieson. This book was unique and showed places to go, when to go, how to do particular activities and what to take. It was the only book available that gave both technical advice and locations for activities. Peter still has his much worn copy.

Linc (Lincoln) Madden was the Venturer Leader at the time. He always had an eye on adventure. A pivotal figure in Peter's development, Linc was the person who made it possible for Peter to develop his skills in the outdoors. He organised the climbing instruction and trips to the Blue Mountains and continually encouraged Peter right through Venturers to his Queen's Scout Award three years later.

'Without his support and influence I may never have discovered the excitement of rock climbing,' says Peter. 'Or caving or challenging bushwalking. In fact, my life might have taken a very different turn without Linc's dedication. Linc was one of those rare "quality Leaders" who gave us a really rich experience in the process. I am sure he enjoyed it too, but without the time he spent we would not have had the opportunity to do any of these things.'

Linc Madden now lives in Queensland. A retired accountant and with a great deal of experience in mining and geological exploration, he understands the outdoors very well and has a great affinity with it. He had come from the country in 1938 and worked at Anthony Horden in Sydney where there was a Scout Troop made up of employees. Of course, they were all over 15 and formed one of the first Senior Scout Troops before they officially came into existence in 1947. All the Scouts enlisted in the Second World War and Linc came back army-organised and with a view that was perhaps a bit hard on discipline. 'That was OK,' he says, 'as long as it was fair and everyone did their fair share of the work. The boys didn't seem to mind.'

Just as Senior Scouts became Venturers Linc became a leader. He was appointed to run the 5th Pennant Hills Unit. Some eighty per cent of the boys came from Normanhurst Boys High School, including Peter Treseder and two of Linc's own sons.

Since 5th Pennant Hills was an all male unit by choice, the physical activities were very strenuous. 'The lads called the mixed units "Coffee Club Commandos",' recalls Linc wryly. 'We were not very popular with Branch Headquarters for our choice, as part of the program change was a policy to include girls at this level of Scouting.'

Linc had some rock climbing experience from the army and teamed up with Rick Jamieson, who was already an internationally recognised climber. Linc also became Cumberland Area Rock Climbing Adviser and, with the cooperation of Sid Marshall, then District Commissioner, incorporated the best of the old Senior Scout program into the new Venturer one.

Peter still clearly remembers his first climb, led by Rick Jamieson. 'This larger than life character led us up the "Unnamed Climb" at Narrowneck in the Blue Mountains. He was a very humble man, scruffily dressed and with eccentric habits. This was a simple Grade 9 climb which he had probably completed dozens of times. His motivation of us, however, was always great. "Fantastic climb! Great climb!" was the typical comment as we made our cautious way up the rock face.'

Rick's eccentricity was famous. One day at lunchtime he took a filthy old comb from his pocket and proceeded to butter two slices of bread and make a sandwich with a whole bar of chocolate. 'We thought he was fantastic!' says Peter.

The rock climbing weekends became a regular feature of Peter's life and he began to spend every weekend away. This was a significant shift in Peter's life, now taking responsibility for his own actions. Mark Foster—later to be Groomsman at Peter's wedding—would get up with Peter before breakfast and go out early to do a climb before 'Scouts Own' on Sunday morning. They always tried to climb something harder than they were supposed to and to get as many climbs in on a day as possible—six or seven while some people were satisfied with two or three. 'We liked to climb on our own,' Mark says, 'as we were obviously pushing ourselves more than the others. You could get stuck in a group where two or three weren't very good or didn't even try very hard.'

There were expeditions all the time. 'We strongly taught the lads that safety was the key,' Linc remembers, 'and Peter responded well on that. But towards the end he was trying to push things further than I was comfortable with. With rock climbing you must have continual experience at all levels, and Peter just wanted to keep on going up the grades as fast as possible. He and Mark Foster climbed together and tried to push each other. They were always looking for the higher aspect.'

One morning Mark and Peter went out early and started to climb Eternity, a Grade 19 climb at Mount Piddington that was well beyond their official capabilities. Peter had, with some difficulty, just reached the top of the first pitch when Linc appeared at the base of the climb, telling him in no uncertain terms to come back down. He and Mark were seriously chastised and Peter found it hard to retrace his steps down the single crack in the sheer rock face.

In June 1974 Peter received his first Rock Climbing badge, signed by Rick Jamieson, Chief Rock Climbing Instructor, Cumberland Area. Eventually Peter went on to become an instructor in his own right, finding the challenge irresistible. And he and Mark continued to climb together for many years.

In 1975 Peter obtained his Rock Climbing Leader Certificate, signed by

David Kinchin, then Assistant Area Commissioner, Venturers, in the Cumberland Area and now Chief Commissioner New South Wales.

Throughout this time there was a culture within the Scouting fraternity that claimed it was madness for Venturers to be climbing grades 18, 19 and 20. 'These were the highest climbing grades in Australia at the time and many people thought that we were crazy,' says Mark Foster.

Peter confirms this. 'Our Venturer Unit was probably the best in Australia for rock climbing, and would be regarded even today as an elite Unit.'

Linc agrees, saying, 'the Unit produced more Queen's Scouts than the rest of the District put together. Clearly we were doing more than the other Units at that time.'

Peter, however, continued to flout the rules, often forgetting or not bothering to obtain necessary permissions or complete activity advice forms unless they were needed to get the Queen Scout sign-off in his Venturer record book. Alongside some expected teenage rebellion was a slightly cynical self-interest. He seemed to regard all authority and regulations as a waste of time and only followed the rules when it was absolutely necessary to progress to a new stage—one which would allow him more freedom in his activities.

His solo expeditions as a Venturer fell into this category and some current Scout Leaders have criticised Peter for setting a bad example. The concept of 'duty of care' has become tougher over the years and while Peter's First Class hikes were attempted in groups of three Scouts, the equivalent standard hiking party today is five to ensure the safety of all members should an emergency arise.

Peter's Venturer Passport records his progress to Queen's Scout level. John Treseder says that he chanced across his log book one day only to discover that Peter had climbed the Three Sisters three times. Peter at the time was 15 and neither John or Dorothy knew he had climbed this rock formation at all!

The expeditions continued, of course, including hikes in the Grose Valley and Blue Gum Forest. He achieved a Bar to the Bronze Medallion in Lifesaving, and completed an environment project which involved measuring water quality in Pye's Creek in the Elouera bushland area.

Through all this Peter remained a bit of a loner, although he was quite popular with the others. Linc remembers that Peter always wanted to go first. 'Even his sister said it,' remembers Linc. 'He was always keen.'

Linc recounts a typical example of Peter's desire to be first—an expedition which went wrong and affected others. 'We had arranged some spelio down at Coolamine Caves in the Snowy. Peter had just got his licence and took his Mum's car. He tore down there ahead of everyone. We found him and Mark Foster sitting beside the car on the Monaro Highway. They couldn't find the way in and wanted to go somewhere else. We couldn't let them do that, of course, and showed them the entrance to the caves area and where they were to camp.'

Peter then whizzed down to Caves Creek and promptly got the car stuck halfway across. He was totally stranded. Linc had to take his sons and another Venturer and drive out and around the long way via Adaminaby to the other side of the creek in order to tow the car out. 'We lost a whole day through Peter's impatience,' Linc says.

In spite of such mishaps Area Commissioner Alan Gamble notified Peter of his Queen's Scout Award a month before his eighteenth birthday in 1975. The presentation was organised by District Venturer Leader, Linc Madden and the 5th Pennant Hills Group and the award made by District Commissioner for Pennant Hills-Beecroft, Sid Marshall, at a public ceremony at Westleigh Shopping Centre on 10 October 1975. 'It was a significant event,' one local newspaper reported. 'Peter was the first 5th Pennant Hills Unit member to receive the award and the first from the newly amalgamated Scout District.'

Linc Madden was quoted in the newspaper. 'To gain the badge a Scout had to make a planned effort and steady progress in scoutcraft. He (Peter) has been an excellent Venturer, excelling in expeditions and rock climbing. By the end of the year he should receive a Rock Climbing Instructor's Certificate.'

As Peter continued to develop these skills as a young adult he began to make more and more of his trips without any support structure and often without telling people much about his plans—a frightening thought to those who know the risks and potential dangers of the Australian bush. This became characteristic of Peter Treseder when he was developing his tiger walking skills. Later, on record attempts, he would arrange support crews—but he still undertook the most hazardous journeys solo.

Chapter 4

Mount Cook in a Hurry

'I am one of those knights who go in quest of adventures. I have left my country, mortgaged my estate, quitted my pleasures, and thrown myself into the arms of fortune.'

Cervantes, *The History of Don Quixote*, 1605

The Higher School Certificate exams were over and Peter had been presented with his Queen's Scout Award. He had also earned his Rock Climbing Instructor's Certificate and wanted nothing more than the opportunity to climb and learn even more. There was nothing much to keep him at home.

Peter and Andrew Lattimore—nicknamed 'Skin' by his friends because he was so skinny—decided to go to New Zealand to explore and climb mountains. They left Sydney with the natural enthusiasm and unconcern of youth. Climbing buddies from Venturers, the pair decided to book into a mountaineering course at Mt Cook in the South Island of New Zealand with a view to improving their skills and experience. Since they had very little money they decided to hitch everywhere to save on bus fares. 'Actually, I had money in the bank,' says Peter, 'but I was too stingy to spend it.'

He was keeping it for the block of land he wanted to buy. A lofty ambition indeed for a school leaver let loose on the world—yet one that the prudent Peter would achieve within a remarkably short time.

The trip started well enough, but Peter soon realised that he and Skin had rather different outlooks on life and the adventure to be enjoyed. Skin was laid back and wanted to take his time. Peter was on the run already, wanting to pack everything into each day. He would get up before sunrise and miss breakfast, getting out to the road to hitch while the good rides were around. Often he would arrive in the next town that the pair had designated by ten in the morning. Skin would stay in his sleeping bag, getting up perhaps by nine and sometimes—as he often missed the best lifts—not even reaching the agreed destination until the day after.

Peter always got fantastic hitches. His technique was to look clean and tidy and to face the traffic head on, making eye contact with a smile and with an open look. When there was competition for rides at major intersections, Peter would always get picked up first. He would never know where he would end up but he didn't mind. That was part of the adventure.

In Christchurch, Peter and Andrew decided the official Motor Camp was too expensive and found an animal pen in the cattle yards next door. By setting up camp there they saved a dollar a night in camping fees—although that didn't stop them using the facilities. At night they would venture over to the site to cook their food, watch television in the communal lounge and socialise with the other campers. Andrew even found a girl he liked! During the day they left their gear in the cattle pen while they explored the town and went rock climbing. One of their first climbs was at Cathedral Rocks.

After a week they split. The different styles of travelling were too difficult to reconcile and Peter was keen to keep moving at a pace which clearly did not suit the relaxed Andrew. The pair agreed to meet for the mountaineering course back in Mount Cook, and to hire their own alpine guide for some lessons in ice climbing.

Over the next few weeks Peter crisscrossed the North and South Islands of New Zealand, running or walking every major tramping track in the country, including the Heaphy, Waikaremoana, Hollyford, Copland, Routeburn, Milford and Tongariro.

Peter still has the map he used on this trip. Brown with age and with every crease stuck together with peeling sticky tape, the double sided map was issued free with the compliments of the New Zealand Tourist and Publicity Department. On a blank part of the map is a list of girls' names and telephone numbers.

Peter met Kaye Smith, Sue Hagg, Anna Dowling and Cheryl Taylor the day he got off a bus in the pouring rain to run the Routeburn Track in the Fjordland National Park. Starting off with the four girls—all medical students on a holiday from The Queen Victoria Hospital in Melbourne—Peter decided to walk, rather than run, this particular track.

Mount Cook in a Hurry

'It was a most enjoyable walk!' Peter recalls with a smile. 'We stopped each night at the huts along the track and the girls slept inside while I stayed outside. The only reason for this was that it cost a dollar a night to sleep inside and I still didn't want to spend my money!'

During this trip he and the girls also climbed several peaks as side trips. One night there was obviously no Ranger around to check on trampers so Peter stayed inside the hut. He left his yellow running shoes outside as was the expected custom. When he couldn't find them in the morning he looked around outside the hut, only to see what looked like bright yellow Christmas decorations hanging in the surrounding trees. The Keas—large native New Zealand birds—had taken his shoes and ripped them to shreds, leaving long strips of yellow hanging from the branches! Peter had no other shoes and completed the next two days of the hike in his socks—tended no doubt by the accompanying girls.

In Queenstown the group went to a restaurant which served a smorgasbord lunch. Peter immediately took advantage of the situation. 'I filled my rucksack with extra food from the smorgasbord,' he says, 'making sure that I had enough to last me the next few days.'

The hitch hiking continued, with Peter taking rides wherever they went, and tackling walks and climbs wherever he ended up. He managed to get a ride from Picton—a small coastal town on the north of the South Island on the edge of Queen Charlotte Sound—across the top of the South Island to the rugged west coast. This was an isolated route at the best of times and hikers often took a week or more to put together the right combination of rides to reach their destination. The man who picked up Peter told him he was going all the way down the west coast—a fantastic ride.

In his sixties, the man drove a Morris 1100 quite quickly along the narrow winding roads. Unfortunately, he proceeded to stop at every pub for a vodka, becoming increasingly unstable on his feet and more and more erratic in his driving. Peter was scared there might be an accident, but didn't dare get out as this stretch of road was notorious for taking days to pick up a lift. Eventually, outside Greymouth, it was too much. Peter got out and started looking for a campsite, thinking he would never get another lift. But, to his amazement, he was picked up almost immediately by a beekeeper who took him down to the town. By this time six fresh eggs which Peter had been carrying in his pack were crushed and leaking all over his gear. He was so tired that for once he decided to pay for a cabin. He got out his wet, egg-covered sleeping bag and went straight to sleep.

Peter found all the people who stopped to be very friendly and helpful. One man took him home. 'I'll fix you up with a woman,' he said, and proceeded to make lots of phone calls. Peter remembers a comfortable bed that night but no woman!

Another time, when sleeping out, Peter was approached by a woman. 'Did you know you're sleeping in a graveyard?' she asked. 'You'd better come home with me.' This kind lady also gave Peter a copy of the famous book *Zen and the Art of Motorcycle Maintenance* which he read on his trip.

A man and his daughter in a Mercedes and towing a speed boat stopped for Peter and invited him to join them. Peter spent a few enjoyable days with them, water skiing.

An older couple picked him up and asked if he would like to join them for a few days. They were on their holiday, they explained. Peter stayed with them at an impressive large white guest house called The Chateau, the couple paying for Peter's accommodation and meals!

It was a dream run and the young Peter Treseder was on a high. Past Invercargill at the bottom of the South Island, he reached the town of Bluff. Arriving late in the day, he was ready to take the ferry to Stewart Island the next day. With nowhere to sleep and the rain falling, he decided to find the harbour and the ferry. Climbing on board he asked a crew member if he could sleep on board. 'Yes,' was the reply. 'Put your sleeping bag on deck under cover.'

The grateful Peter prepared for bed. Just then the chef came on board and after greeting Peter told him not to sleep on deck but instead to take a cabin down below. Later he offered breakfast and said they wouldn't even charge him.

Following a good night's sleep and a big breakfast, the ferry motored out of Bluff Harbour into Foveaux Strait. This can be a rough stretch of water and the journey this day was no exception. Everyone was sick. The crew were busy chucking up over the side but Peter was determined to keep his free breakfast down. He succeeded past Ruapuke Island and the Muttonbird Islands until the ferry reached Halfmoon Bay just near Paterson Inlet, when he heaved it all over the side like the others. 'Later I walked around Stewart Island which had lots of suspension bridges over deep ravines. These made me feel seasick again as the motion was very similar to that on the ferry. I had to walk very gingerly!' Peter smiles.

Back up the middle of the South Island, Peter reached the Arthurs Pass National Park and the town of Arthurs Pass with another good ride. Again, not wanting to spend any money, Peter found a large picnic shelter with tables and benches and plenty of cover from the rain. 'There was a large "No Camping" sign on the wall, but no-one seemed to mind my gear,' Peter says. 'I set myself up with somewhere to sleep and cook my food.'

Leaving the shelter early the following morning, he walked across the main road through the park up to the south ridge of Mount O'Malley. From here Peter hiked up to the 1859-metre Mount Aicken and further up to Blimit at 1921 metres, where he continued his solo traverse of the Arthurs Pass Circuit via Mount Temple and the 1965 metre Phipps Peak. Following Goldney Ridge, he then reached Mount Rolleston at 2275 metres, the highest part of his traverse, and then on to Avalanche Peak, Lyell Peak and Mount Bealey and down to the junction of the Bealey and Mingha rivers at the Department of Conservation Greyneys Shelter from which he had started just two days earlier.

This would have been a tremendous achievement for any experienced hiker. For an 18-year-old to complete the first Australian solo traverse of the circuit was quite remarkable. But Peter Treseder was in a hurry and didn't think much about the achievement as he went on to his next, never looking back.

It was time for some serious ice climbing instruction and Peter made his way back to the village of Mount Cook in the National Park where he met up again with Skin. They made their temporary home in a day shelter. Not far away, guests enjoyed fine wine and food in the plush Hermitage Hotel, the social centre of the village. Located below the Hotel was the

Alpine Guide Centre. This was Peter and Skin's destination as they contemplated the best way to gain more rock and ice experience. Calculating that this strategy would provide them with more personal tuition, the two young men decided to hire a personal alpine guide rather than go on a group course.

In the event, it was a sound decision because the organised groups did not even venture out in the atrocious weather. It was not too daunting, however, for legendary Swiss mountain guide, Max Dorfluegger. Max had an awesome reputation, having made the first solo ascent of the Caroline Face of Mount Cook. Not that Peter and Andrew knew anything about that at the time.

Before they started their intensive training the pair enjoyed Christmas in Mount Cook village. 'We drank weak-tasting New Zealand beer and sang Christmas carols in the local church,' Peter remembers, 'and we felt rather drunk and homesick at the same time.'

Using the facilities around them had become second nature to the travellers, and they made good use of the Hermitage laundries and drying facilities to wash their clothes. There were huge dryers which were used to dry snow-soaked gear and into this went everything. 'Andrew always wore a woollen balaclava which had become a sort of trademark,' Peter recalls. 'He put it in the dryer at The Hermitage and couldn't find it when he took the rest of his clothes out. Eventually, after almost climbing into the dryer, he found a small hard lump of wool. It had shrunk to about 5 centimetres square!'

Andrew and Peter hired boots and crampons and an ice axe each from the Alpine Centre and Max took them out. Their first trip was to the Murchison Glacier. This meant a long hike of more than 30 kilometres through the mountains and across the Murchison River complete with mini icebergs in the water. The group took off most of their clothes and waded across holding up their packs to keep them dry. They continued walking to the terminal face where Max taught them the techniques of self arresting on the ice slopes and how to use ice screws. Peter and Andrew were keen students and learnt many new skills from their personal tuition.

On a second trip their route took them via the Tasman River and the

Murchison River towards the Malte Brun Range. They walked with Max up a wide open grassy slope, climbing about 1000 metres, but were unconcerned about potential dangers as both were experienced bushwalkers. The slippery grass slope, however, caused Max a great deal of worry as he led his young charges higher and higher into the mountains. One slip and the fall would have been long and probably fatal.

The weather closed in even more as they roped up and climbed higher. They built an ice cave in a blizzard at about 2600 metres and Max gave them the option of staying there overnight or pressing on over the peak and back to Mount Cook Village. The decision was made and the trio made their way over the high pass and then glissaded down the slopes on the other side. To glissade is to 'ski without skis', a technique that involves 'skiing' on your boot soles, maybe using an ice axe for support. In practice you also use your backside from time to time. It makes the descent of a snow slope remarkably quick.

Using this technique they reached the Tasman River again by which time Skin was physically exhausted and finding it difficult to continue. Sharing his pack between them, Max and Peter helped him back down to Balls Hut and safety.

From the Malte Brun Pass Peter had seen the Caroline Face of Mount Cook. It looked impressive even from that distance. Max told Peter in an offhand sort of way that he had climbed it and explained the route he had taken. At the time Peter did not recognise the significance of what he had been told—nor the level of difficulty of the climb.

Peter was keen to continue with their climbing but Andrew had had enough. He decided to return to Sydney so Andrew and Peter left the mountains and went together to Christchurch where Peter saw Andrew off from the airport, telling him that he would continue hitching around New Zealand.

Once Andrew was safely on the plane, Peter's dissatisfaction with his own achievements took hold and he went straight back to Mount Cook, hired boots and crampons and one ice axe (at that time he didn't know about using two) and immediately set out to climb the Caroline Face of Mount Cook.

In anyone's terms this was a foolhardy expedition undertaken by an inexperienced and over-confident young man. In hindsight Peter shakes his head and remarks that he was lucky not to have fallen. 'I would never attempt anything like that again,' he says with feeling. 'Even now I can't quite believe what I did.'

Clearly Peter had some burning desire to do something more, to conquer everything in sight and he was too impatient to wait. With his hired equipment and a pack, he headed off and reached the base of the climb.

The High Peak of Mount Cook is 12 349 feet (3700 metres). The New Zealand Alpine Club handbook describes the climb as 'requiring the utmost experience and fitness'. The route takes the climber up the Caroline Glacier, over debris at the foot of the rib that continues right up to Middle Peak. 'There are three rock steps, the middle one being the most difficult and the upper one the most unstable,' the guide continues. 'Above this climb a broken area, then traverse left into a steep ice gully, climb this then gain the rib again and continue to a broad shelf. This is the last feasible chance to escape.'

Using Max's unwitting instructions and the techniques he had just been taught, Peter took off up the climb. He got about two thirds of the way up and realised what he had done. 'I was petrified,' Peter recalls. 'I had no skill to go back and had to continue to the top. There was no way I could go down or back out.'

Peter completed the climb to Middle Peak then across Summit Ridge to the peak. He took a different route down and recorded the climb with the authorities. All his climbs were 'official'—you had to register your intentions and your return via radios at all the huts.

In the next week Peter did two more climbs which were a 'snack' compared with the Caroline Face of Mount Cook. One of these was a second climb of Mount Cook from a different direction. Peter completed this as a return trip in one day which was also considered very quick and unusual. Climbers don't even do that today.

Peter's route took him from the Hermitage Hotel in the village up the Hooker Glacier to Empress Hut and Earles Route to the peak, returning the same way. The first climb, however, was the ascent and descent of the West Ridge of Malte Brun starting from the Malte Brun hut on the Tasman Glacier.

According to experienced mountaineer Peter Radcliffe, New Zealand's mountains are, generally speaking, made of inferior quality rock. This makes head protection essential, and the unwary need to be careful of falling and breaking rock. Climbers usually go in parties of two or more for safety. Peter's solo route took him up the west ridge of Malte Brun, via slabs and buttresses and culminating in a solo traverse of the 'Cheval pitch' so named because it is best negotiated in a 'riding' position. The peak is 2415 metres above sea level.

Why was Peter—who had earned his Rock Climbing Instructor's Certificate only the previous month—in such a hurry? 'My holiday time was running out,' he explains, 'and I wanted to get a few more climbs in before returning to Sydney in time for my HSC exam results.'

Chapter 5
Mickey Mouse Ran up the Clock

'The reasonable man adapts himself to the world; the unreasonable one persists in trying to adapt the world to himself. Therefore, all progress depends on the unreasonable man.'

George Bernard Shaw

Peter arrived home in late January 1976, having established several impressive 'firsts' during his two months in New Zealand. His exam results were good. Hard work had produced straight A's and Peter earned his university place, matriculating to any university in Australia. The choice was his.

Within a few weeks he had started his studies at Macquarie University with a view to obtaining a BA Dip Ed in primary teaching. One of the advantages to the ever-careful-with-money Peter was the teacher's scholarship that came with this course. 'I got paid to go to university rather than having to pay for it,' Peter says. 'And then there were the potential long holidays that came with teaching. I knew this would give me plenty of time to pursue my outdoor activities.'

On his first day at Macquarie, Peter turned up in good clothes and shoes. 'It was the first and only time I ever wore anything respectable,' Peter says. 'From that day on I wore thongs and shorts and a T-shirt. I was not a good dresser.'

Standing around on that orientation day, Peter saw someone walking along with a climbing rope over his shoulder. Naturally he was curious and asked the man what he was doing. 'I'm going to climb E8C', he said. 'Can I watch?' was Peter's reply and the two walked off towards the target building, one of the university's tallest.

Keith Royce was at the time the President of the Sydney Rock Climbing

Club, and well known for his climbing exploits. A mature age student, he had been around Macquarie for some years and did some tutoring as well as his own study. They waited for Keith's climbing companion for about half an hour, talking about climbing. Then Keith offered, 'He's obviously not going to turn up, would you like to climb with me?'

Peter belayed off the concrete seat they had been sitting on, and Keith commenced the climb, using ledges at every storey, until he reached the eighth and the roof. Belaying himself off he signalled to Peter to start his climb. 'I'd never climbed a building before and it was a strange experience in my good shoes and pants,' Peter recalls.

On the way up, Keith had pointed into the sixth storey window. When Peter reached the same level he looked through the glass to see an older man and a young woman hard at it on the desk. He knocked on the window and waved. The man didn't stop but Peter remembers his purple face. 'It looked as if it would burst! I climbed up to the top, scrambling up over each ledge. Uni went downhill for me after that day,' Peter adds. 'The first year was much the same as school and I worked hard to get good grades. But in the second year I lost my way.'

Peter's undergraduate life was not unlike that of his fellow students. Study, part time work, parties, drinking and girls. Except that Peter also continued his expeditions which took priority over almost everything else—including girls!

Wendy claims there were only 'dorky mates and no girlfriends until Beth'. And it was true that Peter didn't chase girls and Beth was his first real girlfriend. He'd rather go bushwalking! This wasn't so much a difficulty in forming relationships, rather a single-minded attention to the outdoors and his real first love—nature—which didn't leave much time for girls.

But eventually Peter met the girl who was to become his soul-mate. Beth and he started a romance that was to stretch for six years before they were married. They met at a Union night in August 1977. Peter was drinking with friends including Andrew Stiff, while Trevor Knight played Beatles' songs and singalong ballads on his guitar. Beth came along with a friend as part of the group. It is worth noting that the only time in his life that Peter regularly consumed alcohol was during his Uni years. As he recalls, 'I may have been blotto on the floor when I met Beth. I used to drink a bit at Uni.'

'We have the same values,' says Beth these days, 'and when we first met we had long discussions about all sorts of things.'

Family values, including the importance of children and a stable home environment, were common topics. Beth and Peter had both taken casual jobs as teenagers and viewed their self-sufficiency as important too. There was little intellectual discussion as Peter was not paying much attention to his studies—and Beth's lack of knowledge of the outdoors hindered conversation on that subject.

Of course, meeting Beth was hardly going to stop Peter's outdoor activities. In fact he started taking Beth with him on some excursions, even though she had no previous outdoor experience. Their first trip was to Colong Caves with the group from uni. They arrived late at night and she had no idea what to expect. 'It was a long way—much further than I thought,' recalls Beth. 'We walked down a big spur and Andy lost a big salami out of his esky, the major part of his food supply for the weekend. It was the first time I had ever encountered leeches and I wore brand new overalls I had bought. I enjoyed the caving but the walk out was horrendous. It was so difficult for me that I threw up from the physical effort.'

It appears that Peter may have been something of a shock to Beth's conservative family. An only child, the daughter of a mother who was herself an only child, Beth was always well dressed while Peter usually turned up in thongs and shorts and a T-shirt, often just before or after training. Beth's mum was a bit wary of him at first, but his relationship with her has matured into one of mutual trust and understanding. At the time, Beth's father was sick, although working, and the house, according to Peter, was 'dominated by women. It was a very feminine house, which was quite alien to me,' he remembers.

Much of Peter and Beth's weekend fun was with the group from Uni. This group varied but, among others, included Greg Charlton, Margaret Charlton, Phil Bourne, Sally Stiff, Andrew Stiff, Rodney Anderson and Michael McAuliffe. Peter organised occasional caving and bushwalking trips with these friends—most of whom were not particularly experienced in the outdoors. They were more like social events than serious expeditions for Peter. The group also went to see films and enjoyed parties, dances and discos together. In other words, behaved just like uni students. At last Beth finally managed to get Peter alone from the rest of the group.

'We went to a wedding at Young,' Beth recalls, 'travelling in Peter's little red sports car. It suffered from the "dreaded drip" where the soft top joined the window. It was so cold we wrapped ourselves in sleeping bags as the heater didn't work. Then the windscreen wipers fell off, the gear stick knob fell off and the passenger window glass fell down into the door, never to be raised again. It was extremely wet. Then the exhaust pipe fell off—but apart from that it was very reliable!'

Peter continued with his serious outdoor activities right through his university days. Dave Drohan, whom he had met on early rock climbing courses with the Scouts, became a regular climbing companion. A member of the Carlingford Venturer Unit, Dave became a good long term friend. Later, he was one of the members of the Rock Squad which Peter and his friends formed as an unofficial rescue organisation. 'I told everyone in the Rock Squad that it was unlikely the authorities would ever use our services,' Peter explains, 'but we were a resource if needed. In fact, a number of us used the skills we developed in rescue situations we handled personally because we were in the outdoors so much.'

Mark Foster had been a student at Normanhurst Boys High School in the year behind Peter and he too was a member of the Venturer Unit. He remembers that he and Peter used to go climbing all the time, when they were at uni. 'We started by doing a lot of Queen Scout stuff together,' Mark says, 'including expeditions and other activities as well as the climbing. This continued right through uni.'

Peter joined 1st Beecroft Rovers with a number of other young men from the Unit including one of Linc Madden's sons. The crew only survived for about twelve months and Peter wasn't the only person to be disappointed with their style. The Pennant Hills boys went along to a crew meeting to discuss the program, and Peter Schofield was their spokesman, outlining plans for the same sort of expeditions they had been used to as Venturers.

The crew was mixed and one particularly forceful female suggested, 'You children sit over there and work out what you want to do while we adults get on with more seemly activities.' They didn't stay long with the armchair travellers.

Although he was still officially a Rover, Peter took a break from Scouting, until Linc asked him to come back to help Venturers. By then Peter was 21, the minimum age you could apply for a warrant as an Assistant Venturer Leader. Linc was District Venturer Leader. Peter had completed his 'Intention to Apply for a Warrant' form, and began assisting with meetings and activities. Then the Venturer Leader had to go away and Peter was left temporarily in charge. Linc arrived at a meeting to overhear Peter telling the boys they would be going canyoning that weekend in the Blue Mountains.

This presented a problem as five boys had not even completed their preliminary rock craft course and Peter had not submitted any paperwork, which needed at least a week's notice. Linc recalls, 'Peter got really pissed off with my decision to cancel the trip on safety grounds and left the meeting. He didn't proceed with his Warrant and never came back to the Unit.'

Peter and Mark's friendship endured however, principally through climbing. 'We were both climbing at the hard end and pushing each other all the time,' Mark says. 'I can remember climbing every weekend of the first semester, probably with Peter, and doing bouldering at Lindfield Rocks to build our strength and technique.'

In Mark's early uni days there was also a walking trip to Tasmania. 'Pete got sick on this trip,' Mark recalls. 'He became totally disinterested in walking, which was very unlike him. After a few days he decided to go home, only to discover it was a tick.'

On another occasion, Mark and Peter went on a Bundeena to Otford walk in the Royal National Park. Not a slow walker himself, Mark understood this was to be a day walk. At the start of the walk Peter announced that he wanted to run it. 'I had come down for a day walk, not a cross country run and was a bit put out by Peter's expectations,' Mark says. 'In the end we agreed on a compromise and we walked and ran the track in turn, finishing by lunchtime.'

During the walk Peter almost trod on a black snake. Mark leapt at him, pushing Peter one way and jumping the other way himself to avoid the snake.

'Another weekend we went climbing in the Warrambungles,' Mark continues. 'We started out at 5am in Sydney in Peter's old Spitfire. We didn't think about petrol and on Bell's Line of Road realised we would soon run out. There was an old servo at the junction of the road to Mount Victoria but it was not open when we arrived at about 6am. I was content to sit and wait until it opened but Peter saw a cottage nearby and went over and woke up the occupants. He didn't even know if they were the servo people! Somehow he managed to get the owner to come over and open up and serve us petrol—and without grumbling. Peter didn't like to waste time.'

Peter was always 'fairly independent' according to Mark and wanted to do increasingly harder things. During his uni years Peter began to expand his variety of expeditions into kayaking rivers and oceans and this left him less time for climbing. Mark believes that Peter decided at some point that he didn't want to climb rocks any more and made a conscious decision to stop climbing. It could have been that Peter had achieved as much as he could with rock climbing and wanted to move on to new challenges.

It was Mark who gave Peter the opportunity for a set of new challenges—the traditional University of New South Wales 'stunts'. Mark invited Peter to join the team—mostly medical students—and he proceeded to play a key part in the stunts for the next few years. Every year the UNSW Student Union issued instructions and challenges to the students for stunts and a 'scavenging list' of difficult objects to collect. It required skill and daring.

The first year of Peter's involvement the team climbed the clock tower at Central Station and turned one face into a Mickey Mouse clock. 'We draped three painted double bed sheets across the face and fixed plywood hands to the clock hands,' Peter says. 'Another time we also broke into the Atomic Energy Commission by scaling two security fences to capture a sign.'

But that wasn't all. The students had a full program for the muck-up week! One of the items on the list was the doormat from the Masonic Club in Sydney. 'We thought that this would be a normal doormat, but it turned out to be as big as a car. We took it anyway, rolled it up and transported it in a VW. We also took every flag in Martin Place and every life buoy from every Manly Ferry at Circular Quay.'

These were well planned commando raids complete with diversions and distractions to keep security guards off the track. 'Often the hardest part was getting all the stuff back the next day without being caught,' Peter says. 'We were careful not to damage anything and we always took all the signs and objects back.'

In the second year the team climbed Government House in Macquarie Street and between two flagpoles hung a huge 30 metre banner which proclaimed 'Ministry of Silly Walks'. The wording, of course, was taken from John Cleese's famous sketches in 'Monty Python's Flying Circus'. There was substantial media coverage.

In the third year however things went badly wrong. The target was a twelve storey tower, the Applied Science building at the university which had a clock on the tenth storey outer wall. The idea was to remove the hands. Unfortunately they were too big to get in through the windows so Peter and Mark moved towards the roof to abseil down the outside. Suddenly there was an armed guard shouting 'Stop or I'll shoot!' 'We just panicked,' says Peter.

He recalls running and running and finally outrunning a growing group of security guards. Although he had recently badly sprained his ankle on an expedition to Mount Solitary, his pain was forgotten in full flight.

The next target was to revisit the Central Station Clock Tower. This time, four faces of the clock were to be covered—a much more complicated and risky venture. They worked out that it required a team of seventeen people. Four to each face—two abseiling and two supporting—plus one odd job person at the top. Neil Treseder remembers painting the Mickey Mouse clock hands on the floor at Westleigh. He was invited to join the prank but declined because his application to join the Police was in train and he didn't want to damage his chances of acceptance.

Getting into the locked building at Central meant climbing onto a low roof, then through a window into the well-secured clock tower, then down to the doors, opening them from the inside to let the crews in one at a time with torch signals. Once they were all in they deadlocked the door and climbed to the roof.

It was run like a full military operation and Peter went over the side with Steve Trémont, an ex commando. After a very short time as they fitted the faces to the clock, they could see reporters in Eddy Avenue and hear sirens coming from all directions. They had a great view of the city and could see Police vehicles in large numbers.

'We didn't know at the time but we were getting live radio coverage. We could hear banging on the door down below, while we were still working on all four faces,' Peter remembers.

Once the signs were fixed the teams made their escape across the roof of Central Station and attempted to abseil off the far side. Everyone except two students were caught. They were arrested, handcuffed, put into paddy wagons, and taken to the old Central Station Police Station. While the officers and security guards—and there'd been about 20 to 30 of them all up, a ratio of two or three to each student—behaved with great seriousness, the students were busy laughing and taking pictures of each other being arrested.

They all spent the night in the cells and in the morning the Union solicitor came to see them. The prank was all over the newspapers and news broadcasts. But in court it was apparent that even the police prosecutor thought it was all a huge joke and there were smiles all around.

As the *Sun* newspaper reported on 31 July 1980: 'Fifteen University of New South Wales students climbed 64 metres up Central Railway's historic clock tower to pin cartoons of Mickey Mouse, Donald Duck, Fred Flintstone and Prime Minister Malcolm Fraser across the clock faces.'

Lawyer K.J. Burke told the court it was listed as an 'outrageous stunt' on the scavenging list of the University's Foundation Day celebrations. The students were charged with offensive behaviour, but Mr J. Flynn, Stipendiary Magistrate, said in view of previous good behaviour he would dismiss the charges after finding the case proved.

Peter obviously needed money to finance some of his expeditions, some of which were a long way from Sydney. He had a small income from his scholarship, but the majority of his money came from his own efforts.

He worked the milk run all through uni, but dropped the fruit shop job shortly after starting his studies. He then found a job that began a lifelong association and an impetus to his own outdoor adventures. On Thursday evenings and Saturday mornings from about 1979 to 1983 Peter worked at Paddy Pallin, the outdoor clothing and equipment store. Paddy himself was still alive then, and was regarded as the doyen of the outdoor equipment scene and a pioneer bushwalker. 'One of my jobs was to make up Paddy's secret proofing formula for japara,' Peter recalls. 'I was sworn to secrecy as this special recipe was considered to make Paddy Pallin's japara coats more weatherproof than anyone else's. I also had to boil the wax and iron it into new tents to waterproof them, and I usually did this at home, ruining Mum's iron in the process.'

In the 1970s and '80s Nick Gooch was the Manager of Paddy Pallin's in Kent Street and he and Peter got talking one day. Peter must have mentioned doing a walk in a day and a half or something and Gooch said 'Oh, Gee, that's pretty fast!' He told Peter he had a list of records in his filing cabinet upstairs and gave Peter a photocopy. It was quite clear that some of Peter's walking times were faster than the records. There were some quite outstanding records set by Warwick Daniels, John Fantini—a legendary character in the Australian outdoors—and Ray Jerrems, all of which have been beaten now, but in those days they included the original 3 Peaks records and others that had stood for 20 years. Nick had recorded them faithfully and the men had supplied him with their times over the years. That's where Peter got his base for the records and got started. He thought he could improve them.

'I remember visiting some of these guys,' Peter goes on. 'I went to Ray Jerrems' house one night and talked about some of the Kosciuszko records.' When *Wild* magazine started, Nick Gooch originally sent the records to the editor for publication, and the original records Peter broke had Nick's name as reporter of the events. Later Peter sent details of his own trips direct to the magazine.

MICKEY MOUSE RAN UP THE CLOCK

Once Peter realised that some of his own times were better than the official records he set out to systematically attempt every record and beat it. But Peter wanted to smash the records, not just to break them by ten per cent or something small, thinking of what people might be able to do a long time in the future. 'I was always aware that I could walk these trips faster than anyone else. I was always coming out quicker. I was always going in and when people would say it'll take you three days to walk to Kanangra, I'd come out in a day and a half. We'd always come out of our trips early—we were never late, because I used to push it a bit. I used to find it reasonably easy to do that.'

This exemplifies Peter's attitude to his expeditions. He is never content to just do better than someone else—he has to completely change the way people look at the activity and the time it takes to complete it. 'It was something I was good at and I just continued to go through the record book, rewriting the times as I went,' Peter explains.

Later Peter became a guide for the Paddy Pallin Blue Mountains Expedition Company—a guided tour operation in the Blue Mountains. The best part was that they let him drive Robert Pallin's Volvo up to the Blue Mountains where his job was to escort paying customers on bushwalks. But they were mostly American tourists and Peter was very frustrated by how slow they were.

Peter now started to branch out with his expeditions. He no longer had any restrictions placed on him by parents or Scout leaders and was sufficiently skilled and experienced to go solo. Characteristically, his expeditions were clearly stepping stones for something bigger, even though most people would have been satisfied with the results as they stood.

During the next couple of years Peter developed his skills in river and sea kayaking while continuing with climbing, canyoning and bushwalking. Many of his trips were not documented however and while he may have broken no records with them, they were frequent and challenging.

At the time and for the next couple of years, Peter was busy locating and descending a large number of canyons, many of which it is reasonable to assume had never before been descended. Claustral and other major canyons that were easier to access had first been descended in the 1960s and this was the new batch.

He started with the first descent of Fortitude and Anembo canyons in the Blue Mountains in March 1976. Basically these were found through a navigation error. Peter was looking for what seemed from the map to be a very big canyon. Twice he took a wrong route—but the upshot was he discovered these two.

Walking along Rail Motor Ridge in an easterly direction, Peter had turned south down what he thought was this big new canyon. As he descended he realised it was too small. This was Fortitude, as yet unnamed. Climbing back up around the canyon, he continued to walk in an easterly direction and then turned south again down another canyon, now called Crikey. Then it was called Anembo, an aboriginal name meaning 'Peaceful Place'.

Crikey is a set of six abseils and is now considered a classic canyon, although very remote. Peter's trip back was an epic hike and he never did find the canyon further east.

The end of May 1977 saw Peter launching his standard fibreglass kayak into the ocean from the Esplanade in Cairns in northern Queensland. His 250 kilometre route would take him up the coast, famous for its crocodiles, and across the ocean to Lizard Island. This was the impetus for the much bigger trips he would make in later years, including the Timor Sea and Bass Strait. In today's terms these original trips are nothing spectacular but, at the time, no-one was attempting these sorts of sea trips in canoes—and sea kayaks, as we know them now, were not even heard of.

Peter's day started early, before daybreak, and continued until just before dusk. 'I pushed myself physically and mentally,' he recounts, 'paddling really long hours.'

The big tides and shallow beaches meant he had to be very watchful of mudbanks and the risk of being stranded in the mornings or being overrun by the incoming tide. He camped each night, dragging the canoe sometimes hundreds of metres up the mudbanks to safety from the incoming tide. On this trip he didn't see any crocodiles, but even so was cautious and a bit afraid, particularly when camping. He camped on Lizard Island, then turned round and paddled all the way back. It was a 500 kilometre round trip, which he completed in about four days.

Peter then immediately took his canoe down the coast and launched it towards Fraser Island, the largest sand island in the world. His circumnavigation took another four days but after the Lizard Island trip Peter regarded it as 'a bit of a holiday. It was very straightforward, in sight of land and I was able to land whenever I wanted to. I camped each night—and saw no crocodiles!'

Shortly afterwards, in June 1977, Peter descended every major cave in Bungonia Reserve. He descended all these to the known sumps at the time, except for Grill Cave which showed unacceptable levels of carbon dioxide approximately 40 metres from the bottom of the left hand branch. He covered all ground between the caves on foot and carried all his gear.

Peter had done all these caves before, many of them a number of times. And his experience had been built up over the years starting with Scout trips. This was the culmination. What else was there to do? He was ready to push himself hard to complete them all in one continuous attempt. This meant being tired both physically and mentally. The trick was to stay mentally alert. 'You have to constantly ask yourself,' Peter says, 'Have you belayed safely? Have you tied a knot in the end of the rope?'

He did, and he completed the descents in two days.

A few months later, in August 1977, Peter launched his kayak again, this time at the Normanby Tin Workings on the Normanby River in Queensland. Travelling north, Peter descended the length of the river to Princess Charlotte Bay. Then, on successfully completing this trip, he travelled to the Coleman River and proceeded to descend east to west to the Gulf of Carpentaria.

By now Peter had done a lot of reading and research about various areas of Australia and had a good knowledge of what had and had not been attempted and achieved. No-one had done these trips before and the challenge was on. 'I felt physically sick all the time from the fear of crocs,' Peter says, 'even though I had no problem. I was really scared, petrified.'

Although reasonably well accessed by roads and fire trails, making escape possible if necessary, neither of these rivers had ever been descended before by kayak. Again that 'first time' motivation spurred Peter on—and provided his introduction to Cape York and crocodiles. 'It was wild country,' Peter recalls, 'and I hitched with my boat both between the two trips and to get out.'

Back on dry land, Peter travelled in December to the southern end of Australia. Once in Tasmania, he found his way to Frenchmans Cap off the Lyell Highway. First climbed by surveyor James Sprent in 1832, Frenchmans Cap is, according to Chris Dewhirst in the pocket climbers' guide, a 'proud and imperial quartzite peak'. Chris Baxter was somewhat more eloquent in 1972 saying, 'You climb close with a friend in the vast white loneliness, the silence rushing up from that sombre, green, unfathomed bush, a thousand miles below.'

The Sydney Route on the sheer south-east face is considered difficult, a grade 15 climb. Pioneered in the 1960s, no-one had tackled it alone and it had become part of rock climbers' mythology, becoming the most popular climb up the main face.

Peter had seen Frenchmans Cap on several occasions and had walked to the peak. He'd seen it again when he canoed the Franklin River and was now determined to make a solo attempt.

The climbing notes give belaying instructions which provide for safety when climbing in pairs or in small groups. These instructions, however, offer no protection to the solo climber, who must rely entirely on his own skill to stay on the rock and not fall to certain death. Since Peter hates heights the 1280 foot peak would have scared him all the way up to the peak. But he was the first Australian, and possibly the first climber ever, to ascend this magnificent route solo.

Not everything went according to plan for the young adventurer during these university years however. Peter was, by his own account, 'a fast driver' at a time when radar traps and drink driving legislation were unheard of. He had a succession of 'bomb' cars, and none of them lasted very long. In them he suffered a number of accidents and more than his fair share of strandings and breakdowns.

One afternoon, in his EH Holden, Peter was driving home from Macquarie University along Sutherland Road in Beecroft. This 'switchback' road runs alongside the railway line and was generally considered to be the 'back way' before the M2 construction bisected it near Epping.

'I had just received a great mark for a philosophy essay on "mind and body" from my lecturer Tanya Bailey and felt really good with a good mark for a difficult topic,' Peter recalls. 'I was driving along Sutherland Road where it has double dips and a big drop. I had always felt that I could jump all four wheels off the ground at the top of the rise and gunned the car up the hill and over the top. As I became airborne I saw a car with a lady driver stopped at the bottom of the hill waiting to turn right. Without her I would have been OK,' he continues. 'I hit the brakes in mid air, which was completely ineffective. I came crashing down on the road, swerved and missed her, rolled the car a couple of times and stopped hanging upside down held by the seat belt.'

The engine fell out of the car but luckily no-one was hurt. The lady was very nice about it and took Peter to her home where he did the right thing and telephoned the police. He was booked for negligent driving and wrote the car off. A tow truck took it home.

Peter's driving started when he was about 14. His friend, Greg Charlton, lived nearby and his Mum had a Simca which Peter and Greg took for illegal joy rides before they had licences. There was a 'drag strip' on a nearby dirt road. 'You'd see this cloud of dust coming down the road,' Peter says. 'The Simca would come flying past, as we timed each other to see how fast we could go!'

'I'm a hell of a lot safer driver now,' Peter adds. 'I know now that a touch of something at speed can send you into a complete spin. The accidents have made me a lot more cautious.'

Many of Peter's trips in those days were some way away from home, and any time spent driving was time not available for the activity. 'I drove with Dave Drohan from Carlingford to Smiggins car park in 4 hours 20 minutes on the old Razorback road, doing 140 kph all the way down,' Peter says. 'It was just the way we drove, chatting all the way down. It seemed quite safe and was a standard sort of trip.'

Ultimately, Peter inherited his mum's white Ford Escort. But by that time it had seen a lot of Peter's activity already. When Mum still owned it, Peter and Mark Foster had taken it to Coolamine caves down a steep, muddy track with bogged 4WDs and even an NRMA vehicle. The little Escort flew past them all. 'We weren't going to stop,' Peter said. 'We wanted to get to the caves to do some caving.'

Peter and Mark did their caving, but couldn't get back up the hill so they decided to go out the other side. 'It was full of washaways and water splashes and we were ultimately bogged,' Peter says. 'I had to go home without the car and tell Mum it would be two weeks before we could get it out. She wasn't too happy about that.'

Often, half the battle was getting the car in and out of places where they went. Whether they were going walking or caving or climbing, they still had to get into quite remote places with terrible roads. On one occasion they took Mum's Escort to Batch camp for Colong Caves. Peter had checked the spare tyre, which was always dodgy, as he knew they could get in trouble on the isolated road. They went in, caved all weekend, came back to the car and saw it had one flat tyre. Peter put the spare on and it promptly went down. They then spent a lot of time driving the other car to Oberon and back to get the spare fixed.

Another time with Mark on a trip to Kanangra the car wouldn't start. Between them they traced the trouble to the carburettor float and fixed it—amazing given that neither of them knew what they were doing!

On another trip the car got a fist-sized hole in the petrol tank. They got to the tar and put a billy under the hole and caught the last of the fuel. They were in the middle of nowhere. They took some tar from the side of the road, melted it over a small stove, gummed up the hole and poured the petrol back, managing to get the car going and reaching the next petrol station. But tar reacts with petrol and dissolves, so they still had a problem. They kept repeating the process until the hole was so well plugged Peter drove the car for another month before getting it fixed properly.

The end for the Escort came one evening when Peter was driving north up the Pacific Highway in the gutter lane at Pymble. 'Grant Clark and

Margaret Lattimore were in the car behind me,' Peter recalls. 'We were heading home after climbing at Lindfield Rocks. I was playing Credence Clearwater full blast when a car came from the opposite direction, cut through the slow moving traffic to turn right in front of me and clipped me as I went past. The Escort rolled down the lane, luckily hitting no other cars but ending up against a telegraph pole.'

Peter found himself upside down again. But his only injury was a small piece of glass in his hand. 'The cut healed,' he says, 'and twelve months later the glass popped out while I was walking in Tasmania.'

Around this time in his life Peter suffered another accident, probably the most serious he has ever had. 'We were into everything and never paid for lessons. We just taught ourselves. I bought an old hang glider from an Australian champion for $30. It was only a glider, not one that could lift. With Greg Charlton, Michael McAuliffe and some others I went to Kurnell on a really windy day. Half way up a huge sand dune I jumped off and got a terrific glide for about half a kilometre. I decided to go back up to the top next time. Meanwhile, the experts were packing up and going home because the conditions were too rough.

'I reached the top and it was so windy it took three guys to hold me down while I strapped in. The whole glider shook. "OK guys, let me go," I said. They let me go and I shot several hundred feet straight up in the air and went backwards. Now this glider wasn't supposed to do that! I pulled the bar back as hard as I could but it wouldn't descend and eventually I lost control completely and was thrown to the ground with a thump by the strength of the wind.

'I was pretty badly smashed around and the wind rolled the glider and me down the beach for a kilometre or so with the others chasing after me to try and stop it. My eyes were full of sand, there was lots of blood all over my face, my nose was broken.

'They caught me and got me to the car. No one knew where the hospital was so Michael said, "I'm just going to drive as fast as I can until a cop pulls me over so we can find out where to go."'

Sure enough, he was soon pulled over and hastily explained the situation.

Peter was put in the front seat of the police car and raced off to hospital. The nurses cleaned him up and his nose was set. The tip of his nose had been ripped open and needed stitches. 'You can see everything on the end of your nose,' Peter says. 'The nurse put two stitches through it without any further anaesthetic and I nearly went through the roof.'

It took a week or more for Peter to recuperate, during which time he made a huge and very complex macrame pot holder which still has pride of place in the front room of his parents' house.

'It's really the only bad accident I've ever had,' says Peter. 'After that we had a ceremonial burning of the hang glider and I've never been hang gliding since.'

Back at home Peter and Neil were still sharing a bedroom. To get some privacy Neil moved in and out of the windowless den in the garage that had originally been built for Peter as a study. Neil would regularly put his bed out there but never stayed very long as it was quite unpleasant without light and fresh air.

Neil also took issue with Peter over his dirt bike which he used to ride after school. He came home one day and it was gone. Peter had taken it to ride to Beth's. 'I was pretty annoyed when I got home to find the bike missing. Then we had a call to go and get Peter and the bike. Peter had been picked up by the police who charged him with riding the bike with no helmet, no licence, and on the footpath. It was poetic justice, we thought!'

This was a typical selfish action for Peter, but completely logical from his point of view. The bike was there and he wanted to go to Beth's. Therefore Peter took the bike. The fact that this might upset someone else's plans didn't even enter his head.

Meanwhile, Peter was becoming increasingly disillusioned with university study. 'During my second year at Uni I started to turn off from the material,' he explains. 'It was very theoretical and I just switched off. My mind was on other things, particularly my outdoor activities, and I started to fail courses because I just didn't turn up for lectures. I was very disillusioned with the course and wanted something more practical.'

He knew he had to end this. 'I wanted to stop the slide,' he said, 'and pull myself up.'

He did so by leaving university and joining the bank, intending to work for the bank for a year, sort himself out and then go back to uni. But it didn't work out that way and he has been with the bank ever since.

CHAPTER 6

TIGER WALKER

'Now, I'm all in favour of long endurance walks occasionally, say once or twice in a lifetime.'

Dorothy Butler, *The Barefoot Bush Walker*, 1991

Peter joined the Ryde Branch of the Commonwealth Bank of Australia as a Batch Clerk in October 1979. A Batch Clerk is the bottom rung in the banking hierarchy. By doing batches and tellers' balances, Peter worked his way up to Examiner then Teller and Teller 1, each a more senior position. 'Some telling positions were very stressful,' Peter says, 'especially on pension day with thousands of pensioners coming in with funny requests.'

In those days tellers were responsible for their own cash. At the end of the day each teller had to have a balanced cashbook and no-one could go home until everything was balanced. 'Most of the time we balanced,' Peter recalls, 'but now and again, such as on a Friday afternoon after it had been very busy, we didn't and the loan staff would have to come down to help us.'

Even back then, Peter had a vision that the place to be was in the loans department of the bank. He managed to get into that area fairly quickly and started to handle loans. His first loan applicant was a very nice looking young woman with an old man. She was there for a personal loan. 'Would you and your father like to come inside?' Peter asked.

But it wasn't her father—it was her husband! Peter was right off to a great start.

He worked his way through the lending area feeling, even 20 years ago, that branch work would have a limited life, whereas loans work would last longer, because it couldn't all be taken over by electronic processing.

There was no further formal study as there had been at university but the bank had internal training for its staff. Over the years Peter completed courses in everything from letter writing to computers, staff management to corporate policy. 'The bank has to make everything as professional as possible,' Peter says, 'so they train everyone in the correct procedure and approach for every part of the job.'

Why did Peter stay longer than his original twelve month plan? 'I hadn't stopped my outdoor activities and, in those days,' Peter explains, 'banks closed their doors at three o'clock. If the tellers balanced, we were out of there by 3.20 pm. I was able to do a lot of after hours training.'

While at Ryde Branch Peter used to run home to Westleigh—some 15 kilometres or so. He would change into his running gear with his office clothes in a back pack and run from Ryde to Macquarie Uni, down to Browns Waterhole and the Lane Cove River, to Lorna Pass across the oval and on to Westleigh and home. This is now part of the route of the Great North Walk, 'a nice piece of bush to run through'. Such training—in the bush and not on roads or running tracks—is one of the reasons Peter is, even today, so adept at running in the bush.

Although working full-time, Peter kept up lots of outdoor activities at the weekends. While still at Uni, he had bought a Triumph Spitfire in racing red. 'I bought the car as a going concern,' he says, 'but "going concern" is a relative term. It was a Mark 1 Spitfire, reasonably rare and rather old. It had been parked in a paddock and found by the parents of a school friend, Jeff Beck. They were in the Triumph sports car club and ran a spare parts business for Triumphs. When Dad and I went to see it it had grass growing out of the seats. I drove it home, did a bit of work on it with chicken wire and putty, painted over the rust and had many years of good fun.'

Often, in the winter, Peter, Mark Foster and others would drive down to the snow on a Friday night, ski all weekend and then come back in time for work on Monday morning. Peter continued to use his connection with Scouts and the group often stayed at the Scout Activity Centre at Jindabyne, bedding down in a hut or pitching a bell tent in the grounds. 'Brian Farmer, who managed the Centre, used to put us up. We bought weekly lift tickets for $25, shared the petrol costs, and enjoyed some very cheap holidays,' says Peter.

Things didn't always go according to plan, and more than once bad weather kept them down in the Snowy longer than anticipated—sometimes with embarrassing results.

'One Friday afternoon,' Peter remembers, 'Mark and I hopped in the Spitfire and drove to the snow. Our skis stuck out of the canvas top of the car and the heater didn't work. We went through a massive puddle going past Lake George and the car stopped. Mark opened his door and water flooded through the car. We got out and pushed it off the road, dried out the distributor and carried on. We drove on to Sawpit Creek where we met two other guys, Grant Hyland and another. It was snowing like anything but we took the roof off the two seater so these two guys could sit with their bums on the boot and their legs in the car. I think they kept their packs on. They were crammed with mountaineering gear, and we all wore full mountaineering outfits, including goggles. We crawled from Smiggins at about 20 kilometres per hour. By the time we reached the National Parks and Wildlife ranger at Thredbo we had a line of cars behind us.'

'You guys have got to be joking!' the Ranger exclaimed as he waved them through.

The group parked at Thredbo Village, which normally doesn't experience heavy snow. But the weather was terrible and they were stuck in Seamans Hut for four days. 'It was damn cold,' Peter says, 'and we spent most of the time in our sleeping bags.'

The hut rattled in the wind and they couldn't get a fire going as the timber was all too big and wet and they didn't have an axe. Every time any of them went outside they were blown off their feet because of the verglass. There was a pole line but they couldn't see from one to next. 'We used a billy for a toilet,' Peter continues, 'and just chucked it outside. On one occasion I stuck my arm outside the door and the billy of shit flew out of my hand and was never seen again.'

But another problem was that Peter had the keys to the safe at the bank.

Eventually the group skied out, reaching Eagles Nest and the lift back to the village. 'But we couldn't find the car,' Peter says. 'Everything in the village was covered in deep snow. We couldn't even find the car park! Eventually we found it then went through trying to find our car under all the snow.'

When they did finally locate it, they took three or four hours to dig it out and dig a trench to the road. Peter had drained the water from the radiator as he had no antifreeze, but the car wouldn't start. Suddenly it fired and blew a welsh plug under the manifold because some water had remained in the block and turned to ice. This was about 4 pm and the local garage lent them some tools, gave them a welsh plug and told them to have the tools back by five. They had an hour to remove the manifold and fix the car with cold hands in terrible weather.

'We got it going then drove with chains to Jindabyne—which was very unusual as you didn't normally need chains on this part of the road. There was much more snow than we expected. We removed them in town, then drove through snow all the way to Cooma.'

Arriving back in Sydney, the Spitfire got to the top of a hill near Peter's parents' place and then bang, clang, the camshaft broke. They rolled down the hill into the garage but the car never went again. Although Peter pulled the whole thing to bits he never got it back together.

Explanations at the bank would be reluctantly accepted after weekends such as this, and Peter would put his head down for yet another week.

All the while Peter had continued to do the milk run early on Sunday mornings for John Kandelas in Westleigh—and this too was to have some impact on his banking career. One day John had a heart attack and was unable to complete the run. Peter was supposed to be at the bank that morning but decided he had to finish the run instead. His boss at the Ryde Branch, Alan Ayres, had at the time a terrible reputation for being tough on employees. Peter simply faced him and explained what he had done. But the reaction was not what everyone expected. Alan merely said that he was pleased that someone working for him had such high personal standards.

Peter continued to walk and explore throughout these years. In June 1979 he decided to ride his bike across New South Wales to Cameron Corner in the far west. 'Cameron Corner was chosen,' he explains, 'because I had never been there.'

It was Peter's first foray into western NSW near the desert country. He had read a lot about where the explorers had been and thought it would be a good challenge. He wasn't sure it was particularly unique, or whether anyone else had ever done it, but this trip was never really designed as a 'first'.

'I pushed it and pushed it hard, which meant being on the bike for up to 24 hours a day sometimes. Maybe with two hours' rest between shifts. I travelled really light. The theory was that it would be warmer the further west I went. I don't think I even had panniers, probably a small pack on my back.'

Peter completed this epic bike ride in just six days on a standard drop handled racing bike with one and a quarter inch tyres. He doesn't remember preparing for the trip very well, but thinks he just got on the bike and rode off, picking up food on the way.

Peter says now that it was a significant achievement but hard to put into context. There were no real adventures, just pedalling and pedalling. 'I pedalled my heart out all the way there and back', is how he describes it. He admits he did get a bit nervous out west towards Cameron Corner because he didn't know what to expect. The road crossed large sand dunes—the dunes run north–south and the roads run roughly east–west. And it was a bit isolated. It was also hard to ride on that type of bike, particularly when there were corrugations. The road ends up on the eastern edge of the Strzelecki desert—which is where Peter ended up many years later when he ran across the desert. 'There was a house at Cameron Corner and that's about all,' Peter recalls. 'I turned around and started to pedal back straight away.'

By now Peter had done many walking trips to Tasmania and was looking for a new challenge. He found it in January 1980 when he took a kayak from the town of Orford on the mainland and kayaked around Maria Island off the east coast of Tasmania, also going ashore to climb Mount Maria.

'It was probably the first time the island was circumnavigated,' Peter says, 'but it was no big deal in comparison with my previous kayak trips. I just picked up a kayak down there, similar to the type I had used before.'

Sea kayaks were still not around at that time, although these areas are all now circumnavigated and there are many tourist trips. Back in 1980 this was a big step forward in terms of what people were doing. A relatively safe trip, it was certainly less risky than Peter's earlier Lizard Island kayak trip. But once again, Peter's motivation was the 'first' ticket.

Back in Tasmania the following year, Peter attacked the Cradle Mountain Track, which he had walked a number of times before. One of the classic walks in Australia, the usual time for a fit walking party is about five days, with extra days for side trips and climbs. In December 1981 however Peter achieved the almost incredible time of 11 hours 5 minutes from the registration desk at Cradle Mountain to the registration desk at Cynthia Bay—a feat which also included ascents of Cradle Mountain, Barn Bluff and Mount Ossa.

'I simply went through it at a run,' Peter says. 'I had learnt how to maximise the efficiency of the run. I ran up Cradle Mountain, via Marion's Lookout. Ducked to the top and back. I can do that in about 20 minutes up and 15 minutes down. I took the big ridge line to Barn Bluff but, instead of the usual way of coming back, I dropped down at the end, maximising the time and not repeating myself. I was back on the track with only an extra hour spent. Mount Ossa is a bit bigger but the track is straightforward. This side trip would have been an hour or so, then I churned through to the end of the trip. It was a gutbuster trip. Nothing very exciting.'

Since then there has been an organised run along the track—without the climbs—that has gradually recorded better and better times. These have put Peter's time in proper perspective, the time for the track now being around 7–8 hours.

Even so, Peter's time was very fast compared with the first race. A race organiser telephoned Peter and questioned him. 'How the hell can you go through this thing and climb the three peaks in 11 hours when our guys are taking 12 without the climbs?'

Peter contemplates his early record and explains that he was 'always acutely aware that the trip would be the first at the time. I'm a bit glib about the records now because they don't seem all that great, but then they were very significant.'

Several years after Peter left Scouting he went off climbing, having become 'a bit fed up with the traditional outdoor stuff'. Mark Foster backs this up, explaining that during his university years Peter just suddenly stopped. He was looking for a change and started orienteering with the Garingal

Orienteering Club with which he competed for a couple of seasons. This was a rare departure into organised competitive sport for Peter, who has steadfastly avoided outdoor activity as a competitive sport. One of the things that struck him about orienteering was that it was all over in 20 minutes. He was used to going away for a whole weekend and being very active the whole time.

'I couldn't just go and compete in one event,' he says, 'so I would enrol in each one and go through the whole day. I wasn't an elite member of the club, but I could buzz round these routes pretty quickly. I used to think it was pretty unfair when they had a good map, say 1:10 000 of Lane Cove, and these guys had been using this map and competing for the past twenty years. I came in as a new person and was competing with people who knew exactly what they were doing.'

Orienteering didn't capture Peter's enthusiasm for very long however and he soon went back to the traditional outdoors with yet another highly developed skill.

In 1981 an invitation arrived from Expedition Leader Earle Bloomfield to join his team on a Japanese Australian Expedition to climb Balls Pyramid. The letter referred to the project as an '... important step forward to better relationships between the two countries'. In the event the expedition did not happen, but the fact that he was invited was important recognition of Peter's skills and reputation.

On top of the bookcase in Peter's sitting room is a wooden trophy. About 400mm high, it was hand made by Grant Clark from a piece of Huon pine. The tall square column is topped with three triangles representing the '3 Peaks' and Dave Drohan has inscribed on it:

'Mightiest of all Tiger Walkers
Awarded to Peter Treseder by members of the 3 Peaks Outdoor Society.'

The four faces of the column detail Peter's impressive achievements in a range of activities under the four headings Classic, Blue Mountains, Regional and Ascents.

'It was my idea to start the club,' Peter says. 'I wanted to create something.'

Traditional clubs like the Sydney Bushwalking Club have a structure, monthly meetings, AGMs and minutes. They put on several walks a weekend and cater for a wide range of skills and experience. 'I didn't want a bar of that stuff,' Peter says. 'I was trying to get away from all that regulation. Even in Scouting I was trying to get away from the red tape. All I wanted to do was get to the outdoors to do things.'

So Peter called some of his friends from Scouting days. 'Keith Williams, Dave Drohan, Derek Stellar, Mark Foster and Grant Clark were there, but it's hard to remember all the original members as there have been so many over the years. We had a couple of meetings to get to grips with the structure of this thing, then we put an ad in the paper and held our first public meeting at the Uniting Church Hall at Pennant Hills. It was on the night that Prince Charles and Diana got married, which is how I remember the date—29 July 1981. Lots of people turned up to the first meeting and we kicked off.

'The club was structured on the basis of Scouting,' Peter says. 'It wasn't just a bushwalking club, it wasn't a climbing club. It was an outdoors club and we called it the 3 Peaks Outdoor Society. Derek Stellar may have come up with the name, after the famous 3 Peaks walk in the Blue Mountains.'

More meetings followed, a logo was designed and members participated in the 'No Dams' campaign. The club headquarters in Thornleigh still has a big banner that was made to march with.

'We used to get ourselves arrested,' Peter recalls, 'marching for the Franklin in the campaign. We were very much involved and supportive of the conservation movement at that stage—and doing a lot of walking.'

The club mirrored Scouting in that it catered for a whole range of activities, not just one. The main function of the club was to meet on a Wednesday night. No minutes were taken; there was no red tape. Members would plan a trip and go out at the weekend. Indeed it was in a sense Peter's idea of an ideal Venturer Unit.

'It was all very similar to the Scouting group I came from,' Peter admits. 'There was a hard core of people very active in the outdoors—say 30 at a time rather than 400 in a big club. In fact all of our members were active. The club built up a good reputation. We had great mountaineers, climbers, tiger walkers, canyons were being explored, the hard bushwalks undertaken.'

One time a meeting was called to develop a constitution because members wanted to join the Confederation of Bushwalking Clubs and you had to have a constitution and some rules in order to qualify. But rules were the last things they wanted. They wrote one—that they weren't going to have any rules—and that satisfied the Confederation and it is still in the constitution today. 'Although there might be a rule to do with insurance now as well,' Peter adds.

The type of people who have joined the club have been independently minded, self motivated people. Never the sort of people who drift to a club for its supporting infrastructure or a regular magazine. 'These guys want to go out and do something,' Peter says enthusiastically. 'They are the infrastructure. There have been some fantastic people through the club and, over the years, a few marriages as well as our share of sadness.'

The importance of the 3 Peaks Outdoor Society should not be underestimated. Always a small club, very successful and very active, 3 Peaks can claim among its members, past and present, an impressive number of key characters in the outdoor activity field. Membership has been self-selecting because of the nature of the club's activities. While this may attract cries of 'elitist' Peter makes no excuses.

'Key people like Dave Drohan, Keith Williams, Nic Bendeli, those characters with a vast experience of the outdoors all went through the club,' he says. 'When you have a good mix of people like that you can do anything you want. The club doesn't teach people, but big clubs have training days. Members need to be motivated. New ones who are self-starters get taken under someone's wing but there are no hangers-on because there's nothing to hang onto! They are all strong characters, all the sort of people you could take on a walk to the South Pole.'

Club members have always been active in search and rescue and in fact the Search and Rescue committee still has 3 Peaks members represented on it. In due course Peter also became Patron and Rock Squad Coordinator of the volunteer Bushwalkers Wilderness Rescue organisation.

Over the years the club has changed with different groups among the membership. Peter's perception is that it is a bit softer at the moment, a group of people who are very keen and doing something every week but with a softer edge to the adventure.

'In the early days,' he says 'we had this group who were setting tiger records, putting climbs up, climbing at the highest level in Australia, mountaineering ascents around the world and discovering canyons. Dave Drohan made the first descent of several canyons and waterfalls in the Wollomombi area. And Dave and I were also setting tiger walking records all over the place.

'We would blitz around some of these walks. Dave was extremely fit, as I was, and he would charge up one of these 1000 metre hills. I would struggle to keep up with him and he'd be walking fast because he thought I wanted to walk fast and yet I was walking fast to keep up with him. We made maximum use of daylight hours. But not everyone wants to do this sort of thing—or has the fitness to do it.'

These days the club focuses mainly on traditional trips, a bit softer, so members can relax a bit more. Peter senses they're content to work within the boundaries rather than push them. Partly because it's harder to find the boundaries, and partly because of the nature of the group. 'That's legitimate,' says Peter. 'It's the same in Scouting. Some will push and others will take it in a more relaxed way. It is always governed by the group of people involved.'

No-one has had much time for membership drives, so the club has maintained its membership level over the years at around 30 to 40. Some from the early days are still involved and the average age of members has probably gone up as a result. It's now about the size of a good Scout Troop or a big Venturer Unit and really can't sustain any more members without an infrastructure.

In any case, as Peter explains, 'new members had to prove themselves before we'd let them take part in a difficult or technical trip. We were always sensible taking them out. We would ask each person if they are really capable of each activity before doing it. As a result, we've never experienced disasters or serious accidents.'

Peter is still a member, but no longer has the weekend time to do things with the club. He doesn't go to meetings any more either, but still maintains a connection with a core of people. 'I do walks and training with some members, maintaining more of an informal link these days.'

A list of all the members since the club began would no doubt however be impressive and colourful, a rich tapestry of outdoor people over time. And Peter should probably be an honorary member.

There are literally thousands of trips Peter has made around Australia that have not been recorded. Those that are represent record attempts, either breaking existing records or making new ones. All were based on a really sound knowledge of the areas before they were attempted as records. Some were done on the spur of the moment, like the 15 minute ascent of Pigeon House. 'I was walking in the Budawangs and decided to have a race. I was really fired up that day!' Peter says.

Some of the passes—like Carlon's Head—came about because Dave Drohan and Peter progressively raced each other, thereby reducing the record. With time it got more serious—the pair even started to leave their packs behind.

Others, like the Benowie Track record, were set because all Peter's training when he lived at home with Mum and Dad was done on bush tracks. It was not called the Benowie Track then; there were just tracks. And the Benowie was pushed through several years later. The Department of Lands came to Peter for advice about how to get down a particular cliff line, and he helped build it. Mark Foster's father was at the time involved with the Elouera Trust which managed the area and the track was a Lands Department project. 'I helped with some staircases, positioning rocks and so on,' Peter says. 'I must have run it soon after it was completed, the first run. That's how my thoughts went—to be the first.'

In 1981 Peter continued with further records for tiger walks in the Blue Mountains. The usual way for runners to do the Katoomba to Jenolan run is along the Six Foot Track. Peter took a different, and rather painful, route.

'Andrew Stiff and I had done a walk in summer,' Peter recalls, 'and hitched into Jenolan. There were a lot of bush fires around and the manager of Caves House tried to persuade us not to attempt the walk. He even offered us a bed for the night if we didn't do it. We took the bed and then did the walk anyway, leaving very early the next morning disappearing down the banks of the Jenolan River.

'We went down from the Blue Pond and onto the Cox's River. We walked all the way to Katoomba in a day, finishing by climbing up Carlon's Head and onto Narrowneck. There were wall-to-wall nettles everywhere. Our legs were covered with these bloody stings and after a while they went numb. When we got home we couldn't sleep and at two in the morning we both got up and stomped around. It took a day or two to go away.'

Peter later used this route for his record breaking run. 'I knew it would happen again. I couldn't avoid the nettles so just ran straight through them. I suffered when I got home.'

The Grose Valley in the Blue Mountains has a fearsome reputation. Even experienced outdoors people like Keith Williams and various Scout troops have had accidents down there or been delayed. It is difficult country even for really good Scouting people and tough outdoors types. And there is a long history of problems in the area. Normally, people going in take four to seven days to walk from Blackheath to Richmond via the Grose. So, when Peter went in and got through in a considerably shorter time—a matter of mere hours—it was a significant leap forward.

Why is it so difficult? There is supposed to be an engineers' track running alongside the Grose River from the Darling causeway, but it is often hard to find. It is quite scrubby around the river although the middle section opens up. As you get down further, Wentworth Creek runs into it and you get into a big, slow boulderish section where you have to go up and over.

Peter remembers that the first time he drank some of the water and got sick and was throwing up. 'That made it a hard trip,' he says. 'And the trail itself is extremely demanding,' he continues. 'You are travelling on a broad scale down a ridge or over boulders. Snakes are a problem. You are moving quickly and quietly and they don't have time to get out of your way. You see a bunch of black snakes when you come through a corner. You're trying to keep yourself safe, make sure you don't have an accident, using your arms. It requires a high degree of concentration.'

Peter had walked this trip before, but probably only once before attempting his record-breaking run of just under seven hours.

'As the guys in the club will tell you, I am known for the very efficient way I do things,' Peter says, in explanation of his tiger walking style. 'I approach it from the risk-free point of view. The more hours you have in the day the better. I get going pre-dawn and start walking in early light, stopping for breakfast. This means I've done half the journey while others will be just getting going. I use my day better, use the breaks better.'

When he's running, there is always danger of hurting himself, slipping, twisting or breaking an ankle. But it rarely happens. 'I'm just very good at it,' Peter says matter of factly. 'People said of me, in those days when I was more agile, that I could walk down a field of boulders with ease, make it look easy.'

And indeed, one of Peter's gifts is the ability to move gracefully over bush obstacles, rather like an athlete's ability to go over hurdles. But is this an innate skill or an acquired one?

'For years I have trained in the bush,' says Peter. 'Training through the same terrain, running home from the bank. Extreme concentration is required—one mistake and you're in trouble. I have developed great skill in bush running. I always look after myself and carry enough gear to survive a night if I get stuck. Some guys now only carry a bum bag with water and a few things. That's too dangerous. Typically I'll have a small backpack with a set of thermals, Gore-Tex jacket, matches and Little Lucifers. Maybe a large plastic bag for cover, but no sleeping bag. And I can survive. They're going to have an uncomfortable night or even die.'

There is a big distinction too between Peter's bush running and marathon race running, whether they are run on roads or through the bush, as is the case with the Six Foot Track marathon and the Cradle Mountain run. 'Even then I am looking after myself, not relying on a team with drinks, 4WDs, helicopters, and the SES. In these organised races if a runner breaks a leg he gets pulled out. Another with a blister gets medical help. There's no risk or personal management. I am combining the two, looking after myself and running, often while navigating. I have to run like an athlete with the mindset of a bushwalker.'

One of the criticisms people make of Peter's tiger walks is that he runs through the bush and never sees anything. This is far from the truth. First, he has always walked through the area before and carefully observed the topography, vegetation and wildlife. He rarely goes into an area specifically to reconnoitre a run. The runs always come after the walks, when he thinks that the route might have the potential for a first or a record.

'I don't go into an area thinking I can do a run to break a record,' he says, 'but when I am in an area I can sometimes see the potential to make a record run through the place and I go back to do that.'

Peter also has a real sense of the importance of what he is doing, and motivates his support teams. 'We're going to make history tonight,' he is likely to say.

He is very aware of putting his achievements in context however. On the return from a successful trip Peter and his support team would feel very satisfied with what they'd done—but they wouldn't feel the need to spell it out to the world, even if they were very aware of their achievement at the time. When they came back they just wouldn't make a fuss about it.

In Peter's own words: 'To push yourself through this sort of thing you've really got to want to do it.'

In a relationship that would have defeated a less resolute woman, Beth Ferguson continued to see Peter. For more than five years they went out together and still Peter didn't pop the question. 'One of the reasons it took me so long to get married was because I wanted to be financially secure first,' Peter explains.

In the meantime Peter often helped Beth's grandmother, Mussie, around the house and backyard in Balaclava Road, Eastwood. 'I really got on well with Mussie,' says Peter. 'She was a bit of a fire-eater but soft underneath. She would come out with these fantastic expressions like "that dirty stop-out" and "that low-down spitting creature".'

Beth didn't understand Peter's record breaking. It didn't mean anything to her at the time. He was just going off on yet another expedition. 'I only started to understand when *Wild* magazine started publishing articles and records. Then the idea sort of crept up on me,' she says.

During their long courtship Beth took two trips overseas. The first was a sponsored choir tour in December 1979 with her mum. They travelled to Israel, Hungary, Austria and London for four or five weeks.

Then in December 1982 Beth departed for Europe and the UK for seven weeks with her girlfriend, Genny Bellamy. Peter began to worry that he might have left his run too late. After all, it had been nearly six years since they met.

One Sunday Peter talked to his father while Mum was out. 'He spoke to me,' recalls John, 'about Beth, who was in London at the time. He thought he might have lost her as it was her second trip overseas. Peter asked me to please go for a walk. On my return he told me that he had telephoned Beth in London and proposed to her. I even got the bill for the international phone call!'

Beth's response to this was that it was 'about time'. She wasn't surprised, she claims, except by Peter's manner. 'I said "Yes" on the phone, then felt rather let down as he wasn't actually there and I had to carry on with what I was doing.'

Beth and Peter bought a house at Wahroonga six months before getting married. Peter's plan had been to pay off the block of land he had earlier bought and sell it before buying a house. But they ended up with both the house and the land, selling the land eventually to Peter's brother Neil who built on it.

The house appealed to the couple. Although it needed a lot of work, it was close to two stations, Waitara and Normanhurst, and was close enough to Mum and Dad as well as Beth's mum. 'And we liked the block,' says Peter, 'because it had lots of trees and birds. That's what really appealed to us.'

The house really needed a great deal of work. 'Unlike people who move into a big new house with everything done for them and with a massive mortgage, we had to do all the work ourselves,' Peter says. 'I built cupboards for the kitchen, bathroom and hallway. We removed an old concrete swimming pool, old chicken pens, and took more than 30 trailer loads of rubbish to the tip.'

Both Beth and Peter still lived at home—and they got both sets of parents involved in renovations. Dot helped with the wallpaper, Dad with doors and the backyard. It seems extraordinary that they didn't live together after so many years of courtship. But as Peter explains, 'it was not quite as accepted in those days.'

But this was the 1980s.

'We were trying to live up to and respect the wishes of our parents, particularly Beth's. There was no real reason to step out of line,' he continues. 'It was the best way; we knew we were going to get married.'

It's a very logical explanation—although one which doesn't seem to take into account that heady emotion when two people love and care for each other enough to want to get married.

'I'm a very logical person,' says Peter. 'You can still do all the things you want without living together. We worked on the house a lot in our spare time and I spent a lot of time in the back room at Beth's place.'

Waiting another six months after six years was then probably not very important to either of them.

The wedding was held at All Saints Church in Parramatta on 7 January 1984. They knew the minister through Beth's church, and liked the church itself. Beth's dad had suffered a serious stroke and was in a nursing home. Paralysed, he attended in a wheelchair and Mum walked Beth down the aisle. Eighty guests came to the reception at Durham Park in Castle Hill.

But what does a seasoned adventurer do on his honeymoon?

On one day Peter and Beth climbed Mount Kosciuszko, went to Tathra for a swim, then went to Pigeonhouse Mountain and walked to the top.

And, in a shop at Hall's Gap in the Grampians, Peter also discovered Leonard Bickell's famous book *This Accursed Land*—his first inspiration for the later Antarctic trips. He couldn't put the book down for two days!

CHAPTER 7

FROM RECORD BREAKER TO SILLY WALKS

'What we do as individuals really matters. Balanced as we are on an evolutionary knife-edge, the actions of each one of us can have repercussions beyond our capacity to imagine. Because we do not understand the physics of consciousness we do not understand how the insights of one might affect the critical mass of a whole. We do not stand alone, we are all enjoined.'

Darly Renee, Geneticist

During his late twenties, Peter maintained his extreme fitness and was regularly making and breaking outdoor records. His sense of adventure had already led him to various sorts of urban explorations and challenges, while his sense of humour and attitude towards any form of authority led him to attempt a series of 'silly walks' that at first seemed out of place in the somewhat serious world of outdoor achievement.

But before this, in April 1985, Peter completed a famous trip, the Blue Mountains Trilogy, in the outstanding time of just 10 hours and 22 minutes. The concept of combining these three classic outdoor challenges—the descent of Kalang Falls Canyon at Kanangra, the journey from Kanangra to Katoomba and the ascent of the West Wall of the Three Sisters—was not new. It required a multitude of disciplines and the idea for the trip came to Peter from a trip Nic Bendeli had completed with Ross Vining in about two days. The standard trip had been done for several years and had become a classic trip in outdoor legend.

To put Peter's time in context, the canyon descent usually takes about a day, with 10 major abseils of more than 30 metres each. The walk is a serious three to four day hike and a group climbing the West Wall of the Three Sisters would probably allow a full day for the ascent. To put these together in ten hours requires a very high level of skill, the ability to move quickly through the natural environment and tremendous stamina. Peter had all three.

'You need the ability to deal with a number of consecutive dangers,' Peter says. 'At Kalang Falls the danger is that, by abseiling quickly, you can make a mistake, fall off your rope and die. You need to carry your gear all the way to Katoomba, moving as fast as a marathon runner, while navigating through the bush without accident, then climb a grade 12 peak, solo, while extremely tired.'

On the run to Katoomba, there had been snakes to avoid in Kanangra Creek as well as the inherent navigation problems and the sheer physical challenge. And there was the danger of falling, as the climb was difficult without rope protection as Peter ascended about 300 metres to the top of the Second Sister—if you have an accident you're dead. 'I did have a rope over my shoulder,' Peter says, 'but all it would have done is to add a bit of padding if I fell!'

To complete all that after the run from Kanangra and abseiling down the falls is tough going. But increasingly over the years Peter has combined a variety of skills and risks in a single expedition. On this trip he had to move very quickly between belay points as he abseiled down the falls. 'You set it up and abseil down,' Peter says. 'Repeat the operation, checking your belaying points very quickly. Most parties would stop to double check everything, and do it slowly. I don't have time to do that so must get it right first time, every time. It is important to constantly concentrate on the safety aspects. People have been killed there.'

The success of trips like this have tended to be the result of a building process. Peter had climbed the West Wall regularly since he was 15 years old, even completing 32-minute circuits during a marathon fund raising attempt with fixed ropes in place over the more difficult sections. The abseil was not new to him and he had honed his bush running skills over many years.

The result, however, made a new record that was way out of the league of any of the previous attempts by skilled outdoors people. Once again, Peter had made people rethink the challenge in the light of his achievement.

He is, however, a little defensive when questioned about his real motives. 'I've strung together these three classic trips, and felt satisfied that I had got away with it,' he says. 'The challenge was for me to overcome some difficulties that are inherent in this problem for myself, which is why these trips have not been promoted to the general public. They couldn't care less about them. There is little social acceptance of this type of achievement compared with, say, golf or marathon running. But in my mind, this is a lot more relevant than an organised race. Some official races now combine some of these elements but with a safety net and I think the social status of bushwalking has changed for the better over the years.'

The following month Peter undertook a trip from Bindook to Katoomba, a somewhat unheard of thing to do for someone in the know. 'I'd been out to do some caving with a group at Colong Caves. Rather than drive back from the car park at Batch Camp, I said I'd run back and meet them at Katoomba. I said I could do it faster than they could drive. Of course I didn't, but still completed it along the hard route in 12 hours. It wasn't exactly the shortest way. It probably took them six hours to drive and they had to wait for me to come through. It was just another nice achievement.'

Miles Dunphy is widely regarded as the father of the conservation movement in Australia. When he was working at Paddy Pallin's Peter was lucky enough to meet him. 'Miles used to come into the shop and always wore a hat and had these beautiful hand drawn maps,' Peter says. 'No one seemed to know who he was and I found that very sad. He was largely responsible for those enormous parks we now enjoy. His concept of the Greater Blue Mountains National Park incorporates what is now Wollemi, Blue Mountains, Kanangra-Boyd and Nattai. It covers a huge area from Muswellbrook to Mittagong, everything we now take for granted.'

As a tribute to Miles Dunphy, Peter conceived a trip—a complete traverse of the Greater Blue Mountains National Park. No one had ever walked the length of the park system continuously, let alone run it. The section from Katoomba south had been done, but no-one had walked from Muswellbrook to Mount Wilson through Wollemi. There were no tracks and it was difficult to gain access.

Keith Williams agreed to help Peter and they set out on a series of weekend walks. 'We were dropped off at Rylstone or Widden Valley,' says Peter, 'and we would work out a route and arrange to be picked up later. We did this for three or four pioneering walking weekends, finding and identifying all the passes through big cliff lines. That's the crux of it.'

Keith and Peter were probably the first ever to link walks together through the remotest section of the park. Subsequently, Peter used the route for a number of runs, such as the length of Australia run, when he linked it in with other routes. This was a critical trip for Peter. The first of the major Australian traverses, it required an enormous level of knowledge before the attempt could be made.

The initial planning process may have taken those four weekends to prepare for the traverse of Wollemi, but the rest was a lifetime build up. 'Even a fitter person could not necessarily do this,' admits Peter. 'They wouldn't have the emotional base, the level of skill as well as the fitness. I know what is out there. The traditional marathon runner couldn't do it. When a running race is set up it is a different thing with drink stations and rescue facilities.'

Peter has a poetic way of describing these major achievements. 'The run is like creating a sculpture,' he says, 'carving a path through the wilderness, utilising all my skills of navigation and fitness. It's almost like leaving a legacy of creation, a painting, except that I'm doing it as an achievement.'

While Peter and Keith were mapping the Wollemi they also planned to attempt a snowshoe traverse of the route from Kiandra to Kosciuszko. 'Keith and I came out of one of these trips in the mountains,' Peter says, 'packed up and went down the snow to do the traverse. But I found that I couldn't concentrate. We got about 10 kilometres into the trip on the first day in lousy weather and planned to head off the next day. I said to Keith, "I can't do this any more." I turned around and came back by myself and Keith finished off the trip. My focus at the time was on the Blue Mountains National Park run to such an extent that I couldn't cope mentally with the snowshoe traverse.'

What Peter and Keith were trying to do with the National Parks traverse was to segment the route for search and rescue purposes in case Peter didn't come out. As usual, this was arranged through Peter's friend, Keith Maxwell, Director of Bushwalkers' Wilderness Rescue. Searching a small amount of bush is a horrendous task and hard enough, but Peter was going to be traversing entire National Parks. If he went missing on a 500 kilometre stretch it would have been the biggest search in Australian history. By segmenting the route it is possible to isolate the area where a lost person might be.

To be fair to everyone, and to keep people informed, Peter would arrange for someone to drop him off and pick him up at the end. People would go in to meet him at various pre-arranged points or he would leave messages. If he didn't come out and meet someone, they could go in and see if the message was there and thus know whether or not he had gone past that particular intersection. For example, one point was an old tin shed on the top of Gosper's Mountain in the Wollemi National Park. Peter would scribble on the back of this shed in chalk 'Peter's come through' and the date and the time. No one ever came in to check this, but he used this spot on numerous runs through the park. If he hadn't turned up at his next checkpoint this location would have been checked to see if he had been through.

'Keith had met me at Carlon's Farm with Paul Fardouly and Cathy Randell,' Peter recalls. 'They had a big plate of vegies waiting.' He had crossed the whole Wollemi Park and the Blue Mountains Park, the first time it had ever been done, and was pretty stuffed by the time he reached his checkpoint. 'Vegies didn't do much for me,' he says. 'Keith might be expert about food and very pedantic—but he's a vegetarian!'

Keith was going to do the rest of the run with Peter all the way to Mittagong. It was particularly cold. They had the meal and walked off in the late afternoon down to the Cox's River in the dark. Peter conked out by the time they reached Kanangaroo clearing, which is private leasehold with sheds for horse riding groups. It was freezing cold, and he had no sleeping bag. As a rule he didn't carry one on these trips—it was too much weight.

Keith however had a fantastic sleeping bag. He unrolled it, promptly went to sleep and snored. Peter lay on top of the table curled in a foetal position, shivering. It was raining and he needed sleep desperately after about four days without any. In the end, he couldn't stand it any longer and at 2am, much to Keith's disgust, got him up and they walked up Strongleg Buttress to Kanangra Walls for breakfast.

A support group had come in and cooked up a big plate of sausages which was much more to Peter's liking. 'The sausages perked me up,' says Peter, 'then Keith and I went right across the southern part of the National Park. Later we slept for a couple of hours at a place to the east of Yeranderie in an abandoned house. I slept between two fires to keep warm.'

The early part of the trip had been mainly jogging through Wollemi, then largely fast walking with Keith. The long, long hours of walking and jogging and no sleep took their toll. 'By the time we were picked up by Beth and Simon Thomas we were both absolutely stuffed,' Peter recalls. 'We did in a couple of days what would take a normal walker a week. We weren't mucking around.'

As usual, Peter and Keith packed up and went home. No-one called the media. They didn't rush out to tell anyone about the trip. 'It's largely a group of friends who support each other, a large network of people who are involved in these trips as backup,' Peter explains.

It had, however, been a ground breaking achievement to cross a whole National Park system in a continuous time. But, despite the achievement, how does Peter explain the apparent contradiction of his ultra-lightweight, ultra-fast trips with the advice given to people undertaking outdoors activities by experts and rescue organisations?

For him there is little dilemma. In this kind of context he supports the idea of groups of three to five, carrying the right gear and, he stresses, not attempting too much. Part of the irony, he claims, is that for the past 25 years he has been one of the leaders of search and rescue in New South Wales. He has completed hundreds of rescues and helped to save many lives and yet, here he is, breaking the generally accepted rules. Out there by himself, running through the scrub, without a sleeping bag. The real difficulty is that if anything goes wrong it's going to go wrong in a really big way, so he has to cover himself as much as he can. Part of that approach is having people like Keith Maxwell and the backup team.

'There is always a balance of what you take,' Peter says. 'The faster you want to go the more you throw out of your pack, but that leaves you without anything to make the trip comfortable. Part of my self-imposed rules were that I couldn't borrow Keith's sleeping bag on this trip even if I wanted to, as that would spoil the "unsupported" nature of the trip. Although on this one I did accept some meals from people so it wasn't completely unsupported like the big desert trips which are. Then I have to carry all the gear myself.'

It should be noted however that Peter has never become lost and needed finding. Nor has he ever suffered an injury serious enough to warrant rescue—and he has always arrived at his chosen destination close to the time he has nominated.

At the beginning of Anzac Day weekend in 1999, Peter was impatient to complete one of the many interview sessions for this book. We finished at lunchtime and that Friday afternoon he travelled to the Blue Mountains, listening to Andrea Bocelli on the car CD player, psyching himself up for the challenge ahead. That challenge was to break his 10 year old record of 14 hours 30 minutes for the continuous ascent of the Classic 3 Peaks—Mounts Cloudmaker (1164 metres), Paralyser (1155 metres) and Guouogang (1291 metres), three of the highest peaks in the Blue Mountains. Tradition decrees that the walker will, along the way, cross Cox's River twice, Kanangra Creek and Whalania Creek and, over a distance of roughly 80 kilometres, ascend and descend some 5000 metres—or about half the height of Mount Everest!

This particular weekend challenge was pioneered in 1958 by a group of the original 'Tiger Walkers'. Led by John Manning it included fellow Sydney Bush Walkers Geoff Wagg and Barry Higgins, who completed the first traverse of the Western Arthurs and even now is a prominent walker. All wore Volley sandshoes, the favourite footwear for experienced bushwalkers around Sydney and even today, Peter's favourite footwear for canyoning. Their time was impressive, all the more so as many of today's tracks did not then exist.

FROM RECORD BREAKER TO SILLY WALKS

The 3 Peaks challenge soon became a test walk for hard walkers to do in 48 hours. It is a standard good hard walk in four days—and a real gutbuster to do in a weekend.

Peter is unable to remember the exact details of each of his trips to the 3 Peaks. He walked it at least once with Dave Drohan to work out the route, and has then run it a number of times, creating a new record on no fewer than four occasions.

In 1966, Ray Jerrems had set out with Warwick Daniels and John Fantini to break his 20 hour 30 minute record set the year before. Jerrems was forced to pull out, but the other two went on, running most of the way to create a new record of 18 hours and 22 minutes, a record which was to stand for 16 years until Peter came along and broke it with a time of 16 hours.

Five years later Peter progressively got his own time down to an amazing 14 hours 30 minutes—another benchmark. Gordon Lee was in the backup crew, and came to end of Narrowneck to meet Peter on his way out. As he came up the rock scramble at Carlon's Head Peter was feeling the effects of flu coming on. He was hot so Gordon threw a bucket of water over him, which didn't help. 'We stopped to see a friend of Gordon's,' Peter says, 'and I couldn't stop shivering. I shivered all the way home in the car and ended up with a week in bed, practically the only time in my life. I had run my body down so much. Often I come down with something within a week of doing a trip because my resistance is so low.'

The route for the 3 Peaks starts where the Narrowneck Fire Trail meets the tarred road, runs along the Narrowneck Plateau, down the spikes, drops into the Medlow Gap, across Yellow Pup Ridge and down to the Cox's River, a drop of about 1000 metres. You climb up Strongleg Buttress which is almost a rise of 1000 metres straight up a very steep ridge almost 45 degrees. The route then takes you along a range where you have to navigate on a compass bearing. Then across Dex Creek, named after Miles Dunphy's dog, Dexter, and on up to Cloudmaker which is the first of the three peaks. From here you drop almost straight down 1000 metres to Kanangra Creek, then straight up another 1000 metres to Mount Paralyser, which is as its name suggests, then straight down 1000 metres to Whalania Deep.

'You then climb this fantastic ridge to the top called Nooroo Buttress,' says Peter. 'It's a steep, rocky climb up out of the mist and just a beautiful sharp ridge line to the top of Guouogang. Then it runs along Gasper's Ridge to Mount Jenolan then down to the Cox's for 1000 metres, then up Breakfast Creek, through Carlons Farm up Carlons Head, up another 1000 metres, then back along Narrowneck to where you started.'

That Anzac weekend Peter hoped there was a bit of leeway in his previous record time. But his training this time was not good. He had been a bit sick beforehand and was suffering from a nagging leg injury. His calf muscle was not working well. Obviously he was generally fitter and younger ten years ago. On top of that he had ridden in a charity bicycle trip and rescued three women on his way back from the mountains the previous week. He went in expecting the attempt would be a disaster.

It was raining on the way up the mountains and it looked as if it would be horrible the whole weekend. Suddenly however the clouds blew away and the bush dried out quickly. Peter started the trip on Friday night and did most of it during the night. Previously, he had attempted the easy stages at night from 2am, then waited for daylight for the difficult sections, then night again for the remaining easy stages.

This time Peter didn't worry about time and just went for it. It was very cold, with a bit of a moon. The trip presented no particular problems, but Peter was not confident of breaking the record until almost the end.

Peter carried a pack with a heavy Gore-Tex jacket on this trip because it looked like bad weather and he didn't want to get really soaked. 'Too much,' he says. 'Thermals and a jumper. Chocolate bars for food and a litre of water. I filled up at the creeks I knew were safe. Those that originate in the mountains are all right, and the hanging swamps hold clean water which comes down in the small mountain creeks. But not the Cox's which picks up sewage from Lithgow.'

The support crew met Peter with bikes at the end of Narrowneck. Sometimes the support crew come out to take photos of the last leg of a trip but can't keep up, so they were put on bikes this time. 'As I flew along

Narrowneck,' Peter says, 'I still felt that I wasn't going to break the record. I was on that fine edge of feeling I was going to be sick, keeping those legs going but pulling back very slightly so I didn't, then when I reached the Narrowneck gate I knew I had a chance, the end was only a few kilometres away. I just ran flat out and my supporters came with me on the last leg up Narrowneck.'

It was a successful record attempt, with Peter knocking off another 11 minutes.

Peter always wears Nike Air Pegasus running shoes. He considers boots too heavy and too painful for his feet. On long runs the extra padding is better for your feet but the centre of gravity is higher which makes it riskier to damage your ankle. And he wears Volleys in wet canyons because the vibram sole is the best grip in the wet.

One day in January 1988, Peter called his brother, Neil, and asked if he wanted to go for a walk up the mountains. Neil said 'yes', but put the phone down thinking, 'Peter doesn't just "go for a walk".'

When they got to Govett's Leap Peter opened the boot of his car, produced two sets of masks, snorkels and flippers and they went down to Junction Rock wearing all this gear. 'We started on the far side of Junction Rock,' explains Peter, 'swam across Govett's Creek using our flippers, masks and snorkels, then followed Govett's Leap track to the car park. If you think about it, it was quite hard to walk up there with that gear on. But I was having a bit of fun, taking the mickey out of the seriousness of some of the more staid outdoor people.'

On the surface such trips are no dumber than anything else Peter does; they are just not generally accepted. Who says that going backwards up Govett's Leap in flippers, mask and snorkel is sillier than anything else? If it was an exercise in fitness that the public accepted over a period of time it would be taken just as seriously.

'Look at anything we do,' Peter says, 'golf, where men and women hit a little white ball with a stick; football, where we kick an inflated leather bag. Spending years training for ten seconds that will decide whether you're famous or not. Synchronised swimming is no less silly than anything else, it's just not as socially acceptable.'

Another example of taking a shot at the outdoors movement is the run backwards up Govett's Leap that Peter did in October 1987. 'Dave Drohan and I went into training. It was really difficult,' says Peter. 'We trained at the Golden Staircase, running up backwards. There was a crowd of Japanese tourists at the bottom of the ladder trying to work out how to climb up. As we climbed up backwards, we were able to see them as, one by one they turned round and climbed up the big steel ladders backwards. At every set of stairs after that they turned round and walked up backwards because they thought it was the way to do it, because we'd done it so efficiently.'

Peter also holds the undisputed record for the first descent of Wollangambe Canyon nude with an inflatable woman! 'She was beautiful, with big eyes that blinked at me,' he says. 'I rode her in the missionary position with these big eyes blinking all the time and she must have been leaking because, each time the eyes blinked, tears came out as well. All the way down the canyon this woman blinked and cried.'

Wollangambe is a very popular canyon, not narrow, with big water holes like a succession of Olympic pools. Peter was with a group from the 3 Peaks Club. 'We all walked down to the beach at the beginning of the canyon,' he recalls. 'There were probably 50 unknown people there all earnestly blowing up their lilos for the trip down the canyon while I started blowing up the woman. Everyone was talking, making a lot of noise, which gradually subsided as I blew and blew and got my woman up to full size and floated off downstream.'

Peter did unusual things with bikes, too! A fantastic ridge comes out of Kanangra Deep called Thurat Spires. You cross this narrow ridge that has a steep drop either side, then abseil down and climb out. Peter took his push bike to Kanangra Creek then all the way up and over the spires. 'It wasn't too bad,' he muses. 'The hardest part was getting it through the scrub which was very tight. The handlebars got stuck. It was my famous bike with drop handlebars. I eventually rode it at least 100 metres down the road.'

Peter also once went abseiling with a sailboard, a nice play on words that actually required a great deal of skill to set up. Photographs were taken by a group of Rock Squad people who set up at Butterbox Point overlooking the Blue Gum Forest. The actual trip was a bit later and went right into the Blue Gum Forest and out at Perry's Lookdown on the other side. Peter carried the sailboard all the way.

Chapter 8
Finding the Bunker

'All men dream: but not equally. Those who dream by night in the dusty recesses of their minds wake in the day to find that it was vanity: but the dreamers of the day are dangerous men for they may act out their dreams with open eyes, to make it possible.'

T.H. Lawrence, *Seven Pillars of Wisdom*

During his younger days Peter had been interested in draining, underground tunnels and so on, and had done a lot of urban exploration. He explored the old train tunnels down near Wynyard where you can still count the missing platforms that lead to never-used tunnels.

He got permission to explore the railway tunnels under Sydney from the then head of State Rail, David Hill. Peter knew his wife at the time, Emily Booker, who worked on the Terry Willesee *Tonight* on Channel 7. She had produced a story on the original harbour tunnel from Balmain which has a trapdoor entrance in a boatshed at the bottom of a property on the peninsula. 'You go down the ladder,' Peter says, 'to an area the size of two rooms which has become a big covered, private swimming pool since it was flooded.'

Hand dug in 1926, the tunnel originally went to Greenwich for tram network cabling. A fissure in the rock caused a permanent leak, which was pumped out for 40 years before being allowed to flood and fill with water. State Rail owned the site and ultimately sold it through an advertisement which offered 'Your own Sydney Harbour tunnel' with the property.

Beth used to go with him on some of these draining expeditions. 'Many old drains from the convict days were just bricked up over natural waterfalls. If you know how to get in you can work your way up some of them under the middle of the city,' Peter explains. 'There is a tunnel from the Ensemble Theatre up to North Sydney. The Tank Stream is now famous and there was a circus rink under the stage at the Capital Theatre, complete with lion pits. As a teenager I had also unofficially explored the old bunkers and military tunnels at George's Head and Middle Head.'

For many years there were rumours around Sydney about a Second World War Control Bunker used by General MacArthur. No one knew exactly where it was, but somehow Peter found out it was near Bankstown aerodrome. After an exhaustive search of the open grounds around there he finally found something interesting in a common area between a block of villas.

'This piece of old concrete was sticking out of one corner of a park area and I thought it might be the edge of the bunker. None of the residents knew what it was,' Peter recalls.

An exhaustive search of the archives in Canberra, assisted by a friendly Brigadier General, unearthed a set of plans which told Peter where the door was and confirmed the exact site. It also confirmed that the door was in someone's back yard.

Peter went out with Paul Fardouly and knocked on the owner's door. His name was David Hoare, and he was Managing Director of Sealy Posturepedic. 'It was a Thursday night,' Peter remembers, 'and we told Mr Hoare that we were sure the entrance to a significant wartime bunker was in his backyard. We asked if he would mind if we came over on Saturday to dig. He said he didn't—and that he would even give us a hand!'

'We turned up on Saturday with tools,' Peter continues, 'and David joined us as we started demolishing his backyard. He has since told us he is a wine connoisseur and had visions of finding the world's largest wine cellar ready built out there.'

The entrance had two big protective buttresses with a path to an entrance between them. They found a buttress but didn't know which side they were on. And there was a heap of soil and concrete to move so they started working on another theory.

From the plans Peter saw that the 12-foot-thick roof had a protective 2-foot-thick concrete overhanging eave. It was likely then that, when they covered the whole thing with soil and debris, that the space below the overhang was not filled up.

'We dug a hole to get under one of these eaves,' Peter says, 'and that gave us access to tunnel into a cavity area where there was no soil. We worked our way along the walls and round the corners to where the back wall was against a a quarry wall. We thought this would be the weakest point. We found a drain at the top, removed part of the drain and crawled through into the bunker at roof level. We then dropped a rope down and got in.'

They found that all the military equipment had been ripped out and there was some obvious evidence of vandalism and graffiti after the war. 'It was quite massive inside,' Peter recalls, 'bedrooms, bathrooms, a generator plant and escape tunnels. It was used to accommodate people for two weeks at a time.'

While it is unlikely that MacArthur himself was ever there, the bunker was used as a radar installation. Original photographs from Canberra showed maps on the walls, but since it was based on a British design it proved inadequate for Australia as it was such a large country.

There were also rumours of an identical bunker at Richmond and Peter eventually found this too, but it was nothing like the first one.

Peter subsequently took two television crews through the Bankstown bunker. First, a Channel 7 film crew Peter knew from some canyoning work made a segment and later, Don Burke used it as a focal point for one of his programs.

Given the publicity it was likely to generate, Peter had obtained permission from the Defence Forces to explore the bunker. Officially they denied knowledge of it and didn't appear to want to know. The local Bankstown Council knew something was somewhere but had no plans or records. They gave permission however on the understanding that Peter shared the knowledge and gave them photographs of whatever he found.

'Some people told us it was full of water and we'd drown if we opened it up,' Peter says. 'Others said it was full of sand. But it was completely empty. Residents also gave us permission, wanting to know what was there. We had to seal it up after to keep kids out.'

Peter's urban underground exploring continued in Parramatta in the western suburbs of Sydney where one of the oldest convict built bridges in

Australia still stands. Lennox Bridge crosses the Parramatta River right on the edge of town and Peter had heard rumours that convicts used to be held inside the bridge and that there may be tunnels under Church Street. 'Paul Fardouly told me,' says Peter, 'that as a kid he could remember an opening on both sides of the bridge and getting in one side which is now concreted in. The other side had been buried by soil and grass. We decided to open it up.'

At 2am one very dark night Peter and Paul accompanied by Dave Stuckey and Fran Rose turned up to dig their way in under cover of darkness. 'We arrived to find bright lights shining on the bridge but decided to go ahead anyway as no-one was around,' Peter recalls. 'Then suddenly, as we dug down about two metres, some drunks yelled out from the bridge parapet, "We won't tell anyone you're burying your mother down there!"'

They reached big thick steel bars covering a small entrance and could go no further that night. So they put a sheet of fibro at the top of the hole, put soil over it and then top dressed the park with the rest of the soil they had excavated.

The tunnellers could not get back until the next weekend and were concerned that meanwhile someone would fall through the fibro and break their neck. 'I went home,' says Peter, 'and made a sort of table to lower into the hole to cover it up. Obviously we couldn't get the soil back as it was scattered all over the grassed banks of the river. I was worried all week that someone would fall through before we got the table in place.'

The next weekend they parked the car and Paul started to unload oxy gear to cut through the bars. Looking round, they realised they were in the car park of the National Bank and that what they were doing could be easily misunderstood!

'Once we cleared the hole again,' says Peter, 'we lowered Paul head first, holding him by his feet.' Then the bars came out, one by one. 'I've got it!' exclaimed Paul as he passed a red hot bar to Peter who threw it into the Parramatta River where it sizzled before sinking in the gloomy water, followed by another, then another.

They climbed inside the bridge and found some short tunnels which could have held four or five convicts—but no tunnels to Church Street.

'When we came out,' Peter says, 'we lowered the table in place and stuck four centimetres of soil on it. At least no-one would fall through.'

Months later the Council was considering moving the entire bridge stone by stone as it caused some problems when flooding occurred during heavy rain. They decided to have an official look at the inside first as they had also heard the same story about tunnels.

At a public ceremony, with more than a hundred people present, the council engineers started to dig—only to find first Peter's makeshift table and then the remains of the cut bars. Someone had beaten them to it! The green keepers who had been wondering about the top dressing suddenly realised where the soil had come from.

'I only found out from the press stories,' says Peter, 'as it was supposed to be an historic occasion and no-one had an explanation. This is the first time the true story has ever been told.'

During 1985 and 1986 Peter turned his attention to some classic trips in the Snowy Mountains, during both summer and winter. There is a long history of famous trips to the Snowy from the 1930s on, as people gradually improved the times for skiing and running. These included the Thredbo to Kiandra and Perisher to Kiandra trips. Legendary skier Robby Kilpinen set a record time in 1964 from Perisher to Kiandra which stood for 20 years until Dave Hislop, one of the best cross country skiers this country has ever produced, broke it.

Peter had walked and run this area extensively over the years and was looking for an edge to beat the running record. He went to St Ives to see Ray Jerrems who also held some early records. Ray had knowledge of tricky linkages between valleys that Peter thought he could use to shorten the trip, and he kindly passed on his knowledge.

Indeed Peter went on to bring the time down to just over 6 hours, remarkably a few minutes faster than the ski record. 'Dave reckons he can knock another two hours off,' Peter says, 'given the right snow conditions. You must have good snow conditions for the whole trip to make a record-breaking ski run and it is too difficult to ski unless you can also navigate. But Dave has a broad outdoors experience and can ski fast and navigate.'

Not many people have run across this sort of country. The Institute of Sport has some organised runs around that area but they are quite contained as the athletes lack bush navigation experience. So the runs Peter does are still quite unusual. He set new records for both Thredbo to Kiandra and Perisher to Kiandra on foot together with an impressive 'Figure of Eight' trip that took in the whole area.

He followed this in winter with a snowshoe traverse from Kiandra to Perisher. This trip built on the abandoned trip with Keith Williams who, after Peter pulled out, was probably the first to complete it on snowshoes.

'I wanted to do something different,' Peter says, 'and I'm not a good skier. So I asked Paul Fardouly to make me a special pair of racing snowshoes, with the back cut out so my feet can stay closer together when I'm running. This enabled me to achieve a time that was about double the time of my run in summer.'

All this experience was building up to Peter's traverses of the entire Australian Alps which were completed in 1989 and 1990.

Peter had been canyoning for many years, discovering some and exploring those already known. A vast amount of information circulated by word of mouth; none of it was published although now it is freely available and tracks into and out of canyons have been developed and even signposted.

Then, in January 1986, Peter made a continuous descent of six major canyons on the northern side of Kanangra Walls. He had a great knowledge of all these canyons which are among the biggest and most dramatic in the Blue Mountains. Not as tight or as dark as some of the others, they all had big drops. Each would take a normal team a full day and it would still be an effort to be proud of. There were big drops of 50 metres inside waterfalls, and the canyons involved big walks in and out, with navigation required since these canyons were rarely visited in those days.

Peter simply wanted to string them all together in one trip and he worked out an efficient route between them. It was important to work out how to get back up the ridge line to do the next drop. For example you climb up Cyclops Buttress then drop down Thurat. 'It's a very rocky buttress,' he says, 'with scrambling and climbing that I really like. It gets you up to the top quickly like climbing a mountain. It's fantastic country, big relief.'

This was to be the first time the canyons were completed continuously in a single weekend. It was a significant jump forward in terms of what people had achieved. 'You have to carry two ropes,' explains Peter. 'It's tiring to pull down one rope and set it so many times. You must concentrate on doing the right thing even though you're very tired. You must focus on detail all the time to make it safe.'

Walking between the canyons and carrying all his gear, Peter made the descents in a continuous 37 hours and 30 minutes. The sheer scale of the enterprise should not be underestimated. 'You'd have to string together three or four 50 metre abseils,' he recounts, 'landing on small ledges half the size of a kitchen table, then another, then another. All with a bloody great waterfall thundering down beside you. It can all be a bit overpowering when you're tired.'

Claustral Canyon was Peter's next target. The best known and easiest to get to canyon, Claustral presented slightly different challenges. He made various attempts in various conditions in 1987 simply to see how fast he could get through. 'I arranged support teams at the top of the canyon and went for an out and out race record in a round trip,' Peter says. 'The standard for Claustral is a day trip. A quick trip is six hours, my best time is less than 2 hours. It was a process of refinement,' he explains. 'Short cuts included carrying shorter rope. Mine was 20 metres—just long enough for 10 metre drops, not 50 metres. I jumped the first abseil, went hand over hand on the next drops, not attached with an abseil device. Dangerous, perhaps, but a "controlled risk". I had tested the water depth and obstacles over many trips. This also helped when I did the rescue, as I had jumped the first abseil before at night. And the hand over hand was possible down the girl's rope because I'd done it before; I knew exactly how big the drop was.

'My best time of one hour and 23 minutes sounds ridiculous, but it's just efficiency,' Peter says. 'I'm through the first abseil in seconds, where it takes others 15 minutes or more. People talk and spend time looking around—I don't. If you concentrate you can overcome the safety difficulties. But one mistake and you've had it. Claustral is cold and big.'

A few months later, a group of Peter's friends were discussing Claustral and thinking about the hardest way to do it. 'Well, it has to be midwinter when it's freezing,' Peter says. 'It has to be at night when you can't see, and has to be done in the nude!'

'Now, that was a really serious trip,' Peter remembers. 'Not like some of the other fun trips or silly walks as we call them. All you are wearing is a head torch, 20 metres or rope and sandshoes. If you have an accident or the head torch goes then you stop and die, because the only thing that keeps you alive is to keep moving. It's a bloody cold place.'

Once again Peter arranged for a team to help in the attempt. 'I have a memory of driving up the first time with Paul and Cathy,' he says. 'I got out of the car, took off my clothes and then said it was too cold and we went straight home again.'

The second time was called off too. The wind was so strong it blew the little 4WD around in the wind on the way up. 'I got out and took my clothes off then again told the team that it was just too cold to do this and we went home.'

The third time Peter drove up with Steve Davis. It was still midwinter, the same year, but conditions were slightly more favourable and Peter felt he could do it. Steve was backup. He got a fire going, Peter took his clothes off, Steve took photos and off Peter went. He would come through to look for him if he hadn't turned up after three hours—but that may not have been soon enough if he had met with an accident.

'People wonder how I did it,' says Peter, 'or look on it as a lark. It wasn't. It was on a much finer margin of safety, it has to be right. The water is so cold it takes your breath away. You can hardly breathe, then you get out and the air feels even colder as you move through it. Once you make the first couple of jumps and the first abseil there is no choice, you're committed to go through. There's just no way to get back up.'

The nude trip through Claustral catches a lot of attention, and is part of outdoors legend. 'Scout groups always ask me about this one,' Peter says.

'Perhaps because many of them have done it themselves in summer in wetsuits and have an idea of how difficult it would be.'

Peter has tried to work with a couple of television crews to film a trip through Claustral so people can see what it is like. Until the introduction of digital cameras, the equipment presented a problem. One such attempt was with TV host Larry Emdur, but the technical problems made it impossible to complete. Bulky and susceptible to moisture, the big Betacam cameras were very hard to handle. 'I was told by the producer,' Peter says, that if you had to choose between saving yourself or the camera, you'd have to throw yourself over because the cameras are worth $80 000 each.'

Full wetsuits would be worn during filming, but Peter comments on the extreme cold. 'Standing still in the water for up to an hour is a very demanding process.'

As canyoning has become more popular, and tracks in and out more clearly identified, so the number of accidents has increased with a need for rescue in difficult conditions. While Peter may have worn just a pair of Speedos or hiking clothes when tackling canyons in the early days, he now prefers to wear a spring wetsuit or a full wetsuit for any rescue. 'It's no joke standing around in chest deep, freezing cold water,' he says, 'while trying to rescue someone who's hurt or stuck.'

Chapter 9
Unsung Hero

'Only that which is good and true will endure like a rock and no wanton hand will ever venture to defile it.'

Ludwig van Beethoven

In terms of the hierarchy of trips, Scotts Peak Dam to Federation Peak is the classic hard walk, the one experienced bushwalkers test themselves on. It is a challenging walk that traverses the rugged country of the Arthur Ranges in Tasmania. Typically, bushwalkers with heavy packs would set aside two weeks to traverse the area, although some notable walkers have cut the time down to a few days.

In January 1988 Peter travelled to Tasmania specifically to do this walk in a record time—and with the idea of combining a rafting trip down the Franklin River. 'I was of a view the time could be reduced to a day,' Peter says of the heart stopping trip. 'From Scotts Peak Dam, across the Western Arthurs, up Federation Peak and back to the Dam, all in a day. No one had ever done that.'

There's a bus that goes out to the dam every second day and Peter took it. The bus dropped him off and he did a test walk up the Western Arthurs. To retain his fitness for the attempt the following day he was walking as slow as he could, but even at that speed he quickly caught up with—and passed—another group. That gave him inspiration!

'The next day I wanged it. Without stopping and carrying only a small daypack I left the Scotts Peak Dam car turning circle and took the traditional route to Federation Peak via the Western and Eastern Arthur Ranges, returning to my starting point via the Eastern Arthurs and Arthur Plains. I knew that I had to get the bus back or stay out there for another day,' Peter says. 'I could see the bus pull up, and knew I was running out of time. Charging across a big flat boggy plain with lots of button grass, I made it just before the bus left, covered in grime and mud. I also broke the 24-hour barrier by about half an hour.'

The bus took an exhausted and filthy Peter back to Hobart. 'There was another bus leaving for the Franklin River that afternoon, but I had no gear for the river trip sorted out,' remembers Peter. 'And the bulk of my personal gear was out at Sandy Bay caravan park. I knew that Mark Fowler, an old friend, ran a business called Open Spaces above Paddy Pallin's in Criterion Street, Hobart. Mark used to be the factory manager for Paddy Pallin's in Sydney. I knew he had rafts.'

Peter hadn't seen Mark for five years but rushed into his shop. 'G'day, Mark, how are you going?' he asked. 'I need a raft for the Franklin. And I've got to get back to Sandy Bay now and get my gear.'

Mark gave Peter an inflatable raft—together with a good paddle that belonged to someone else by mistake. Taking these with him, Peter rushed back to Sandy Bay, had a quick shower, packed his gear and was ready in time to catch the bus to the Franklin with his newly acquired raft. The bus dropped Peter and his gear at the Collingwood Bridge on the Lyell Highway.

The standard Franklin trip takes 10 to 16 days in a raft, a little quicker in kayaks. Peter had completed the trip a few years earlier with a group of six or seven including Steve Trémont, Michael Floyd—otherwise known as 'Pinky'—and a few others. This had been one of the first half dozen raft trips down the river and was fun while the weather held. 'It was a relaxed trip,' Peter remembers, 'and it was nice to watch the women swimming naked in the river each night!'

But the rain started as Tasmanian rain does. 'On that occasion I didn't have a wetsuit,' Peter says, 'and I got colder each day. It was raining heavily one morning and Steve said "Put your tent back up, we're staying here for the day." As the river was rising constantly and the rain wasn't going to stop I told Steve in no uncertain terms that I was going on and left with most of the party.'

By the time of Peter's solo raft attempt, the Franklin had been canoed in less than a day. But kayaks are a lot faster, whereas a raft simply goes where it's taken by the downstream current and takes longer. Peter wanted to reduce the time for a raft to a day.

'I got out of the bus and laid the raft out,' he recalls. 'Most appropriately it was called "Moses". But I had forgotten to bring a pump and had to inflate it by mouth. And I had a life jacket but no helmet.'

Launching the raft, Peter began the paddle down the Collingwood River to the junction with the Franklin. He then paddled all the way down the Franklin to Butler Island on the Gordon River. But he didn't break the kayak record.

To navigate a raft down the river in such a short time meant risking the real danger of some particularly big sets of rapids. 'Usually, you need to portage around one huge set which is very time consuming—up to half a day,' Peter explains. 'I didn't have that much time and just went through.'

'I was scared,' he adds. 'I had seen these rapids before and knew how big and fast they were. There's really not much margin for error. And even though I didn't break the 24 hour barrier I was quite pleased with what I thought was a reasonable time.'

These trips were reported in the media. The Federation Peak time caused a bit of criticism ranging from comments like 'this is not bushwalking' and 'tiger walkers wreck the wilderness experience' to positive comment such as 'he's moving so fast you won't see him'. And some who supported Peter's achievement pointed out that he moves with such speed through the bush that he actually makes minimal impact on the environment and other walkers.

'Talking to outdoors guru Dave Noble,' Peter reports, 'indicated to me that my successful trip destabilised the pecking order of serious outdoors people. It seemed to upset some of them that their precious "test walk" had been reduced to a day by this stupid young bloke who had come along and wiped it out. I think some people were upset by that notion as if, in some way, it shouldn't be allowed.'

'A gruelling solo run through 1500 kilometres of some of Australia's most rugged wilderness has made a Sydney bank officer favourite for the title of the country's toughest athlete.' So reported the *Australasian Post* on 19 February 1987 on Peter's run from Mount McKenzie in Barrington Tops to Walhalla, Victoria.

Peter had set off from Barrington Tops in November 1986—a silly time of year for running through the Blue Mountains and Barrington Tops on account of the high summer temperatures and the risk of bushfires—but better timing for the high country further south. Peter was looking to further extend his ever increasing expertise by covering these big classic bushwalking areas quickly.

As usual, he had set up food dumps—one every 500 kilometres—and had arranged support through Keith Maxwell, Director of Bushwalkers' Wilderness Rescue in New South Wales. The trick was to isolate and segment the areas in case of the need for rescue. Nick Eichhorn, from Bushwalkers' Wilderness Rescue, took him to McKenzies Hut where a few people saw him off.

In his presentations Peter recounts an anecdote from this run that raises a few laughs, but which nevertheless emphasises the dangers facing a solo bush runner. 'I had been running for about an hour and a half through the Mount Royal Range when I leapt over a large dead log,' he begins. 'As I was in mid-stride a snake leapt out and bit me on the dick! Now, what's the cure for snakebite, I thought. Luckily the cut and suck method is out. That's right, you bind the affected limb with a stretch bandage, lower the limb and wait for help. So there I am, standing in the pouring rain, my shorts around my ankles and a stretch bandage in my hand, wondering what to do.'

It seems that the snake was a non-poisonous green tree snake and, apart from lots of swelling which made it awkward to run, Peter suffered no long term effects. He just carried on running, completing the first stage of some 300 kilometres right into Wollemi without a single break.

The scrub was atrocious and difficult to get through. And there was a second snake attack at Nayock Creek, a beautiful rocky based creek in Wollemi. 'I was wearing grey gaiters,' says Peter, 'and a red bellied black snake threw itself off the rocks and attached itself to my gaiters. It wouldn't let go until I picked up a stick and flicked it off.'

Peter then encountered problems on the Colo River with flood water, and was washed downstream 200 metres. He was so tired by the time he got to the Colo River that it didn't seem to worry him. He just drifted down and got out where the water had taken him.

There was some very difficult navigation between Gosper's Mountain and Mount Wilson. The long flat ridges made it difficult to work out where Peter should drop off to get where he wanted to go.

At Kanangra Walls Peter was met at Coal Seam Cave on the side of Kanangra Walls by Keith Maxwell, Robert Pallin and Quentin Chester. This welcome trio had cooked up a pan full of sausages which Peter washed down with Coke. 'That's the sort of thing I look forward to,' says Peter. 'I'm not very scientific about my food on these expeditions and I hadn't eaten very well until this point.'

Peter then pushed on southwards, reaching Sawyers Hut where snowshoes had been stashed with food and other alpine gear. He remembers there was more snow than he had anticipated and almost pulled out at Kiandra. But he traversed the whole of the Australian Alps, travelling day and night. There was atrocious weather on the Bogong High Plains and navigation on the alpine track was more difficult than he expected. 'There were too many conflicting fire tracks and it was very difficult to work out where I was,' he recalls. 'It's not what you'd call wilderness.'

On the alpine track Peter was surprised by dingoes. 'They came into a dugout when I was trying to sleep,' he says. 'It must have been their home! I didn't carry a sleeping bag to save weight, so the dugouts were the safest place to shelter from the elements.'

Mount Hotham provided the next 500 kilometre break. 'At the beginning I was moving two or three days without a break,' Peter recalls, 'but towards the end I needed to stop every day.'

The end was Walhalla, a small village tucked into the hills which marked the end of the Alpine Track. Peter remembers it was drizzling with rain and he was wearing his trademark red jacket. Ensuring a new and impressive tiger walking record, his achievement changed forever the standards against which outdoors hard men measured their success. Peter had crossed all the traditional bushwalking country from New South Wales to Victoria in one continuous trip. But it was not without some pain and the ever-present danger of injury. '1500 kilometres in 10 days equals an average of 150 kilometres a day,' Peter says. 'On these long trips my knees bother me, they get very tender.' Despite twisting an ankle on Tessellate Range, Peter completed a very successful and history making run.

On the strength of this success Peter decided he could run the whole length of Australia. Through the generosity of sponsors including *Australian Geographic*, Paddy Pallin and Commonwealth Bank, he was able to comprehensively plan the whole trip. He needed more than 500 maps, some 150 of which were used in the actual run. Peter would sit at a card table, reading maps and making notes. 'Beth ran the household.' Peter recalls, 'while I spent months ploughing through this huge stack of maps working out the route.'

As a result of such detailed planning exercises, Peter has an encyclopaedic knowledge of a vast area of wilderness. All the maps are filed in cabinets in his garage. Frequently he is called on to advise groups—ranging from Scouts to Duke of Edinburgh Award hikers—about the best possible routes to take, and *Australian Geographic* regularly refers its members to Peter for advice. The easy access to a full set of maps is also useful in search and rescue situations. 'In the old days,' Peter says, 'I used to call Robert Pallin and we would drag ourselves all the way into town to open the shop to find an appropriate map, sometimes in the middle of the night.'

Peter's detailed planning sheets look as if they could be recording complicated military manoeuvres. Each meticulous landscape A4 page is full of handwritten detail for navigation and rescue purposes—including the map series and scale, distance and cumulative distance, the rise and fall and cumulative rise and fall in metres and the map references under days indicating targets and actual distances travelled. Map references for food dumps are also included together with a description of the proposed route, complete with major features such as roads, mountains and rivers. There are also written notes for converting magnetic variation. 'The simple things are what you forget to do when you are really tired,' he explains.

The final document for this expedition included seven pages of closely handwritten and exact notes. On the back Peter had written: 'Buck up, do your damnedest and fight, it's the plugging away that will win the day'— the mantra from Mawson's Antarctic expedition. There is also a Kipling quote from 'If' taken from Shackleton's book and a further quote: 'What have we come to conquer? Only ourselves.'

Peter explains that he keeps these inspirational notes written into his packs and other places to look at when he feels really terrible during a run.

Peter aged 9 (left) with brother Neil and sister Wendy.

Peter as a Wolf Cub in 1966.

Confident in his abilities, Peter was able to show younger Scouts the techniques of climbing and abseiling, even at the age of 15.

Peter receives his Queen's Scout Award from the Chief Scout of New South Wales, Governor Sir Roden Cutler VC, AK, KCMG, KCVO, CBE.

Climbing in the New Zealand Alps at the age of 18, Peter quietly started a lifetime of adventure and record breaking.

Search and Rescue training included bush navigation and communication skills which Peter undertook while he was still a teenager.

Peter emerges from the bush near Kanangra, exhausted after his three-day canyon marathon that almost cost him his life in 1989.

Crossing the deserts on foot is a lonely pursuit. Peter training in the Simpson.

Peter on a Search and Rescue training exercise. Constant practice ensures that rescuers have the highest level of technical skill.

Peter abseils off the southern pylon of the Sydney Harbour Bridge with 81 year old Dot Butler.

Peter making a speech at his brother Neil's wedding.

Peter with his wife Beth, and daughters Marnie (right) and Kimberley (centre).

Peter involves the children in outdoor activities such as canoeing.

In the headwaters of the Jardine River on Cape York. Large crocodiles were encountered a few hundred metres downstream.

Peter in the headwaters of the Charnley River in the Kimberley.

Peter during his 5500 kilometre run from Cape York to Wilsons Promontory.

The concept of the length of Australia run was twofold: to focus public attention on National Parks and wilderness areas of eastern Australia; and to provide encouragement to young people that the great adventures and challenges can still be had in our own backyard. Peter's chosen route would use traditional bushwalking routes as much as possible and stay away from so called 'civilisation'. He was to complete it solo, with search and rescue coordinated through the NSW Federation of Bushwalking Clubs, which would rely on Peter reporting his own progress through a series of prearranged contact points. This had the benefit of segmenting each 500 kilometre stretch into manageable areas for search and rescue purposes.

With so many maps required for the whole trip, Peter organised for sets of maps to be left at the food dumps. It had taken some time to establish the ten dumps, all the way up to Cape York and back down to Wilson's Promontory. Each of them contained four day's food, clothing, head lamp batteries, maps for the next section and specific environment gear. Peter's diet was to mainly consist of food which required no cooking, with some dehydrated food and at least one tinned meal for consumption at each cache, since a small stove was left at each dump too so Peter could have one hot meal.

Originally Peter had planned to make this trip in September/October but was unable to take leave from his job at that time. He finally left earlier, in June that year, at short notice. An inauspicious start was a day's delay due to vomiting caused by a virus.

Peter was to start the run at the northernmost point of Cape York. He flew out of Sydney on a Thursday afternoon and spent the night between connecting flights sleeping on the footpath under an awning outside Cairns airport after security threw him out. He was woken in the morning by a Japanese tourist. Peter caught his connecting flight and was then driven the last 80 kilometres up to the top of the Cape.

In September 1988 *The Bushwalker* reported on what Peter was to call 'the Australian trilogy'. 'On Thursday 2 June, Peter flew to Cairns on what he hoped to be his greatest test to date—to run from the tip of Cape York to Wilson's Promontory.'

'A trip such as this,' the article continued, 'requires tremendous planning especially when you wish to keep away from man-made intrusions. Thus Peter had to investigate many routes in country with which he was totally unfamiliar. Eventually, by following part of the proposed national horse trail, using walking trails in 58 National Parks and identifying "green corridors" linking those parks, a suitable route was identified.'

In fact, Peter navigated his own route through a large proportion of the wilderness areas, only using established tracks where they matched his most efficient route. Basically this meant following the old telegraph track down to Cairns then keeping roughly parallel to the coastline. Nearing the north of Brisbane the route moved inland and down through the New England National Park. From Barrington Tops he would be repeating his run of November 1986 through the Blue Mountains, over Kosciuszko and the Alpine Track to Walhalla and then on to Wilson's Promontory.

'I swam the Jardine River at night,' Peter remembers, 'where the Aboriginal ferry runs during day. I had taken this route following the telegraph line south along the old road, rather than the new bypass, as I needed to be near creek beds for water in the heatwave conditions. Some tourists had also advised me that they had observed drought conditions throughout the Cape country.'

'The thought of crocodiles worried me,' Peter adds, 'as I swam the 75 metre river in the dark. The current swept me down some way as I crossed and I felt very vulnerable. I knew the crocs were there from my research, particularly from Ron and Viv Moon's books. Crossing the river also reminded me that Ron had written that no-one had ever canoed the length of the Jardine River, and that provided the impetus for my later trip by canoe.'

Apart from encountering lots of snakes on the road and coiled around fence posts, Peter also had to contend with other hazards on the track—and he was stung by a wasp in Daintree National Park. 'It's not surprising then,' as *The Bushwalker* continued, 'that he should encounter feral pigs grazing beside the road, numerous reptiles (taipans, death adders, tiger and black snakes), wasps, stinging trees and lawyer vines as well as the unaccustomed heat.'

It took him about seven days to run down to Cairns, making him possibly the first to run down the length of the Cape.

For Peter far north Queensland was a real surprise. 'It's just so vast and lonely,' he says. 'And very difficult country. The Gympie plants sting you if you brush against their big flat leaves. It's very painful and the lymph glands swell up. I slept in my running clothes and had to put up with mosquitoes and sand flies.'

He did however have the pleasure of seeing beautiful brolgas standing in the lagoons of Lakefield National Park. But when you're running you get tired, and one of Peter's main problems was that he found himself getting very depressed. 'Depression caused by fatigue mainly' is how he puts it. 'I found that I was going past that breaking point where it was getting almost impossible for me to keep on going because I was extremely fatigued. I was having to look after myself, in a kind of strange environment—a hot environment—and having to navigate at the same time. I was constantly having to think where I was going.'

To avoid thick rainforest Peter followed the Kuranda Railway which led him through rugged but beautiful terrain with great gorges and waterfalls. At one point he was half way across a bridge on what he thought was an abandoned railway track when a tourist train suddenly appeared before him. Peter was stuck in the middle of the viaduct with nowhere to go—so he climbed over the side and hung on. The tourists were all looking out the windows at a waterfall on the other side and Peter thinks that only one small girl saw him.

It became colder the further south Peter travelled. As he got closer to the NSW border the water in his drink bottle would freeze overnight. The food dumps provided him with progressively warmer clothing but loss of body fat made it harder for him to stay warm.

Suffering from depression through fatigue and loneliness, Peter's physical condition was also deteriorating. And the weather forecast was not encouraging. 'I almost pulled out then,' Peter says. 'It became obvious it would be foolhardy to push through the snowfields. You have to do Cape York in the dry season, but that means the high country is under snow. The further south I went the colder it got. I tried to sleep in my Gore-Tex but it was too cold. The combination of lack of food, lack of sleep and running 18–19 hours a day with only about 4–5 hours sleep made it increasingly obvious that it would be silly to go on. I couldn't control my shivering, and didn't want to die in the snowfields.'

Peter made the decision to maintain his current pace and link into his previous run at Barrington Tops and pull out then. *The Bushwalker* article picks up the story. 'Realising the general run down of his body, his depressed mental state and the extra motivation needed to meet his daily goal made him realise that he would not be able to complete the entire journey as a single effort. So too did news of heavy snow falls during June. All of these factors convinced Peter that to continue would increase the risks to a level that even his abilities and training might not cope with. So to avoid concern to others and danger to himself, when nearing Toowoomba Peter rang Beth and she agreed to pick him up at Barrington Tops. He arrived some four hours late at 2.00pm that day after some 40 hours nonstop running.'

Beth had driven to the Barrington Tops meeting point where Peter had made an appointment for 10am a week earlier. That he was only four hours late is quite remarkable—but even so Beth was a bit upset when he wasn't there on time. 'There was no media,' Peter recalls matter-of-factly. 'I ran in, got in the car with Beth, drove home and got some fish and chips. It was a nice way to finish a trip.'

The Bushwalker concluded its report. 'As a result Peter failed in his goal of running from the northern most tip of Australia to the southern most tip of the mainland in a single effort. That it was required to be completed in three sections—the Trilogy as Peter now calls it—is still a magnificent achievement.'

Lincoln Hall later wrote about the trip for *Australian Geographic*. '"Of course I get scared," said Peter Treseder. "And I get lonely and depressed. Before every one of my big runs I feel sick with nervousness.

'"A run like this is 90% in the head and only 10% in the body," Peter maintains. "It would be so easy to give up or give in to despair. Queensland is a mighty lonely place when you're in the middle of it with only a small daypack containing waterproof clothing, maps and compass, half a litre of water, almost no food and no sleeping bag. I knew I'd be in serious trouble if I slackened my pace and did not reach my dumps within a day or two of schedule. The challenge is to keep all these factors under control in your mind, while running hard continuously and navigating from maps. When I felt like a break I'd slow down to a walk for a while. That way I could keep going for 18 or 19 hours at a time."'

The following month, August 1988, Peter completed the final leg of the journey—from Walhalla to Wilson's Promontory—in the rain and wind. About ten kilometres from the end he badly twisted his ankle and had to hobble the last bit. Peter had been running through the night and had a head torch on. In the early morning he saw the lighthouse which stands at the end of the promontory.

'As I reached the lighthouse,' Peter remembers, 'I realised there was a huge fence cutting me off from the end with a sign claiming it was "Commonwealth of Australia Property". I decided to climb the fence and was immediately bailed up by two enormous and fierce looking Doberman dogs, which barked and barked. The keeper was really annoyed until I told him what I had just done. It turned out that he was an *Australian Geographic* subscriber. He became very friendly and invited me in for breakfast! Sitting in his kitchen and later from the top of the lighthouse, I could see across Bass Strait which gave me the idea for the kayak crossing.'

A locked gate at the visitor car park some twenty kilometres back up the track meant that, after this incredible feat of completing the length of Australia trip, Peter then had to walk back up the road to where the tourists leave their cars. 'It was a bit annoying after 5500 kilometres,' says Peter.

But the overall statistics for the trip were impressive. Peter ran for a total of 41 days at an average 135 kilometres per day, totalling some 5500 kilometres. The cumulative rise and fall during the trip exceeded 120 000 metres and Peter crossed 58 national parks.

One of the Australian Bicentennial projects in 1988 was called 'Unsung Heroes and Heroines'. The idea was that one Australian would be selected to represent every year since 1788. These were to be ordinary Australians who had achieved extraordinary things but had not received huge public recognition.

Beth answered the ad which appeared in major metropolitan newspapers and put forward a detailed submission on Peter's behalf. A shortlist from more than 4000 nominations was drawn up and a researcher interviewed each shortlisted nominee, together with family and friends. Detailed reports were written. Finally 200 Australians were selected—including Peter.

The Australian Bicentennial Authority handed over all the research material on these 200 people to Greenhouse Publications who produced an official book containing a brief biography of each. The Bicentennial Medal and a copy of the book were presented to them in a ceremony at Government House by His Excellency Air Marshall Sir James Rowland AC KBE DFC AFC, Governor of New South Wales. 'It was a pretty big deal,' Peter recalls, 'a real honour to be up there with 199 great Australians.'

Writing all too briefly about Peter in the official book, Lois Hunter describes his Cape to Cape run. 'Peter Treseder is probably the least orthodox of long distance runners, travelling so fast and so hard that one suspects he has not time to experience the much-celebrated loneliness that is supposed to be a part of the run.' Somewhat ironic, given Peter's own recollections of the trip.

CHAPTER 10

NEAR DEATH IN MURDERING GULLY

'It is through action that man steps forth from the repetitive universe of the every day where every person resembles every other person; it is through action that he distinguishes himself from others and becomes an individual.'

Milan Kundera, *The Art of the Novel*, 1986

Katoomba to Mittagong has been a classic walk or run for many years. Before the Bicentennial Track was opened, the standard route was to follow your way from Katoomba to Yerranderie via Narrowneck, the Cox's River and Scott's Main Range, then go across the Sheep Walk down to the Wollondilly, then along a series of fire roads down to Burnt Flat Creek then up to Wanganderry Station and Wombeyan Caves Road and finally into Mittagong.

'I can't remember how many times I've done it,' says Peter. 'My best time for the original route was in 1984 when I broke my own record, completing the trip in 15 hours 26 minutes.'

Robert Sloss had the original idea for the Bicentennial Track and formed a committee to establish a walk with huts and bridges along the lines of the Cradle Mountain track. There was an uproar from several quarters as no-one was keen on creating a formal track through the wilderness.

But Robert persisted in establishing a route. The key was in clearing a track in the upper reaches of the Nattai River up towards Mittagong which would allow the walker to come to Yerranderie and, instead of following the Wollondilly south, to cross it and go up over Balloon Pass and follow the Nattai into Mittagong and Lake Alexander.

Once Robert had established the track with markers, there was some competition to see who could walk it first. Tony Powell and Peter took out the honours, completing the 140 kilometres in about three days. 'It was a fair walk in quite rough conditions,' as Peter remembers it. 'Tony and I were conscious that we were completing the first walk.'

In his early forties, Tony was a friend from the 3 Peaks Club and had a lot of experience walking and canyoning with Peter. 'We knew that a few other parties were going to attempt the walk the following weekend,' Peter says, 'so we just went right out and did it. I wanted to be the first!' Robert recorded it as the first official walk of the Bicentennial Track and these days leads trips along the track with a standard time of about eight days.

'There wasn't much of a shift for me to want to run it,' says Peter. 'I arranged a trip in March 1989 and set out from Katoomba Police Station. Bruce Clausen, my training partner from the bank, came in with Tony at a spot where the Starlight track hits the Nattai, a place called Macarthur's Flat. They ran the last 20 kilometres with me to Lake Alexandra and kept me going along that last hard part.'

The Grose River area has always enjoyed a mystique. The trip from Blackheath to Richmond has often resulted in overdue walkers because people tend to underestimate the difficulty of the terrain. Veteran bushwalkers Max Gentle and Dot Butler first did the trip many years ago.

Dot had come up with the idea of *The Sydney Morning Herald* trip. In the 1930s most people worked on a Saturday morning, so Dot and her companions would catch the train from Central Station just after midday on Saturday. In those days it was a slow trip up to the mountains. To save time Dot would have stashed her bushwalking clothes in a locker at Central, changing from her city work clothes before boarding the train.

The party would get to the mountains by mid-afternoon. Dot had a packet of sausages and bought fish and chips wrapped in *The Sydney Morning Herald*. They then walked to the Blue Gum Forest, ate the fish and chips for tea, slept in *The Herald* to keep warm, then used it to start a fire the next morning to cook the sausages! They would complete the trip in a day.

'Dot has been a hero of mine for as long as I can remember,' says Peter, 'and I did the re-enactment as closely as I could as a solo trip in December 1989.

Dot was out there doing it right back in the 1930s, pushing the boundaries all the time. The only difference was that *The Herald* is no longer used to wrap fish and chips!'

In 1988 when Search and Rescue had needed to raise a great deal of money to buy urgently required radio equipment, Peter suggested a 'climbathon' at the Three Sisters in the Blue Mountains. His ability and profile would be a big advantage in raising money for an organisation he had been involved in for many years and which received no official funding. Peter had done such a thing before with Mark Foster, when they made 12 ascents in eight hours for another fundraiser.

They rigged the side of the West wall with ropes and Peter connected himself to them with a Gibb's ascender. A team of people, including Grant Clark, set up the ropes. But Peter was the only person climbing and was sponsored per ascent by many supporters. In addition the support team set up bucket brigades all around the Three Sisters to collect money from members of the public who were watching.

'It was a bleak day and mostly raining,' Peter remembers. 'I built on the knowledge and experience from the previous climbathon. There is some danger, because you're pretty high, but it's quite safe so long as you remember to change over to each new bit of rigging.'

Peter had arranged for a few of the team to take up specific positions on the wall and around the circuit to look after him. The allotted time was, once again, 12 hours. This time however Peter flew around the circuit, up the west Wall, over the top, down the stairs and back up the Wall again no less than 22 times at an average time per circuit of just 32 minutes.

Remember, this is a climb that most climbing parties allow a day to complete! Not surprisingly, Peter's efforts helped to raise around $20 000 —which included a generous donation from Dick Smith. 'It was so successful,' Peter says, 'that we approached the local council for approval to do another one. But they knocked us back as the National Parks and Wildlife Service were involved by then and they didn't want us bothering the public.'

Peter can't remember how many times he has climbed the West Wall of the Three Sisters, but he does remember one other memorable occasion. He and Andrew Stiff had the idea of creating the world's biggest Christmas tree. So they acquired a lot of those yellow roadworks lights that blink. They stuffed 30 or 40 of them into packs and dragged them to the base of the Second Sister. They then spent all night hauling them up the wall, the packs gradually getting lighter. At regular intervals they would place another light and turn it on, before moving up the wall to the next spot. 'Eventually we finished and went round to Echo Point,' says Peter. 'There we could see our 1200 feet high Christmas tree, blinking away on the other side of the valley.'

In February 1989 Peter saw an opportunity to 'capture' another river. This time his sights were set on the Macleay in New South Wales. 'My sister was living in Kempsey,' Peter says, 'so there was a focus on this area as a family. The trip followed on from one that I'd done with Steve Trémont—my Franklin River companion—Beth, Paul Fardouly, Cathy Randell and others.'

On that trip Peter and Steve had walked from the Blue Hole, Armidale, down the Garra Gorge to the Macleay River at George's Creek. Here they met the others and canoed to Bellbird where they ran out of time. But it gave Peter a good grounding about what the place was all about.

The Macleay was the first in a series of reasonably accessible rivers that Peter explored. 'These are big rivers,' he says, 'but disappointing with high pollution, mainly agricultural run off. It makes the water nutrient rich and encourages growth of all sorts of unpleasant stuff. You wouldn't want to drink it.'

For his solo attempt, Peter positioned his canoe slightly higher than George's Creek, starting his run in the centre of Armidale at Dumaresq Drain which eventually runs into the river. He canoed down to Kempsey and pulled out where the main bridge goes over the river. His brother Neil brought him a bike which he pedalled all the way to South West Rocks to complete the journey.

Fittingly, a photograph Neil took of Peter holding his bike aloft at the end of the trip was later used as a poster for Australian Geographic shops.

Near Death in Murdering Gully

Over the years, Peter had gained much experience in canyons and continually pushed himself to bigger and harder achievements. He conceived the idea of the 'big daddy' of all canyon trips in 1989. The idea was to start from the northern extremity of the canyons beyond the Zig Zag railway on the Newnes Plateau and work his way across to Kanangra. He would go through one after the other, all 26 selected canyons, and cover all the ground in between finishing at Kanangra Walls.

The trip from Newnes to Kanangra Walls is a tough enough bushwalk even without the canyons. There is a great deal of ground to cover through quite difficult country. To include a descent of all the canyons is a major undertaking. It ended up becoming three and a half days of solid canyoning for Peter, and nearly cost him his life. 'Bob Cavill took me out into Newnes and got me started,' Peter says, 'while Bob and Steve Irwin and some others arranged to pick me up at Kanangra.'

As usual, Peter had arranged various sign off points so the support team knew where he was. 'I made a phone call, for example, from Mount Wilson,' he remembers, 'and met one of them somewhere else. There are a few places where you come out into civilisation and can make contact.'

How do you do such a trip efficiently? 'You don't need ropes for all of the canyons,' Peter says by way of explanation. 'You arrange it so you can drop gear at one spot and pick it up for the next canyon where you need it, without having to carry it all the way round. You must also be efficient in terms of the route you might be following.'

Claustral Canyon is a good example. The usual way to complete Claustral and Thunder canyons is to do each one from the top to the bottom. However, Thunder Canyon is located to one side of Claustral and the finish for both is the same. Peter started Claustral in the usual way from the car park, then climbed up the side of Thunder Canyon to the top and made a normal descent into Claustral and completed that. Both were achieved without him having to go right around to the start again.

In other words, Peter's extensive knowledge of canyon terrain—together with meticulous planning—enabled him to use passes to link the canyons together to traverse them efficiently. And his knowledge of where the passes might be was crucial to the success.

Everything went well until he reached the last stage at Kanangra. By this stage Peter had been traversing canyons for almost three days solid without any sleep or break—an endurance feat unparalleled in the sporting world. He was wading up Kanangra Creek in fast water up to his waist. It was very difficult to get up and he was extremely tired and finding it hard to concentrate. Rain had swollen the creeks and the weather forecast was for more. Peter knew only too well that many canyons become totally impassable after heavy rain and that fatalities have occurred when canyoners have been trapped by rising waters and drowned.

At the final canyon, Kalang Falls, Peter's support team planned to come in and film him, establishing themselves with climbing equipment before he arrived. As he made his way up Kanangra Creek Peter tried to turn left up Murdering Gully, which he had done many times before. It was the standard route. But for some reason he missed it—presumably because he was too tired and cold, it was raining, he was wet through and the creek was in flood. 'I realised I was in the wrong spot,' he recalls, 'and didn't know where I was. I dropped my pack once and it took me ages to get it back. I was lucky to find it.'

Eventually Peter found another way up, although ultimately he still found himself where he shouldn't be. It was too vertical and he couldn't get down again without abseiling. He was trying to force himself up when he came across an 11mm blue water rope hanging down in the gloom. He presumed that he'd crossed Murdering Gully and was closer to Kalang Falls and that the rope was one Bob had set up to film him.

Using his remaining strength, Peter climbed up the rope hand over hand. It was a 50 metre rope and every muscle was burning as he reached the top. To his horror he saw that the only thing securing the rope was a knot in the end which was held fast in the fork of a small tree. He had climbed 50 metres in extreme danger of falling off the face of the cliff.

Peter left the rope there and scrambled a bit higher. By this time it was dark, he was tired and he still didn't have a clue where he was. 'I sat on a little ledge half a metre wide in the pouring rain with my Gore-Tex jacket and leeches for company all night,' he says.

Experts say that you tend to lose 25 per cent of your ability to think straight every 24 hours without sleep. By the end of three days you have perhaps 10 per cent of your normal faculties left. 'That's just how you feel,' agrees Peter, 'you start to stumble.'

At about 9am the mist cleared long enough for Peter to work out where he was. He was able to set up his abseil rope, get down, find his way to Murdering Gully and walk out. By the time he arrived the others were getting really worried. And he never did find out where the rope came from!

Peter has been involved in Search and Rescue for years, feeling that there was a distinct need for a small group of fit, skilled people to be able to go in and do canyon rescues. Police can easily rescue people from cliffs, run a truck up to the edge, set up their equipment. But as canyoning became more popular, special skills, years of experience and lightweight equipment were what was needed.

Peter formed the Rock Squad, now recognised by the State government as having achieved the standard for qualification required by State legislation. Indeed, this group's recognition marked the first time any actual qualification had been sought under the legislation. 'I have always maintained that the politics of rescue would mean we would be unlikely to be called upon by an official rescue group,' Peter says, 'but our expertise would be out there in the field in the bushwalking and canyoning fraternity.'

In fact, individual members of the Rock Squad, including Peter, have been involved in a number of rescues that have only been possible because they were there and had the necessary skills.

'We now go for reaccreditation every three years,' he says. 'It starts with a three hour written theory examination on mechanical advantage systems and other subjects. You must know where the forces are being applied to the system and where it is weakest and how much it will bear to make rescues safe. Testing our personal mobility skills is next, up and down ropes, and the group dynamics of running a rescue. We do this through the Volunteer Rescue Association—a section called the Australian Lightweight Vertical Rescue Instructors—run by two friends, Philip Toomer and Judith Bateman. For 20 years these people have given up their time to build people's skills to help make the bush a safer place for everyone.'

The Great North Walk runs from Sydney Cove to Newcastle for a couple of hundred kilometres. Friendly with John Eggleston, the project manager for the Lands Department who was building the track, Peter had walked it in stages before it was constructed and given John some help with details of the route from his own extensive experience. 'John subsequently helped me with the run,' Peter says. 'When I ran the whole length in May 1990, parts were still not finally constructed although there were track markers. I was keen to get in and do it first.'

Peter took the route from Newcastle down to Sydney. He wanted to do the whole trip under his own steam. Most people take a ferry across the Hawkesbury and Sydney Harbour. But in the early dawn light, Peter swam across the Hawkesbury from Patonga to Brooklyn, all the time worried about sharks.

'Beth and Mum and the family were having a Mothers' Day picnic at Lane Cove when I ran through the park,' he remembers. 'But I was pretty tired by then and didn't stop. When I reached Valencia Wharf at the end of Valencia Street in Hunters Hill, I used a sea kayak to paddle down the Harbour to the Man O'War steps at the Sydney Opera House. I had special permission to land there. Sitting in the sea kayak after running so far was very uncomfortable. My bum was chafed and very sore. When I got out of the kayak I could only hobble up to Macquarie Place where the track officially starts or finishes.'

The Great North Walk usually takes an experienced bushwalker about a week. Peter completed it in just over 32 hours. John Eggleston documented the run for the Lands Department. Peter recalls that every so often John would pop up at strange places to flash a photo. Then a few kilometres further on he would reappear. Needless to say Peter was pleased to be the first person to officially run the length of it.

A few months later, in August 1990, Peter traversed Kosciuszko National Park on snowshoes, thereby continuing to build on his previous trips in both summer and winter.

The following year he used all this experience to complete a snowshoe traverse from Canberra through the mountains to Victoria.

'Looking back,' he says, 'there's a build up of length and intensity in these trips. I had experience on other smaller trips across Kosciuszko National Park and from Kiandra to Perisher on snowshoes. But I understand this was the first time the whole of the Australian Alps had been traversed in one go.'

Peter decided to use snowshoes because he didn't think he was a good enough skier. In fact he thought he'd wipe himself out skiing. Some of the areas are heavily wooded and you need a great deal of skill to negotiate them. For him, snowshoes were a better bet, even though they are strenuous to use—and even though, strangely, Peter does not wear boots, even with snowshoes. 'I used running shoes,' he explains, 'wrapping them in a plastic bag.' And his 'racing snowshoes' are specially adapted for speed with cut outs at the back to avoid catching them as his feet cross over from back to front.

The trip covered the whole area from the northern to the southern extremities of the generally accepted winter snowline. Starting at Honeysuckle Creek Tracking Station in the ACT, the eight day trip ended in Victoria at Walhalla. 'I was very pleased with the time,' Peter says. 'Most of the ground was under snow and I didn't have a tent. I camped in dugouts on the alpine track and stayed in the occasional hut. I took very little gear except a light sleeping bag and food which I didn't have to cook.'

Once again, Peter had set a new standard, building on his already extensive knowledge and understanding of the terrain to employ a different set of skills. It is this multi-skill approach and his ability to survive and perform in difficult conditions that continues to set him apart from other outdoors people.

Chapter 11

Crocodile Country

If you can force your heart and nerve and sinew
To serve your term long after they are gone,
And so hold on when there is nothing in you
Except the will that says to them
'Hold on'

Rudyard Kipling, If

When Peter read in one of Ron and Viv Moon's books that no-one had ever navigated the entire 270 kilometre length of the Jardine River, he was captivated by the idea. He thought about it again while worrying about crocodiles as he swam across the river on his length of Australian run. Before long he was hooked.

'When I got back, I called Ron Moon on the phone,' says Peter, 'and asked him if it was true that the Jardine had not yet been canoed. "No, it hasn't," he said. So I asked him if he would like to organise an expedition. Ron said he would and the expedition was born!'

All of the organisation was done over the phone. Peter raised the sponsorship money from *Australian Geographic*, the Inflatable Boat Warehouse provided the canoes and Paddy Pallin provided food and equipment. Ron organised support from *4×4 Australia Magazine* and also brought vehicles, invaluable expertise and his brother Dave as support.

Ron, an experienced four wheel driver, bushman and author, knows wilderness Australia very well. His brother, Dave, is equally at home in the bush. 'The first time I met Ron was when he picked me up on the side of the expressway going north,' laughs Peter. 'We had the canoes and gear, loaded it all up, then picked up his brother, Dave, on the way and headed north.'

Peter and Ron seem to have the same attitude on trips. Get in, get it done and get out—safely. The two are now good friends. 'It was a really safe feeling to be with these guys,' Peter reflects. 'Their expertise in fixing broken vehicles, welding from battery power, extracting vehicles from bogs and navigating through wilderness country was invaluable.'

The Jardine is the largest perennial river in Australia. It is also the only river with its whole catchment area protected within national parks or reserves. 'It is important to recognise the nobility of the river by Australian standards,' Peter says. 'As incredible as it may seem, the only disturbance in the whole of its catchment of 2507 square kilometres is the unformed road that follows the telegraph line to Cape York and a few minor roads, now mostly abandoned. There are no feral or grazing animals except for a large population of pigs, no agriculture and no timber has been cut commercially. This is an unprecedented situation in the civilised world.'

In a magazine article in *4×4*, Ron describes the river as 'rising in the low jungle clad hills that make up the Great Dividing Range in this section of Cape York, the Jardine beats a tortuous path through all the points of the compass before swinging to its final destination on the west coast of the Cape, just 40 kilometres south of the most northerly tip of Australia.'

The Jardine is a sandy based river which literally bubbles out of the sand in the rainforest. Their aim was to walk into the headwaters where it starts and follow it all the way to the ocean.

Apart from Ron and Dave Moon, the expedition also included Steve Irwin, Peter's friend from Search and Rescue and Warwick Blayden, a bushwalking companion. The group drove straight through to Cairns in Ron's Toyota Troop Carrier. They did the trip in just two days, changing drivers regularly, but stopping only for fuel. They then made their base at a house at Clifton Beach which belonged to a Search and Rescue colleague. After some final preparations and intent poring over maps they drove up to Cape York, via Musgrave Station. Camping was basic, using the internal part of two-man lightweight tents to keep out the mosquitoes.

When they reached the mighty Wenlock River it was still in flood after a late wet season. The only way to cross was by using a raft constructed from four rows of seven 44-gallon drums, held on each bank by cables to save it from being swept downstream. A vehicle would be driven onto thin branches supported by the drums and pulled across by people in the river, mindful of the ever-present danger of crocodiles.

In these wilderness conditions everyone helps everyone else and the group was no exception, helping others and accepting help themselves. 'We got bogged,' says Peter, 'and used a hand turfer winch to get ourselves out. Then we assisted another vehicle on what passed for the main road, which was underwater at that point. It had bogged on a side track.'

Captain Billys Landing Road leads off the main Development Road up the Divide on the eastern side of the Cape. Peter remembers driving along this road and thinking he didn't want to get out of the vehicle. It was stinking hot, with mossies, flies and an impenetrable wall of jungle to get through. Fallen timber had to be cut out with a chain saw, winches were needed to get the trees out of the way. The remote roads were slow and time consuming. They had continual problems with punctures, using an inflatable balloon jack off the exhaust system. At the last camp he and Ron were discussing with Dave where they would come out on the river later. They really didn't know.

As the group travelled further into the jungle they camped on the road itself. There was no other traffic—and there was nowhere to go off the road.

Eventually it was time to walk. Everyone had the same amount of shared gear, including the inflatable canoes and paddles. But a photograph taken of the four together with their rucksacks containing personal gear shows Peter's looking half the size of the others'. It probably weighed less than 15 kilograms while the others held a good 20 or more.

Peter explains that they took the inflatable canoes because they thought they might have to walk for up to a week before striking water. As Ron remembers it, while their packs were heavy, the paddles proved to be the most awkward piece of equipment—they kept getting tangled in the scrub, bringing the group to sudden, unexpected halts. And since they had taken only ten days' food, mainly freeze dried, the pressure was on.

Dave had turned back with the support vehicle on his way to the agreed meeting point down river as soon as the four had set off on foot.

'They got a gun?' the Aboriginal ferryman asked him, his brow furrowed by years of squinting into the sun, and possibly a touch of worry.

'No,' replied Dave, knowing they had decided not to take guns because a crocodile attack would be over in seconds and there was more chance of them shooting each other than a crocodile—a decision even Ron and himself, who were very familiar with guns, had agreed with. 'It's a national park.'

'Huh! Big old man crocodile, he don't know that! He eat you all the same.'

With that reassurance Dave, the pick-up man, returned to his lonely vigil on the banks of the Jardine River in far, far north Queensland.

With limited food and water supplies and no radio contact with the outside world, the others knew they had to find the headwaters of the river fast. They thought it might take several days but then, after a day, they saw the water bubbling out of the sand. It was not deep enough for canoeing, so the party inflated their bright yellow Dolphin inflatable boats and pulled them through to avoid carrying everything. The jungle was thick, the water was crystal clear, fallen logs were everywhere. It was very hot, with lots of flies.

Ron takes up the story. 'Launching our canoes we had set off down river only to be stopped within 100 metres by the first of many log jams. Hauling, sweating, carrying and cajoling our boats and equipment through mazes of twisted logs was alternated by brief bursts of paddling on the free flowing stream.'

Overhanging vines and vegetation made the journey dark and mysterious but still, according to what they'd been told by experts, they did not expect to see crocodiles for at least 150 or 200 kilometres. The national park rangers and everyone else had said they were not to be found in the upper reaches.

Disaster struck suddenly on the first day as Warwick's supposedly unrippable canoe hit a sharp, broken branch, suffering a gash about a metre long. The mending kits were very small, with only small patches and two small tubes of glue. The group spent hours fixing the rip by taking cushions from the boat to use as a patch and using all of one of the precious tubes of glue. Obviously the experts who claimed the boats wouldn't tear had never been in this type of country. Here, pigs root around the base of trees and, when the monsoons come, the soil gets washed away and the trees fall in the river.

The very next day the other boat was also ripped—and was mended in the same way. After that they had no glue left and couldn't afford to get more rips. They swam with the canoes through pools, occasionally getting into the boats where the water was deeper. They tried to look after them, carrying the canoes under and over fallen branches, taking immense care. One more rip and they would not have enough canoes for the whole party and they hadn't even got to the main part of the river where they must canoe through crocodile country. Then the unexpected happened.

'Steve and I were walking the boat around a corner,' Peter remembers, 'and a huge crocodile launched itself off the bank across the water in front of the lead canoe. It scared the hell out of us. It was obvious it had pissed itself so we had scared it too. It had probably never seen a human.'

From the slide marks on the bank Peter estimated that this one was probably three to four metres in length.

'What the hell do we do?' cried out Steve.

'Stuffed if I know,' replied the expert, Ron Moon. 'I've never been so close to them before!'

The stress of manoeuvring the canoes around obstacles, when they had to be in the water with crocodiles, began to tell on everyone in different ways. Steve came down with a bout of diarrhoea and was sick for a couple of days. All of them were suffering from nerves at different levels, although everyone was pretty calm. 'Warwick never came back on another trip,' Peter admits. 'And I felt nauseous all the time but said nothing. It was beautiful country but we were on edge because of the risk.'

Peter had not told the others that he had ever been up in this country before. 'I wanted this trip to be a real first for everyone,' he explains. 'The thing was to keep it all fresh for us all, including myself.'

It was difficult to judge their progress. 'We could only guess at our position and our rate of travel,' Ron wrote in *4×4 Australia Magazine*. 'Creeks and even quite major streams joined our river with seemingly no correlation to the map. At our second night's camp the river was 10–15 metres wide and we passed at least one major island where the river had branched and then reunited without even a hint of it on the map. Along the banks the vegetation changed between magnificent virgin rainforest, tall heathland and drier sclerophyll forest. Fish flashed across pools and shallow sections while birds and butterflies added a splash of colour.'

The group set up camp only half a metre from the side of the creek. They couldn't get in any further, and by now there was a real danger from crocs.

As Peter, Steve, Ron and Warwick made their way down the river it got deeper and wider. When they reached the point where two branches of the Jardine meet, they knew the worst was over. In fact in one photograph Steve and Peter seem quite relaxed, lying back in their canoe, being taken down by the current, their bodies almost on the waterline. Nevertheless, it wouldn't have taken much of an attack from a crocodile—just a nudge or a bite—for the boat to be destroyed.

Towards the end Peter and his companions were walking the canoes over big sandbars. The river was really wide and shallow and Warwick even tried some fishing when they made camp.

Completing the river safely and without incident, the four met up with Dave. He had set up camp under a shelter and placed a sheet of corrugated iron between him and the water as he too was paranoid about crocodiles.

With a sense of relief the paddlers packed up their boats and drove to the Cape York Wilderness Lodge where, in their official 3 Peaks Club Jardine River Expedition T-shirts, they were given a free meal in exchange for Peter delivering an impromptu presentation to the other guests!

For a pleasant finale, they decided to take a brief tour around Cape York in the 4WD. Coming back across the still flooded Wenlock, Ron thought it was now shallow enough to drive through—but the car started to float. Ron quickly opened the windows and let the water in to provide ballast.

With an improvised snorkel, he kept the engine running. Water came in one window and out the other, while the others used snatchem straps to pull the heavy Troop Carrier across the river and out of danger.

'The Jardine was a really significant achievement,' remarks Peter of the trip. 'A lot of people said it couldn't be done. It's a magnificent river that, surprisingly in 1989, no-one had ever canoed for its whole length. This prize had got away for so long. We had the privilege of being the first, with the whole thing pristine. There are not many countries in the world where you could do that.'

This trip also signalled the start of Peter's serious public speaking as he started to work the story into bank presentations. He had been talking to John Martin at the Commonwealth Bank about the clients they got in to talk about economic matters. 'I told him they all get bored and only come out of respect for him,' Peter says. 'He was a bit of a lateral thinker and had set up a company dining room with proper silver service that was used all the time to wine and dine clients in the North Sydney Branch. So I suggested that we might get some clients in and I could talk about crocodiles. He agreed to give it a go and everyone became very enthusiastic.'

The idea worked, the clients loved it and Peter carried on, making new presentations after each trip—marketing to the clients in a soft sort of way. It was the first time Peter started to include some of his philosophy in his slide shows. 'I started talking about focusing on goals, doing things for the first time,' he remembers. 'It wasn't very well thought out at that stage.'

The following year, Peter decided to attempt the full descent of the Archer River and invited the Jardine team along. This time the canoe team comprised Ron, Peter, Steve Irwin and Dave Dickford replacing Warwick Blayden. And there was a bigger support team including Ron's wife, Viv Moon, their son Trent and Ron's brother Mick, a real tough guy who had spent almost his whole life in the army including several tours to Vietnam.

Viv was in charge of the 4WD trailer, which had cooking facilities built in. She has a great reputation for cooking and even produced fresh bread every day.

The Archer River is towards the south of Cape York but was flooded completely at the mouth towards the western side of the Cape. Peter's aim was to walk over the Great Dividing Range and through the jungle to the headwaters. The park ranger told them however that it was particularly bad where they wanted to be pulled out. The trip would be impossible if they couldn't get the support vehicle in.

Peter believed he owed it to his sponsors to achieve something. He had again arranged sponsorship with *Australian Geographic*, Paddy Pallin and the Commonwealth Bank. And there were new sponsors too: Australian Native Fisheries, Canoe Specialists and Waves Overseas Sales. Peter immediately started to look for another objective.

'There was a fair bit of tension in the group,' he remembers, 'as we had lost our aim, and were trying to refocus. My view was that the sponsors didn't give us the money for a holiday. I needed to come back with something we had achieved. At the same time there was some pressure from the party that we should just give up and do something softer. It took quite a while to refocus the group.'

The target they finally decided upon was the Dulhunty, which flows into the Gulf of Carpentaria at Port Musgrave. Looking without success for an old mining road indicated on a map, they decided to look up the map maker who lived at the tip of the Cape, several hundred kilometres away. On the way they thought they might as well bag another river which had never been fully explored—the Eliot, which runs north into the Jardine. Peter believed they could get access to the headwaters, making a full descent possible.

The group was well-equipped with two four wheel drive vehicles plus trailers. It was very remote country and they needed to be totally self-sufficient. When the party reached the Wenlock and crossed by the oil drum raft, the combined weight of the vehicle and trailer almost totally submerged the raft with a real danger of losing everything if it tipped. Luckily it maintained balance, reaching the opposite bank in safety.

The party navigated in to the upper part of the Eliot River from the dirt road by walking on a bearing. It was difficult in flat jungle country to judge distance so Ron used an old army trick of counting paces and tying a knot in a length of string to judge the distance travelled. 'Ultimately we found the creek,' says Peter. 'We had a much needed drink then walked on until we could use our rafts.'

The creek suddenly expanded. In their bright yellow inflatables—which were nothing more than kids' toys you could buy in any camping shop—they saw huge and beautiful pitcher plants, fantastic formations and waterfalls. They followed the creek down through a series of cascading falls a metre or so high which they had to walk around to make sure the inflatables were safe.

Eliot Creek is hemmed by steep banks and jammed with wood in its upper section. Further downstream it runs across flattish rock and Peter was confident there were no crocodiles at this level because of the waterfalls.

'We met the support crew in magnificent country at Twin Falls, walled in by waterfalls,' Peter recalls. 'Our plastic Canadian-style canoes had been brought in by vehicles and we changed over for the serious part of the journey.'

Soon the creek became a bit canyon-like with rocky sides. They came across more beautiful waterfalls but didn't want to risk a capsize. By now there was the ever-present danger of crocodiles, so they portaged around almost every fall.

Steve and Peter tried to canoe one waterfall where they knew the water was deep enough but lost it—and Peter lost his camera overboard. 'I had to dive down very quickly to get it,' he recalls. 'This was prime crocodile country and we were starting to get on edge. We could see slide marks on the banks.'

In one memorable incident the canoes were close together and a big crocodile came aquaplaning across the river towards them, head out of the water, eyes looking straight at them. It submerged just beside the canoe. It was a very scary moment. 'Let's get the hell outa here,' Ron Moon called out.

Peter took many photographs of crocodiles up close. 'They would surface just beside the boat but taking photographs without good equipment was difficult. I would start to shake,' he remembers. 'The biggest croc I have seen in the wild was about six metres. It was like being in the water with a dinosaur, especially when you look at it through the water beside you.'

The group canoed safely down to the Jardine to the place they had previously canoed. As they had no need to go further unsupported they tied the canoes to the support inflatable which had a motor and were towed to the next point.

By now the expedition was beginning to fall apart as some members clearly did not want to continue. But Peter still felt the pressure to go on and do something new. 'So we decided to do the first descent of the Dulhunty,' he says, 'but had to work out how to get ourselves out at the end.'

The Dulhunty River runs roughly east to west coming out at Port Musgrave. They found the map maker and then located the old mining road to give them access to the exit point for the canoe trip. They had almost reached the old mining camp along the road when they came to the last creek before the Dulhunty joined the Ducey.

'Getting bogged was a new experience for me,' Peter admits, 'but it was as much part of the expedition as anything else. I have a strong memory of crossing creeks with a huge bow wave in front of the vehicle and boggy, slippery exits needing maximum skill. There was a sign on one creek crossing which said, "Water level can vary 4–6 feet in pot holes. No fishing."'

It took three days to clear their way through the abandoned track to a suitable area for the canoe trip to finish so the expeditioners could be picked up near the end of the river. Severely overgrown, the track was hard, hot work. 'We had to cross a little creek near the end on the way back after finding the spot and got the vehicle well and truly bogged,' Peter says. 'It was sideways and the tide was coming in. We tried everything. We tried the turfer winch and broke it, snapped a bolt inside. Then we tried to set up a "Z" pulley to gain mechanical advantage. Steve was in the vehicle revving it up when the steel cable snapped, throwing the turfer winch by his head. We were still stuck.'

After some hours they used the other vehicle to drag the bogged one backwards to the wrong side of the creek by building a causeway with lots of small branches. They eventually got back through just before the tide covered it in several feet of water. Then, once again, they walked in to the headwaters from the main dirt road, this time from a point approximately 40 kilometres south of the Heathlands Ranger Station. They navigated to the top of the creek in the usual way, Ron pacing them with knots.

They had decided to walk the whole upper section of creek as they were very disappointed with the performance of the rubber boats. 'The strain was terrible,' Peter explains, 'with some of the guys not really wanting to do it because of the crocodile issue. How to keep them motivated, keep them going was my biggest problem. As with all my trips I was the driving force, but I had to have Ron's cooperation. I just couldn't do it without his support. Dave, at this time, just didn't want to be there at all.'

Ron later wrote in the *Northern Sun* that the group 'followed a dry channel less than 50 centimetres wide which soon collected a steady trickle of water. By mid afternoon the group were at their canoes, which they had paddled upstream the day before from the Overland Telegraph Line crossing point of the Dulhunty.'

The stream became a real river, reinforced by the waters of the Bertie and Cholmondeley Creeks, all named by explorer Frank Jardine, and the paddlers pushed on downriver in their plastic canoes. Everywhere was hanging rainforest, very dark and mysterious. To avoid crocodiles they camped a fair way from the river in thick scrub. At one point a snake fell off the branch of a tree and landed right between Ron and Dave as they canoed. An old tinny was seen wedged several metres up in a tree—washed down in the wet season. 'I even considered taking it to help deal with the crocodile problem,' says Peter.

This was their worst experience with crocodiles to date. The crocs bumped the bottoms of the boats repeatedly, an aggressive action which Peter knew could precede serious attacks. 'A menacing head would then appear right next to our boat,' says Peter. 'It was a scary sort of river, like a tunnel, very spooky. We manoeuvred the boats around trees, and sometimes had to be in the river which was very dangerous.'

Feral pigs, often in groups of 30 or 40, waded in the shallow water, although most took off when they saw the boats. On one occasion a couple of large pigs charged down the bank towards them, but thankfully took off and turned away as soon as the other boat came around the corner.

By the time the paddlers met up with their support crew at the prearranged spot the guys didn't want to go any further. They were by now entering prime crocodile breeding country, with marine swamps and mangrove thickets—nurseries for baby crocodiles—and, as the river widened up into the Gulf of Carpentaria, no identifiable river banks.

Peter however was still keen to finish the trip. He and Ron agreed on a compromise. They would take the inflatable with the motor provided they could work with the 3 metre tidal rise and fall to get down and back in time. If the tide dropped too far they would find it impossible to get back up the river over all the exposed logs in shallow water. When they started out at 6am the next day, the river had dropped only about a foot or so. 'Ron gunned the boat down the river,' Peter remembers. 'It was really exciting stuff. A couple of times he turned the boat to check it had enough power to get back up against the tide.'

As they reached the end of the river in the Gulf, Ron did a wide turn to go back upriver. On the apex of the turn the engine suddenly died. 'I paddled madly against the current to get us to the side where we could grab a tree,' says Peter. 'The tide was rushing us out into the Gulf of Carpentaria and we didn't like either the idea of being stranded until the incoming tide, or the prospect of having to paddle all the way upstream.'

Ron finally got the motor going, and they raced back up the river, just managing to scrape over the last trees before the tide dropped completely. 'I saw the only dead crocodile I have ever seen,' says Peter. 'Floating upside down, it was about 5 metres long. That was very unusual—the only thing that could have killed it was a bigger crocodile.'

For this trip, as much as for any other, Peter's research was thorough. 'I had read as much as I could,' he says, 'about crocodile attacks, when and where they occur, trying to define a pattern, identifying warning signs and learning about their behaviour. Then I just hoped like hell that the crocodiles had read the same books!'

On the way back from the Cape York trip Peter phoned home and spoke to his father. 'Congratulations, you're going into Group Credit,' said John.

'What the hell is that?' asked Peter.

It was a promotion and, unusually for the bank, it was one Peter had not even applied for. 'The normal promotion process,' he says, 'is that you put your name forward and the selection process starts with those people. But, in this case, I had just been selected.'

Peter had been in charge of a team of corporate lenders at the North Sydney branch of the Commonwealth Bank working under John Martin, an inspirational manager and something of a legend in the bank. Now, he was to work in the city in a new credit area that was being set up by another legend, John Edwards, a man with a fearsome reputation for his toughness and integrity.

CHAPTER 12

SOLO ON CAPE YORK

An explorer is an explorer from love, and it is nature, not art, that makes him so.

Ernest Giles, *Australia Twice Traversed*

The Archer River was still unexplored so Peter organised with Ron and Steve to go back the following year to complete the Cape river system. 'No one really wanted to do it,' Peter says, 'and ultimately they all pulled out on me. But I had my sights on completing the trip and decided, as I used to in Scouts, that if no-one would come with me I would do the trip on my own. I wasn't going to let this thing slip, even though I couldn't get anyone to go with me. I'd gone a long way down the track with organisation and sponsors.'

'I had a month's leave in June 1991,' says Peter, 'but the arrangements fell apart only a month before the due date. So I had to put the Archer trip together very quickly. I brought my planned Hinchinbrook Island trip forward to the last two weeks and decided to concentrate on the Archer for the first two.'

Peter had very quickly recruited Keith Williams and Ian Brown for the Hinchinbrook Island expedition, together with Greg Randell. Peter flew to Cairns but didn't have a boat. 'The first thing I did was to hire the cheapest car I could find,' he says, 'but forgot about roof racks for the canoe. Then I drove around looking for a cheap canoe, finding one at Clifton Beach to the north of Cairns.'

The car was a VW beetle with a roll back roof and Peter rolled it back and stuck the canoe in behind the seat, sticking right up out of the roof. With the canoe like a sail he drove slowly through Cairns and up to the Atherton Tableland along winding roads into Mareeba. Peter had decided to bag the Mitchell River too.

'Obviously I didn't want to leave the car up there and pay all that rental,'

Peter says, 'so after leaving my canoe in the upper reaches of the Mitchell I drove the VW back to Cairns. Then I hitched back up to where my gear was stashed.'

As journalist Glenville Pike reported in the *Northern Star*, 'He flew to Cairns, purchased a canoe and had it in the headwaters of the Mitchell River between Mareeba and Mount Molloy in two days. In another he had returned to Cairns and run from Mareeba to where he had cached the canoe in the Mitchell. He then canoed down past the Cooktown Crossing.'

The Mitchell River is 650 kilometres long and has one of the biggest catchment areas of any river in Australia. Discovered in 1845 by the explorer Leichhardt, it is one of the great rivers of the north. There is no settlement apart from Kowanyama for the whole 650 kilometres as any homesteads are well away from the river because of flooding.

The river is relatively pristine. But navigating his way through the early stages of the river was very confusing at night, which is when Peter did it. There was however plenty of water in this ever-flowing river, fed mainly by the McLeod River's rainforested source on the western side of the coastal range just north west of Mossman.

A property developer had in recent years cleared many square kilometres of the country in order to build the biggest privately owned dam in Australia. Consequently, the river was full of bits of timber that had been pushed into it from the clear felling. At the time there had been a lot of protests and the local Aborigines were also concerned that the topsoil would be washed down the river in the next monsoon, ruining their fishing. Peter had asked permission from the Kowanyama settlement to do this trip through their territory. 'I wrote to them as I always do,' he says. 'The white manager had said he would take me out if I needed help.'

Peter knew there was a fairly large set of waterfalls on the Mitchell at a place called Gamboola. Ron Moon had mentioned it and warned him. There were freshwater crocodiles in the top of the river too and salties some way down, but Peter didn't know where. Generally they're not found together because the salties eat the freshies! Peter canoed down and found the falls—and indeed that's where the salt water crocodiles started.

'There were a couple of incidents,' Peter says. 'The first when I was going round a bend in the river with a metre high sandy bar on one side of me. The crocodile was sunning itself on the bank and, when he was aware of me coming down river, he slid off the bank and landed on the front of my boat as I paddled around the corner.

'The boat tipped bow down, throwing me up in the air, his thrashing tail catching me on the chest as he tried desperately to get away. I was thrown out of the boat and scrambled quickly up the bank where I realised the crocodile had pissed itself in fright. That made me feel a bit better as I think I'd pissed myself in the boat too!'

The boat went floating off down the river, before jammimg itself on the opposite bank. 'That was no good to me,' Peter says, 'as I had been thrown out of the boat with nothing. All my gear was in the boat, on the other side of a crocodile infested river. I didn't feel too happy!'

Peter walked back up the river for some kilometres and crossed where he felt it was safer. Then he trekked all the way back down the other bank until he was able to retrieve the canoe, on the lookout for crocodiles the whole time.

After that Peter decided to wear a small backpack with survival gear in it in case such a thing happened again, a practice which was to save his life.

There was no room for camping equipment in the small kayak so Peter would snatch a few hours sleep beside the boat on the bank, preferably where he couldn't see any crocodile slide marks.

One night he was resting by the river and was chased up a tree by a wild pig. 'I seem to have more trouble from pigs when I am on my own than when I'm with a group,' he muses. 'And this one just chased me right up the tree and wasn't going anywhere. I'd done a St John Ambulance First Aid course that the bank organised just before I left and learnt how to tie a collar and cuff sling—so I used one to tie my hand to the tree so I wouldn't fall off.'

The tree overhung the river and there were crocodiles in the water. Peter could see their eyes at night as they waited for him to fall out of the tree, while the pig rooted around the base of the tree waiting for me to climb down. 'I just hoped that if I fell asleep the sling would stop me falling. I was stuck there for four or five hours until the pig finally went away.'

It took Peter about four or five days to complete the trip to the Gulf and he had no more incidents with crocodiles on the way down. When he got there he met two men who had been fishing and were on their way back to Weipa in a Shark Cat. He was behind in his schedule and asked them for a lift. Everything got loaded into the bottom of their boat and they took him up to Weipa where he met a couple of American tourists from Carson City. This couple were looking for a place to fish and Peter needed to get over to the upper reaches of the Archer. So he suggested that Port Stewart had great fishing. 'Now, I didn't know whether it did or not,' Peter smiles. 'I'd been out there once with Ron Moon but really I had no idea.'

This move, however, gave Peter the opportunity to make a quick descent of the Stewart River which runs from west to east from the Divide, the rivers on the eastern side being quite short.

'The Americans drove me around to Coen in their four wheel drive,' Peter recalls, 'and positioned my canoe where I wanted it. I ran from there up into the headwaters in the McIlwraith Range just east of Coen, ran back, picked up my canoe and paddled the Stewart River to Port Stewart in a day. It was a long day, with lots of crocodiles in the river. When I got back to Port Stewart sure enough these guys were there. Luckily they were happily catching fish and having a good time and they agreed to set me up for the Archer.

'We drove along a fire trail to Peach Creek, an upper tributary of the Archer in the McIlwraith Range rainforest some 20 kilometres north east of the Coen airfield. I knew exactly where I wanted to go as I had been there the year before with Ron. We drove towards some tin mines and I stashed my canoe where the road crossed the creek. We drove back around to Coen, then I ran back up into the McIllwraith Ranges, a pristine rainforest area. I remember seeing a rare green tree python. Then I made my way down through beautiful cascading rocky sort of country along the upper part of Peach Creek down to the plains, picked up my canoe and paddled 300 kilometres down the Archer River.'

This was really remote country and the rangers had warned Peter there would be lots of crocs. When the river floods they go all over the alluvial plain and, as the water level drops when the dry season comes in, they concentrate back onto the river itself, moving quite long distances across country.

Peter admits he was very nervous having to paddle at night on a very tight deadline. He was well into the two weeks he had allowed for the rivers and Ian, Greg and Keith were due in Hinchinbrook for the second two weeks of his leave. He had to get down there and yet here he was heading off into the middle of nowhere in the Cape area.

'It's eerie at night,' Peter recalls, 'as the crocodiles make this sort of barking sound, their eyes glowing redly. Obviously, there are just as many around during the day but you don't see them so much as they are so well camouflaged.'

Barramundi in the river, flying foxes in their millions, scrub fowl and feral pigs were Peter's other companions. His plan was to get out at Aurukun, on the northern bank of this huge bay. He had come into the southern side following the natural course of the river and followed it right down to the Gulf of Carpentaria to complete the descent.

Peter was on his way back up to a suitable spot where he could cross to Aurukun, feeling pleased with his effort and just keen to get out of there. He was planning to leave the canoe with the Aboriginal people for the kids and to fly out on a light plane.

'That's when the crocodile grabbed the end of the boat and started tossing it about like a matchstick,' he says. 'I fell out, panicked and swam like crazy about 50 metres for the shore, dreading that the already aggressive crocodile would let go of the boat and chase after me and kill me. I was really, really, scared.

'I never saw the crocodile during the attack,' Peter continues. 'By the time I got to the shore I was aware the thrashing had stopped and the crocodile was probably heading after me so I got well away from the shore and up on the bank. I could see my boat with almost half a metre of the back bitten right off. I guess it was in the crocodile's belly.'

The damaged canoe drifted off down to the Gulf of Carpentaria, never to be seen again. By now Peter was on the bank, but the danger was far from over. He was hundreds of kilometres from civilisation—and once again on the wrong side of a crocodile infested river. Crocodiles, he knew, hunt with great skill and patience. When one sees its prey on the bank of the billabong getting a drink at night, for example, it will come up on the other side, only its eyes showing and without a ripple. Then it will sink down and repeat the process across the billabong, always keeping its prey in sight. Eventually it will get within a metre where it will see you silhouetted against the sky above the bank.

Crocodiles have massive great tails which they thrash from side to side to give them extremely fast forward motion. And they have enormous energy over short periods of time. They'll grab prey, drag it back into the water and roll and thrash to drown it. Then they can do what they like with the body. They bite chunks off, swallow it whole and digest it in the stomach. They don't need to eat very often so they stash the carcass somewhere in the mud, going back to it whenever they need a feed. Usually the meat is rotten by the time they finish it.

'I wasn't keen on becoming crocodile food,' says Peter flatly, 'so needed to get right away from the river.' Fortunately, following his Mitchell River experience, he had a pack on his back with a little food and some water. 'As I tell my audiences at this point,' Peter recounts, 'I had always wanted to run across Cape York, although not quite under these circumstances! I had no choice but to run back about 250 kilometres.'

It took a couple of days. He collected water from the creeks as he ran. The shadows of the trees concealed lots of snakes. One night he startled a camp of Aboriginals. They welcomed him into their camp and called him Byamee, meaning 'spirit man'. Earlier they'd seen him go down the river in the canoe and then he'd come on foot from the other direction. The Aborigines were really impressed with the sort of distance he had covered—hence the name.

Peter completed the run to Port Stewart where he found the American guys yet again. 'By this time they just thought I was the real Crocodile Dundee!' he laughs. 'They gave me a lift to the Development Road where I hitched a ride down to Cardwell and met up with Ian Brown, Keith Williams and Greg Randell, ready to start the Hinchinbrook traverse.'

By then Peter had canoed three rivers, a total of 1035 kilometres, and run 250 kilometres across Cape York—all in eleven days.

CHAPTER 13

SPIRIT OF ADVENTURE I— HINCHINBROOK

'Pervading all is the feeling that here nature has excelled itself in its portrayal of splendour and strength, leavened with the ever-changing beauty of sunlight, shade and colour, so that yesterday's impressions are as different from today's as tomorrow's surely will be.'

Arthur and Margaret Thorsborne, *Hinchinbrook Island—The Land Time Forgot*

One of the world's largest island national parks, 393-square-kilometre Hinchinbrook Island lies about 5 kilometres off the Queensland coast at Cardwell between Townsville and Cairns. This is where Peter met up with Ian Brown, Keith Williams and Greg Randell to start the Hinchinbrook traverse. While Peter, Keith and Ian were experienced companions on tough and challenging expeditions, Greg Randell was a bit of an unknown quantity. Untested, he was the brother of Cathy Randell, partner of Peter's friend Paul Fardouly from the 3 Peaks Club.

The first time Peter saw Hinchinbrook was when he had been driving up to Cape York with Steve Irwin to do one of his early river trips. 'I had just handed the driving over to Steve,' Peter recalls, 'and he told me to look out the window. These fantastic peaks were sticking up out of the clouds off the coast to our right. At that time I'd never heard of Hinchinbrook Island, I didn't even know it was there.'

The island skyline is dominated by 1121 metre Mount Bowen, which towers over a rainforest wilderness and mangrove lined shores. Once Peter's curiosity was aroused it didn't take him long to discover that no-one had walked the backbone of the island from the northern to the southern tip. The East Coast Track was very popular and people had climbed some of the prominent peaks like Mount Bowen, but no-one had traversed from one end of the island to the other. 'I couldn't believe in the 1990s that no-one had ever traversed it,' Peter exclaims. 'I just thought, I'm going to do this.'

Captain Cook had discovered the island in 1770 and named it after Lord Hinchinbrook. The Aboriginal people on the island were a separate group from those on the mainland, and were known as the Bandyin after the peaks of the islands. They built huge stone automatic fish traps on the beaches. Cemented in place by thousands of years of oyster shells, these traps are still washed by the tides every day.

The four explorers caught the regular ferry which takes people to the start of the East Coast Track. The ferry captain agreed to help them get to Hecate Point which is the northern tip of the island. It couldn't get too close to the shore so they were put ashore in a small boat.

It was extremely hot and humid as they unloaded the boat and climbed to the top of the watershed. They had quite an amount of water in their packs because no-one had been able to tell them whether there was any water up there or where they would get it from.

Peter's presentation about this trip opens to the rousing music of 'Nessun Dorma' and a succession of breathtaking slide images of the island, each dissolving into another even more stunning view. Majestic mountains and beautiful ocean views are followed by captured images of sparkling creeks and free flowing waterfalls. Untouched, thick rainforest vegetation extends to the top of the peaks in an unbroken vista of lush green. Hinchinbrook Island was like a secret kingdom and one could only imagine how its Aboriginal inhabitants had lived.

The series of unconquered saddles and rising peaks presented a challenge Peter and his team could not resist. 'It was a real challenge,' Peter says as the music rises to a crescendo and the screen fills first with long range shots of the whole island, then closer views of fantastic rugged country.

Peter's presentation continues as the constantly changing slide show and music build powerful emotions in his audience. This is the first of his professional presentations with audio-visual effects and philosophy honed by his friend and mentor, Tim Lamble.

Peter refers to a book on the island, *Hinchinbrook Island—the Land Time Forgot*, by Margaret and Arthur Thorsborne, whom he credits with saving the island from development and securing it as a national park. The island has no permanent residents; Margaret lives in a beautiful rainforest lot opposite the island. The East Coast Track is now named in Arthur's memory and Margaret continues to stand up for the preservation of our environment. Her last big campaign was directed against the dredging of Hinchinbrook Channel and the destruction of mangrove swamps for a resort development. She appeared regularly on Australian television screens, a little old lady with a big message and a determination that matched that of the big financial interests.

'Ian, Keith, Greg and I stayed with her before and after the expedition and Beth and Marnie have stayed there too,' Peter recounts. 'She has this magic little cubby house place in the rainforest on the mainland, overlooking the island. It was into this world we stepped.'

Despite the warm and humid climate the group had reasonable gear in case of bad weather. They really didn't know what they might find up the top. The party had also anticipated quite large rock climbs and taken ropes for this eventuality. Appropriate dress included shorts, shirts, gaiters and leather gloves. A pair of garden secateurs named 'the badge of courage' would be handed to the leader to help get through the scrub.

'The scrub was probably the worst we have ever seen,' Peter says, 'and we had to snip our way through. But the reward was that, from the ridge line, we could see on the eastern side scattered islands out to the horizon and, on the west, the mainland coast and swampy creeks turning and twisting down below.'

The party walked for about eight or nine hours a day. Mostly the weather was good but they did encounter a few misty days. 'It was very rocky,' remembers Peter, 'and we had to climb up fairly steep ridges to get to the top of some of the peaks.'

The island is only about 50 kilometres long—a distance Peter would regularly run in half a day on some of his trips. But their best distance after nine hours struggle through the tangled vegetation was just 8 kilometres. 'Our worst day,' Peter recalls, 'was 1 kilometre travelled after nearly eleven hours' hard work.'

Navigating was difficult as the only map available was not very accurate and the scale too small to show many features. Many of the deep canyons were not even marked. The route was often decided by climbing trees and using binoculars. The group did, however, enjoy camping spots with million dollar views. 'We stretched a tent fly between the trees and shrubs on the ridge line so it provided the minimum of shelter,' Peter says. 'There were no tents to damage the undergrowth. Our aim was to walk in and walk out without leaving any evidence of our trip. We had great views—but we were exposed to the weather.'

Since Peter had just completed his two strenuous weeks in Cape York canoeing and running, not only was he tired, but he had been operating at a different speed. 'I had to adjust myself to the different terrain,' he says. 'My psyche came down to a kilometre a day. It was a really big shock. The defining factor was the scrub. We had to dig and tunnel our way through it. You can't walk over it, it is so incredibly dense. I would say it was the most sustained lousy vegetation any of us had ever struck.'

Photographs taken from above show only arms aloft and a hat penetrating the head-high undergrowth, untouched for thousands of years, as the group pushed their way through. Huge fig trees with buttress roots lead to thickets of lawyer vine—so named because once it gets its spikes into you it doesn't let go. The barbs caught in their clothing and on their skin. The tough leather gloves were wrecked. There were banksia and casuarina trees all intertwined. 'We couldn't walk over the vegetation,' Peter explains, 'because we didn't know where the ground was. We weren't on solid ground so we had to tunnel and cut our way through to avoid accidents. The first person had a difficult time, and we took it in turns to lead with the secateurs.'

At one point the map showed an easy ridge at an angle of around 50 degrees, but in the saddle there was an unmarked gorge which had to be descended and climbed again. Some other big descents off the ridge lines meant that the four used ropes to lower their packs and abseiled down, old fashioned hand over hand style. Going up was often more straightforward than going down as it was easy to get stuck on cliffs, without any route down clearly identifiable.

The scale up close was enormous and to gain access to the major part of the traverse the party had to climb a big band of rock. Peter led this section which took them vertically a couple of hundred metres. There was also lots of rock scrambling which Peter particularly enjoyed.

Water was a constant problem as it was so hot they needed to consume a lot. They usually collected it at night, by camping in gullies or ducking down the side of saddles to creeks far enough to get fresh water. Sometimes they used the map to try to find these spots but it was not very accurate. Nevertheless, they didn't have any problems finding enough water.

Because the expedition had a clear intention of not creating a path they also took cooking stoves and didn't build any campfires. Where they camped they didn't cut down any vegetation and the flattened grass would pop back up in no time once they were gone.

It is a tribute to the skill of these four adventurers that they achieved their target without incident and in safety. Ian Brown wrote in his account of the South Pole expedition that Peter wanted to pull out of the Hinchinbrook Island trip at a particular point—something Brown couldn't understand. Peter sheds light on this incident by explaining that, by the time they had traversed half the island, Greg Randell was really struggling. There was a once-only opportunity to pull out—and Peter offered it to Greg by publicly offering for them all to call it a day. 'My gut feeling,' recalls Peter, 'was that by giving him the opportunity to pull out without losing face I would release the tension and pressure on him, taking it on myself.' And indeed this is exactly what happened, with all four members of the team completing the expedition.

The island had probably not been fully explored because it was such difficult country to navigate and travel through. There were real dangers in unmapped territory and a walker attempting Mount Bowen off the tourist trail had lost both his legs in an accident.

As they came down off the end of the last mountain they traversed down a creek and came across something quite unique. At first they thought it might have been wasps—there was clearly a swarm of something. As they walked closer they could see that every tree, bush and rock was covered in moths. Billions of them, all up and down the trees. The moths came off in military precision from the bottom, creating a snowstorm of moths, getting up behind their glasses, in their ears and eyes. 'We couldn't see where we were putting our feet,' recalls Peter. 'It's amazing, the power of a simple little thing like a moth multiplied millions of times.'

It was a million to one chance that the group should encounter such a phenomenon. On their return several scientists at James Cook University in Townsville became very excited about the discovery when they heard of it.

The traverse was completed in nine days, finishing at George Point in the south of the island. Before they took the ferry back however they walked to the East Coast Track and made their way back up the island to have a quick look at the resort in the north. That there was no marked track for this northern section was of little hindrance.

Along with Paddy Pallin, *Australian Geographic* and The Athlete's Foot, the Commonwealth Bank had provided sponsorship for this trip which Peter partly repaid through his exciting audio visual presentations to bank clients. Tim Lamble helped with the first of these professionally produced shows, which was based on the three Queensland river trips and the Hinchinbrook Island traverse. 'I knew of Tim's work,' Peter says, 'and just called him up and asked if I could come round and meet him. He's helped with all the shows since then, providing inspiration for the themes and direction for the emotion-building combination of audio and visual images to capture the attention of the audience and put them in the right frame of mind.'

Peter's philosophy starts to shine through in this particular presentation. He makes much of the way in which the trip started. The glance out of a car window, coupled with the power of the spirit to make the expedition happen.

'We succeeded,' he says, 'because we had a vision for the future and we weren't scared of failing. We just got on with it. I believe we can all develop the power that makes us all strong so we can do anything.'

All of Peter's presentations have an image of him and his companions showing the Australian flag—in one case a pillowcase borrowed from a German tourist—at the completion of their journey. He pushes the Australian theme a lot—but claims to have more of a world view than a nationalistic one. 'I am proud of the spirit of the Australian people,' he says. 'It seems to exemplify what we can all do. If we can do it, you can too.'

Peter was awarded the first of his three *Australian Geographic* Society's Silver Medallions in 1991. His association with *Australian Geographic* had developed over many years through generous sponsorship and articles about his trips in the magazine. In the early days Dick Smith sponsored some of Peter's expeditions and the organisation was well aware of his exploits.

The Silver Medallion was awarded for Peter's Spirit of Adventure and for his long term involvement in search and rescue work. In his acceptance speech, Peter thanked Dick Smith and made a strong point about responsible risk taking. This was particularly relevant as around that time there had been talk among some New South Wales politicians about charging people for rescues. But first, Peter entertained the gathering.

'In 1988, the Bicentennial year, I completed a series of runs from the top to the bottom of mainland Australia. I traversed 58 national parks from north to south, a total distance of 5500 kilometres, averaging 130 kilometres a day for 41 days.'

Peter then went on to relate the incident when he was bitten on his penis by a snake. The incident makes a funny story and the successful completion of the run proves that world class adventures are possible in our own backyards. 'But what would have happened if the snake was poisonous and I required rescuing or had died?' Peter asked. 'How would society have viewed my adventure?

'When I was growing up, I learnt at school about people like Scott, Mawson and Kingsford-Smith. Their achievements to me at the time seemed to be so great that in my mind they became almost superhuman—God-like. They appeared to me to be larger than life and as a normal person I could never hope to emulate them. As I matured and was successful at my own adventures I realised that their achievements were not beyond my grasp and that they were, indeed, just ordinary people like you and me. They did, however, possess a vision for the future, were prepared to work hard to achieve it and were not scared of failing. They possessed the spirit of adventure.

'Adventure exists in the outdoors, in the arts, in business—everywhere. One of my fundamental beliefs is that anyone from any walk of life possesses this spirit and can achieve anything that they set their mind to. I also believe that if everyone worked towards these ideals, society in general would be better off. Ordinary people striving for greatness. We all, therefore, have the capacity to make a positive contribution to society.

'But adventure, by its very definition, has an element of risk involved. It must be remembered that occasionally, while striving towards a particular goal, people are going to make mistakes. Society has to be prepared to pick up the pieces and provide encouragement where needed. It must not dampen the individual or group spirit.

'This award is therefore dedicated to the hundreds of men and women who are involved in bushwalkers' search and rescue, who are prepared to pick up the pieces, at no cost to the community and so encourage the spirit of adventure.'

Peter had started to canoe a series of non-remote rivers, and had tackled the Macleay first. He now set his sights on others.

The Nymboida River flows into the Clarence River and is regarded as a classic white water river in New South Wales. Peter started in the New England Plateau well above the headwaters of the river. He went up as high as he could and came down on foot to Platypus Flat where he had stored his canoe.

Platypus Flat is where the commercial rafting trips begin for an exhilarating ride down river. 'I'm not a great canoeist,' Peter admits, 'and this is a classic white water descent. Some rapids I had to portage around, others I went through in a kamikaze fashion.'

Peter made it through the rapids and into the Clarence and followed the whole length down to the breakwater at Yamba. He then paddled back up a short distance and pulled out.

'Dolphins swam along with me for about an hour,' he recalls. 'Five or six of them swimming and diving alongside the canoe. They kept me going and it was a great way to finish the trip.'

Peter had been going for three days solid, paddling through the night, even through some of the white water. The only light he had was from a head torch and he went through some of the rapids and walked around others. He 'wasted a fair bit of time' because he couldn't see where he was going—but he kept moving. 'That's my usual way of doing these trips,' he explains. 'Just keep moving, even if it's a bit slow at times.'

Food supplies were in Peter's backpack for the upper section, and stashed in the canoe for the river itself. Canoe Specialists at Beecroft had lent Peter the kayak. 'I always used the skirt on the kayak,' he says, 'and was able to do eskimo rolls in those days. I think I wore a life jacket but no helmet. I would have known the risks but very rarely use a helmet for anything.'

Peter had gathered a lot of knowledge of the northern part of the Blue Mountains National Park over the years and decided to string the Seven Peaks of Wollemi together. In April 1991 he tackled them. Unlike the southern section, the Wollemi doesn't have the same tradition for trips like the 3 Peaks walk. Perhaps the major difference is that there are no tracks between the peaks in the northern part.

'It is very remote country,' says Peter. 'Going into Mount Mistake, for example, you cross a series of wide ridges and it's difficult to know where to turn off. It's difficult to navigate and traverse and people typically would take days to get in and out.'

Starting at Grassy Hill on the Putty Road, Peter took in Mount Savage, Mount Barakee, Mount Mistake, The Maiden, Parr West, The Island and Parr South in his round trip, returning to his support crew in just 16 hours. 'A significant trip,' Peter comments, 'taking in a number of the major features for the first time in a continuous loop. There were no particular problems but the navigation was hard—as well as the actual walking.'

Marnie Treseder was born at the Sydney Adventist Hospital on 17 October 1990 and Peter was there. 'It was one of the times I felt really scared,' he admits. 'Really scared. It revolved around this thing we had created that couldn't be walked away from. I went through a whole range of feelings. I was scared for Beth about the birth but more than anything about this thing we had created.'

Peter had attended prenatal classes at the Sydney Adventist Hospital and Beth gave him books to read. 'I read this bloody great book on pregnancy on the train because I had no idea what it was all about,' he says. 'That made it easier at the birth because I then understood more, knew what to expect. In the end I felt quite comfortable about the physical aspect. But I was nervous about the outcome. Was it a he or a she? Would it be healthy? What about the ongoing responsibility?'

Beth maintains that Peter stayed calm and that she was unaware of his nervousness. 'It was a straightforward birth,' she says, 'in the beautiful surroundings at the San.'

After an indication that it was time, Beth had gone into the hospital, spent the day in hospital watching TV and Peter joined her after work. He wanted to know what he could do but there was not much action, so he went home. After a couple of hours he got the call to go back. Beth's labour started at about 9.30pm. 'It was all very tense,' Peter remembers. 'When Marnie popped out she was given a quick clean and given to Beth then I took her off and gave her a bath. She was determined from the moment she popped out, she seemed to have a determined quality about her,' he says before adding, 'the next day I was really stuffed.'

He went back to work and Beth stayed in the hospital for a week, Peter visiting every evening after work. When Beth came home, her mother, Anne Ferguson, was there to help while Peter used most of the daytime of his week-long paternity leave to train for his next expedition.

Peter had been away for a month up in Cape York during Beth's pregnancy and his more local expeditions had continued up to September with a run from Binna Burra Lodge to O'Reilly's Guest House in the Lamington National Park behind the Gold Coast.

'Peter was not there to help,' insists Beth. 'He knew my mum was around and took advantage of the extra week's leave to do things. I seem to remember he came and went. The only time he was at home he was asleep on the beanbag with Marnie asleep on top of him. She would quieten down lying on Peter's chest.'

In November, a few weeks after Marnie's birth, Peter ran the Hume and Hovell Walking Track over three days. The concept of the track was thought up by John Eggleston, a project manager for the Lands Department. However, the politics of that organisation dictated that he would be given management of the Great North Walk while his concept was handed over to someone else. But his interest in the Hume and Hovell continued and he was able to assist Peter with maps to get his run set up as the track was being completed.

'I had done a series of day and weekend trips with various 3 Peaks members in order to set up the run,' Peter remembers, 'though not as many as for some trips because the track is substantial and generally well marked. It has stiles over fences and established camping grounds.'

The run started at the marked tree at Albury and followed the mostly marked track all the way to Lake Burrendong. Keith Williams was stationed at the Sport and Recreation Camp on the northern end of the lake and had agreed to give Peter a hand with canoes to traverse the lake from the south. As usual, Peter wanted to ensure that he completed the entire distance under his own steam.

'But I had asked Keith to give me a hand,' Peter says, 'and he was waiting for me at the southern end of the lake when I came down off the high peak of Wee Jasper. It was very steep, the track took me down to the road, then down to the lake. I was stuffed after more than 300 kilometres of running.'

Keith is a canoe instructor, highly skilled and expert in a variety of craft. By his own admission Peter is no expert canoeist and was worried as soon as he saw the canoes that Keith had brought along. 'They were TK1s,' Peter says, 'which are very fast, flat water racing boats, very long, with no sides and very tippy. Even if I was fit I would find it hard to sit up in them. I knew as soon as I saw them I was going to have problems.'

Peter had a bite of lunch that Keith had brought along then tried out the canoe. 'I kept falling over every 3 or 4 metres,' he remembers. 'I just couldn't stay upright. I thought this is going to end right here because I won't be able to get up the lake. Every time I fell out I had to drag the canoe back to the shore and start again, then I would fall out and have to try all over again.'

Keith, meanwhile, was easily paddling about near the lake shore, waiting for Peter. Eventually he got it going but discovered that once he was moving he couldn't stop or he would fall out again. There was nothing for it but to start off and make as much progress as possible.

After paddling for a couple of hours, Peter's legs had gone to sleep and he stopped at a little island for a rest, dragging himself up the shore. Once he got the feeling back in his legs, he got back in and paddled on to the other end of the lake past the sport and recreation camp. He had some problems with the waves from powerboats and only just managed to get there before dark.

While Keith packed up the canoes, Peter started running. The rest of the track follows a fire road and then the main road into Yass. 'After Keith packed up all the gear he drove behind me in his car,' Peter remembers. 'I ran in his headlights, while he sat behind me, snacking away in the comfort of his warm car.'

Peter ran another 30–40 kilometres, about the length of a normal marathon, to finish the run at Cooma Cottage in Yass. The whole trip had taken an hour less than three days.

Chapter 14

Conquering Bass Strait

'This is ours together,
This nation—
No need for separation,
It is time to learn.
Let us forget the hurt,
Join hands and reach
With hearts that yearn.
Your world and mine
Is small
The past is done.
Let us stand together,
Wide and tall'

    Jack Davis, *The First-born and Other Poems*

As Beth Treseder read in *The Sydney Morning Herald* of Saturday 25 January 1992 of her husband's award of an Order of Australia Medal in the General Division, he was on his way to completing a double crossing of Bass Strait in a borrowed sea kayak.

Starting out that Thursday morning about 7am, Peter had set the 5.5 metre *Greenlander II* straight towards Tasmania, ignoring the generally accepted and safer paddlers' route via the islands. His starting point was Tidal River, on Wilson's Promontory in Victoria—his target Cape Portland on Tasmania's north eastern tip. By canoeing directly to Flinders Island and avoiding the Hogan and Kent Groups he would shave some 30 kilometres off the journey.

Bass Strait lies in the centre of the roaring forties. It is renowned for its rocky islands, outcrops, shipwrecks, unpredictable weather and tidal currents. There are unconfirmed stories about two Victorians who swam in to a beach in Tasmania after abandoning their boats in huge surf, and of a Tasmanian who died in an attempted surf landing near Port Welshpool, but it is not clear who completed the first kayak crossing of the strait.

In 1980, the colourful character, Laurie Ford, had arrived in style on the mainland to preside over the first sea instructor kayak course, having paddled from Tasmania. Several of the trainees then paddled back with him after the course. Earle Bloomfield used a crossing in 1986 as training for an adventure he was planning in Greenland. Peter Treseder was to follow with his trip a few years later.

'I guess it was just a logical extension of some of the kayaking I had done in the past,' Peter explains. 'The Timor Sea trip or some sort of remote trip was in the back of my mind. So I spoke to Larry Grey at length on the phone and others in the sea kayak club in Sydney about how they had done it.'

The traditional route is to island hop around an arc of islands. You can usually see from island to island. They vary in size from impressively big with sheer cliffs to very small and craggy and they are mostly difficult to land on. You have to know where to go. Most paddlers will get to one island and stay overnight. If the weather is good the next day they will go on to the next island, if it's bad they stay where they are. It is a relatively safe trip for an experienced sea kayaker unless the weather changes quickly and you get stuck between the islands.

The canoe Peter had borrowed from Ian Brown was well-equipped for the journey, with waterproof compartments for supplies and a hand bilge pump. He had decided to balance the risks. 'It's a bit like climbing a mountain. You can get up to the summit fast with certain risks or you do it slowly with a big party and take longer with the different risks that implies. I chose to go straight across. The risk was that I would be a long way from the islands and, if a really big sea came up like it did in the Sydney to Hobart race in 1998, I wouldn't be able to handle it. It's basically a higher risk but you get it done quicker.'

Peter used a standard bushwalker's Silva compass to navigate by during the day, and at night relied on the beams from island lighthouses. He had obtained all the marine charts and memorised the sequence of light flashes on all the lighthouses. By day he could see where he was going but even

Not all of Peter's expeditions have been serious. Here in the Blue Mountains with brother Neil, he creates one of his 'silly' records.

Peter, Keith Williams and Greg Randell traversing Hinchinbrook Island in 1991.

The famous abseiling trip in the Blue Mountains.

Peter rode his inflatable woman in the missionary position all the way down Wollangambe canyon.

A design combining the best elements of previous carts, Peter's desert cart weighed 260kg at the start of the Simpson crossing in 1996.

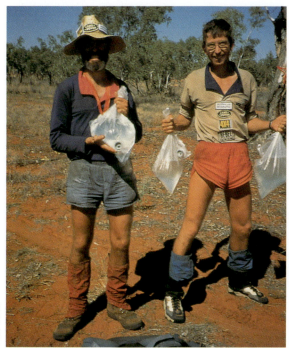

The last day of the Simpson crossing was 80 kilometres on foot with backpacks. This is all the water Peter and Keith had left when they arrived at the finish point.

Peter (right) discussing the British attempt on Batu Lawi with the Pak Ukat village headman in the long hut.

From left: Peter, Morie and Dave at their bivouac camp between the two peaks of Batu Lawi.

Peter at Cape Byron about to start his record-breaking East–West traverse of Australia in 1995.

A typical vision of Peter at speed in the bush.

On Captain Billys Landing Road at the headwaters of the Jardine River. Notice Peter's small pack size relative to his companions. From left: Steve Irwin, Warwick Blayden, Peter and Ron Moon.

Training in the snow with his 'racing snowshoes'.

Peter training with snowshoes on the soft sand – a reasonable substitute for snow.

Peter and Keith set up camp on the Ronne Ice Shelf, Antarctica.

Carrying Scout Group name tapes on his journey to the South Pole, Peter is proud of his Scout background and is actively involved in motivating Scouts and their Leaders.

so the drift and tides were a problem as they are so unpredictable.

Peter paddled all the first day and that night non-stop. Still feeling strong after reaching the northern tip of Flinders Island in 25 hours, he paddled on to Cape Portland, completing the 230-kilometre journey in 38 hours. He had to get to Tasmania before it got dark. The last four or five hours were a desperate struggle to get across and Peter just made it by nightfall.

There were no incidents during the trip except for a big fright when a whale surfaced right beside him. 'This huge great thing came up beside me like a Russian submarine,' Peter recalls, 'and swam along with me for an hour or so.'

Finding time to do these trips is always a problem. For the strait crossing Peter had tacked three unused rostered days off onto the long weekend, giving him a total of six days to drive down to Wilson's Promontory, complete the double crossing and drive home again. A few of his workmates in the bank knew of his plans, but some did not altogether approve.

'John Edwards called me into his office,' Peter remembers, 'and told me he thought I was being irresponsible. He said the least I could do was to let the authorities know what I was doing. Now I was in a bit of a quandary. If I went to the Land Sea Search Centre and the Water Police they would probably tell me not to go.'

Some of the other senior staff at the bank were boaties, with ocean experience. They persuaded Peter to take an EPIRB (Emergency Position Indicating Radio Beacon), a positioning device you attach to your wrist and flick on if you need rescuing.

'Dick Branson lent it to me,' Peter says. 'They all thought I was nuts doing this thing. But I agreed that if I was taking the EPIRB I should tell the authorities. What I did in the end was phone them and tell them I was going to do some canoeing around some of the islands off Wilson's Promontory. I just neglected to tell them one of the islands was Tasmania!'

After he got back Peter reported in and the man he had spoken to had a great laugh. He thought it was a fantastic trip. But, by then, he also knew it had been completed safely and pumped Peter for information about the conditions.

Peter admits he had been petrified about the weather. He had watched the weather charts for months before he made the attempt, studying the patterns—and made a promise to Beth that if the weather was bad when he got down to Wilson's Promontory then he wouldn't go.

In the event, however, the weather as Peter started out was very good—and it held all the way to Tasmania and almost all the way back again.

'I wouldn't have done it if I had thought it was irresponsible,' says Peter of the return trip. 'I could have pulled out at various points and didn't need to make the double crossing. In the end I did so because I couldn't afford to pay for the canoe to be flown back to Melbourne. It would have cost a fortune that I wasn't prepared to spend, so I paddled back.'

When he'd landed in Tasmania it was dusk and, as usual after paddling for hours, Peter couldn't walk. He lay in the sand for a while then dragged the boat up and slept for a few hours. Starting off before daybreak the next morning, he made it to Flinders Island. By now he felt very tired so rested for a couple of hours. Then he headed straight back to Tidal River as the weather had begun to deteriorate badly. His final six or seven hours through the night were a real struggle. The next day brought storm conditions so his luck had just held. He had been blessed with a patch of almost perfect weather.

At Wilson's Promontory Peter grabbed an hour's sleep, drove back to Sydney and promptly went to work the next day. There were congratulations all round about the Order of Australia and letters and messages came in from all quarters. 'I was overawed,' Peter says. 'It was fantastic.'

The award had been made for Services to Bushwalking and, as the Governor said at the time, it was unique. 'Peter Sinclair, the Governor of New South Wales, impressed me with his knowledge and the way he had a quiet word with everyone,' Peter says. 'He knew about my Trilogy run and was spot on with his comments. He said at the presentation in April that it was quite unusual, being drawn from such a huge base of people involved in the activity.'

After his initial nomination for the award, a number of Peter's friends and colleagues had been interviewed to check the references. They included Ian Gibson from Paddy Pallin, Howard Whelan from *Australian Geographic*, representatives from the bank and members of various search and rescue organisations. The award was made in recognition of his contribution to the sport at the cutting edge, for his long term involvement in search and rescue and for his motivation of other people.

'It was a real honour to get it,' he says.

By the middle of the year Peter was looking for a new challenge. He chose the remote Kimberley region of Western Australia. 'I wanted to go to a different area of Australia and I had no experience of the Kimberley,' he says by way of explanation. 'It has completely different geography to the east. And, of course, I also wanted to do something for the first time.'

He spoke to Malcolm Douglas, a well-known Australian documentary film maker and bushman, who had experience in the Kimberley. He met up with him in Sydney where Douglas had a house at that time. He told Peter that he had briefly seen the bottom part of the Isdell River and it was the best looking gorge he'd seen anywhere, but didn't have time to do anything more.

On the strength of that discussion Peter put together an expedition to be the first people, apart from perhaps indigenous Australians, to traverse the entire length of the Isdell River from top to bottom, the Charnley from the bottom to the top and the Manning River from the top to the bottom—a 650 kilometre circuit.

The team comprised Ken Wilson, a doctor and friend of Peter's, Keith Williams and Tony Gavranich, a local guy recommended to Peter. 'I thought he would be a good asset,' Peter says. 'He helped us pull the expedition together.'

Kimberley country is very remote and the party would not be able to carry their food for the whole 650 kilometres. Peter wrote to Norforce, an intelligence gathering unit operating in the northern part of Australia and based in Darwin. Essentially it comprises a small professional group of soldiers who utilise a vast number of volunteers including the Aboriginal people. Peter asked the Commanding Officer, Lieutenant Colonel J. McRoberts, for sponsorship and for help to get food and transport into the area. Most of the food for this expedition had been purchased by Tony in Derby and the group needed to get from Darwin to Derby, then go into the remote country where they would need food dumps. Much to Peter's delight McRoberts said yes and allocated three vehicles and a team of drivers. 'These are yours,' he told Peter. 'They'll do what you want.'

When Keith and Peter walked into the Norforce base at Larrakeyah Barracks in Darwin in straw hats and Keith wearing expedition sandals, the army guys were astounded. They didn't believe these eastern softies would be capable of such a trip. 'You've got to be joking,' they scoffed. 'You guys will never do it, you're too soft!'

Somewhat incredulous when they first met him, they'd asked Peter if he really was the man who had completed all these expeditions they'd read about. It was the Clark Kent factor at work again!

The three expeditioners, including Ken, spent a couple of days at the barracks. They got chatting with a few soldiers including Tim Daniels in the Army Survival Unit. This unit had produced Major Les Hiddens, the Bush Tucker Man, who had done a lot of work mapping natural food resources to enable army personnel to live off the land if it ever became necessary.

One of the critical things about this trip was to be able to traverse from the end of the Isdell River near the mouth across to the Charnley so the party could go upriver. The army guys at Norforce were well trained with all sorts of equipment and resources. They'd been in the region a few weeks before and didn't make it. They each bet Peter and his team $100 that they wouldn't make it either. 'We were a bit worried because if they didn't make it what chance would we have?' Peter recalls. 'But we accepted the bets.'

Peter approached this expedition in a completely different way to the army. They had protective clothing, Peter had his red shorts and volleys. He was intent on travelling as light as possible and relying on precise navigation.

The resulting presentation on this expedition is one of the most beautiful and moving that Peter has assembled. The focus was his impressions of the Aboriginal people. 'I can remember feeling their spirit more strongly in the Kimberley than anywhere else,' he says.

Peter starts by walking on stage with clapping sticks as didgeridoo music rises over emotive slides of the scenery. Rich, red quartzite rock, pristine waterways, native wildlife and tidal flood plains are interspersed with images of unique Aboriginal artwork rediscovered by the party. There are no people in the first few minutes, just stunning scenery. Unseen for hundreds of years, the beautiful cave paintings show animals and people, representing 50 000 years of aboriginal history. Dorothy Treseder's voice overlays the music, reading the poem quoted at the beginning of this chapter.

Today there are no Aboriginal people there. 'They gave us permission to walk across their land at the well-run Mount Barnett Station,' Peter tells his audience, 'and told us there was plenty of water up there.'

Norforce provided three nearly new Land Rover Defenders with professional army drivers. These turbo diesel powered vehicles were built to exacting Army specifications and performed faultlessly. 'I felt completely safe with these drivers,' Peter says 'charging along tracks at high speed and drifting around corners. The soft tops let the dust in everywhere and it was very noisy.'

Critical to the success of the journey, the dumps were set up first. Food was stored in white cloth bags hung in trees out of the way of feral animals. Peter's concern about water grew as they reached the headwaters of the Isdell and found only rivers of sand. Eventually they found a waterhole, but were concerned about water quality. Keith tested a hand pump water purifier. 'We had to navigate very precisely between waterholes or we would run out,' says Peter.

The group made their way down the river, keeping to the rocky ledges on the sides. Peter was the leader, driving the expedition. Keith was relatively laid back and Tony was quite relaxed. Ken was the navigator and cook and would have been happy to spend more time in this wonderful country; he was not so interested in the goal Peter had set. Peter and Keith were keen to get the trip done in their usual efficient way and at one point a fair amount of tension developed between Keith and Ken, although in retrospect Peter thinks it was probably over something fairly silly. 'We were totally isolated in this area,' he says, 'with no radios.

It was probably even more isolated than the South Pole trip—and we were away for a month.'

While the party had tried lots of different bush foods including grevillea tea, Keith was the fisherman during the expedition. He would catch enough black bream in five minutes to feed them all for tea. He would just throw in the line and pull out the fish, half a kilo each time. A photograph shows him with a huge grin holding up a prize catch. The river had never been fished before, except by its original inhabitants, and was a fisherman's paradise! Ken, meanwhile, cooked up lots of interesting dishes from their stores, while breakfast was the standard muesli and powdered milk.

A routine developed. They would get up very early, walk at first light to midday, rest for about three hours in the heat of the day, and then walk until about 7pm. This gave them an opportunity to make use of the waterholes. 'I had more baths than I've ever had on a trip,' says Peter. 'We picked a place which was less likely to have crocodiles and took turns watching out so we could enjoy the water.'

As they descended, the waterholes got bigger and were separated by substantial waterfalls. Theoretically there were no crocodiles up high, but they took no chances and did not swim in the 5-kilometre stretches of water they found between the falls.

The group walked as far as possible, using the rocky ledges to work their way downriver. As the river became navigable they prepared their rubber boats—the same sort of children's yellow rafts Peter had previously used—and paddled down through narrow gorges.

'Camping in the gorges was great,' Peter enthuses. 'We'd pull the boats over, stop on a rocky shelf, watch the stars at night and build a fire from driftwood.'

The camping was basic, too. They used a sleeping bag with a mozzie net over the top. Keith had a specially made lightweight protective swag to keep the flies off. He hated flies and would even sit completely enclosed in his bivvy bag during the midday break.

He had also suffered with bad blisters at one stage, burning blisters between his toes caused by the heat coming off the rocks and through his volleys. 'It was a lot hotter here than Cape York,' Peter says. '30–40°C dry heat. You could feel it coming off the rocks at night. Without water you're gone in this harsh country.'

Walking on the side of the gorge you can get bluffed out and have to go back. And you don't want to swim the big sections in case of crocodiles. While there were a few crocodiles—freshwater at the top, salties in the tidal reaches—the only incident was when they came across a baby freshwater crocodile about the size of a large lizard trapped in a pool. 'We moved it to safety,' Peter says, 'otherwise it would have died where it was.'

The beautiful quartzite gorges evoked a very spiritual atmosphere, connecting back to the Aboriginal ancestors. Vast and pristine, the whole area was like the beginning of time, untouched and unspoilt. Some of this section required scrambling up rocky cliffs which Tony and Ken found hard, while Keith and Peter enjoyed it. 'We came across a series of five superb gorges,' Peter recalls. 'Really narrow waterways and huge walls. It was exciting to be the first people to explore this area for at least hundreds of years. In a good wet season the water would be roaring through.'

In this upper area, the party came across a huge boab tree. It was so old, its curious formation of the trunk and branches looked rather like a rhinoceros. 'We sent a photograph of the tree into *Australian Geographic*,' Peter recounts, in a competition to find the biggest boab tree in Australia. 'The photograph shows four people standing in front of the tree and they don't even cover the width of the trunk!'

They had to walk down the mud flats, being very careful that no crocodiles were hiding anywhere. They could see their heads out of the water as they went down in the tide, but they weren't taking any chances.

At Walcott Inlet where the land opens up into a huge tidal area they dumped the rafts. Tony had organised for someone to pick them up later by boat. The party had picked up from their food dump before they reached the estuary and these supplies had to last a long time until the next one up the top of the Charnley.

In this section, which the soldiers had bet they could not cross, there was lots of big dry open country and flooded tidal areas. It was offputting walking through the massive cane grass, and they were always looking out for snakes. But even worse were the loose cattle—bulls particularly. They had come from old cattle stations, and the animals had not seen people for years. The party would suddenly come face to face with one. Keith had a theory that you could stare the bulls down. But the rest of the group would take off and try to climb small spindly trees while Keith was trying his theory out. Most of the time it didn't work and he'd have to join the others up a tree.

The four successfully navigated their way to the Charnley, mentally collecting their $100 bets. Walking up the Charnley with the tide out, they needed to consider the risk of soft mud and the possibility of a crocodile left behind in a wallow. Navigating upstream from billabong to billabong and water reach to water reach, they made their way slowly to the headwaters. One night they stopped quite late at a billabong and just went to sleep. In the morning they looked around and discovered an Aboriginal burial site above the billabong with full skeletons laid out on the shelf. 'It was quite spooky,' says Peter.

Once at the headwaters and collecting from another food dump, the group made their way down the banks of the Manning River and back to Mount Barnett Station without incident.

'On no other expedition had I felt closer to the Aboriginal people,' Peter says. 'I could feel their spirit, see them walking the landscape, fishing the rivers. I could see their hands at their places of worship and developed an enormous respect for their skills. They had lived in this landscape for 50 000 years but I would be dead within two days if I didn't have all the modern conveniences in my back pack. They depended on the earth. They cared very deeply about their environment. Otherwise they would not have been able to live in harmony with it for so long.'

Tempered with this experience are Peter's feelings of sadness at what we have lost. 'If you contrast these rivers with the Macleay and Clarence Rivers which we've stuffed up you can see what this country was like,' he says. 'All this knowledge was also being lost. Traditionally passed down from one generation to another, we now have a situation where whole generations are being wiped out and the continuity broken.'

Towards the end of the expedition the group hitched a ride with two grandmotherly Aboriginal women who had children with them. They told them that they each had had twelve children, all of whom died through alcohol related illness, accidents or fights. These women were now caring for their grandchildren, and trying to instil some of what they knew before it was too late. 'But 50 000 years of knowledge is fast disappearing. Look what we've done in just the last two hundred years,' Peter adds.

Peter recounts such incidents in his presentation as part of his theme of bringing these two cultures together. 'Each culture can teach a lot,' he says. 'We can learn how to live in harmony with nature, they can learn how to live in a modern society. As the poem says, "it's time to learn and stand together".'

Sometimes Peter's belief in people's abilities to change things comes across as a little naive. But there is no doubt he is able to press the emotional buttons that do lead to action. Tim Lamble and he are concerned that there is an emotional response but feel that when people leave they do nothing. 'What we try to do is to get them to take some action,' says Peter. 'I ask them "What do you care about most?" I ask them to do something that night, take some action in whatever direction they believe.'

Chapter 15
Spirit of Adventure II

'I look at the world and human life sometimes seems like an impenetrable blackness, full of cruelty and suffering. Undaunted, however, I look at the human spirit and find something of love there. Something that cares and shines out of the dark universe like a star of hope. And in the shining of that light I feel the dreams and prayers of all beings. In the shining of that beacon I feel all of our hopes for a better future. In the shining of that human heart light there is a strength to do what must be done.'

Peter Treseder and Tim Lamble

Making his way rapidly from Robertson in the New South Wales Southern Highlands to the Warrumbungle National Park, Peter started 1993 with one of his combination trips.

In just over four days in January, he rafted and canoed the entire length of the Hawkesbury–Nepean River to Broken Bay then paddled his sea kayak up the coast. Burying his canoe in the sand on the beach south of Newcastle, he rode a bicycle he had carried on the canoe up to the Warrumbungles, making a solo climb of Crater Bluff to complete the trip. It was another opportunity to put together different skills and overcome a variety of physical challenges.

Returning to the beach to retrieve his canoe, Peter located the spot only to find it covered by towels and several topless girls enjoying the warmth of the sun! 'I asked them to move so I could dig my canoe out,' remembers Peter, 'but they didn't seem to believe me and refused.' Undeterred, Peter started digging around the towels with his hands, revealing part of his canoe. 'The girls then got up and helped me enthusiastically,' remembers Peter.

A couple of months later, in March, Peter and Beth took Marnie on holiday to the peaceful and relaxed Norfolk Island, off the New South Wales coast. Beth was six months pregnant and interested mainly in relaxing and shopping, which didn't suit Peter at all.

'I wanted something a bit more dramatic,' he recalls. Peter made contact with Chris Buffett, one of the descendants of the original Pitcairn Islanders who settled the island. They went to a barbecue at his house and he helped Peter to plan a trip. 'The island is relatively flat, but you still need to have a logical route,' Peter says.

Peter suggested circumnavigating the cliffs of the island. The island is 1600 kilometres north-east of Sydney, covering 3455 hectares of mostly volcanic origin. Some parts are open ground, some headlands and coastal stretches are privately held. The imposing cliffs are lined by the famous Norfolk Pines.

Running in a clockwise direction around every headland and bay, Peter set out from the jetty at Cascade, crossing over boundary fences until he reached his starting point just over three hours later. He remembers being chased by dogs a few times and, along the way, he had climbed the only two peaks on the island, Mount Pitt and Mount Bates.

To celebrate the 50th anniversary of the New South Wales Youth Hostels Association a few months later, Peter helped to organise a 50 Peaks Challenge. On the weekend of 17–18 April 1993 some 75 teams set out across the State to climb 50 NSW and ACT mountain peaks. By the time these teams started, Peter was six days into his own challenge—to climb all 50 peaks himself in one continuous trip.

'It started with a phone call from Janet McGarry, the Marketing Manager of YHA,' Peter remembers. 'Janet asked for my support to develop the concept of the 50 Peaks event and she thought I might add some useful media exposure.'

Peter agreed and a team met for a number of planning meetings as the final list of 50 peaks developed.

Starting on Saturday 10 April on Lord Howe Island, Peter climbed Mount Gower, a beautiful rainforest clad peak. Despite all his experience however, the organisers made him go with a guide up Mount Gower. The guide took Peter up and back. 'It was just a walk really,' maintains Peter, 'with some exposed parts.'

The time started as soon as Peter tackled the first peak but his main concern was the travelling time between peaks. Fiona McCrossin, writing in *The Bushwalker* in August 1993 describes the challenge. 'Peter's plan involved a route that covered the peaks in a logical driving sequence but this, as he discovered, is not necessarily the most logical way to walk them. Having returned from Lord Howe, he headed west through the Colo-Wollemi National Park, then north through the Warrumbungles to Mount Lindesay near the Queensland border. A long drive south brought him through the Budawangs followed by a 16-hour run in one day through Kosciuszko National Park which knocked off nine peaks in one go.'

Peter remembers that he flew back to Sydney, hopped into his car and started to climb the peaks one after the other. Some he ran between, but the car was used to get between most of them. He admits that he knew he needed some help with Mount Lindesay, so he got his friend, Barry Davies, the Recreation Officer at Binna Burra Lodge, to meet him and they climbed it together.

The support crew drove Peter between the peaks and accompanied him on some of the ascents. Peter, however, completed some peaks during the night while his crew slept in the car. He found it quite a lonely experience at times, but never considered giving up.

A few scattered peaks were bagged including The Rock at Wagga Wagga and Mount Imlay near Bega, then the team headed back north through Kanangra. Peter had climbed Mount Cloudmaker and scaled Mount Solitary at dawn on Sunday 18 April. He was due at the base of the Three Sisters at 9am for the final climb with 82-year-old mountaineer Dot Butler and Steve Irwin, and had to sprint all the way around to meet the deadline.

'I was ten minutes late,' Peter recalls, 'feeling dizzy and sick. Well-known mountaineer Greg Mortimer was ready to go up with Dot if I didn't arrive, but gave me a big hug and told me to go on.'

Peter however, needed to rest for half an hour before starting. The trio successfully climbed the Second Sister, raising the YHA flag on the summit. This inspirational photograph was used on the cover of the YHA Annual Report for that year and was widely used in the media, achieving the publicity the organisation had sought.

Meanwhile Peter had completed his challenge—the ascent of all 50 peaks in eight days. During the trip he had run 600 kilometres, covered more than 5000 kilometres by car and climbed 22 553 metres.

Towards the end of the trip Peter and his support crew had experienced problems with the car, including multiple punctures. 'Our old family car took a pounding on some terrible dirt roads,' Peter recalls ruefully. 'We went pretty fast in poor conditions to maintain our schedule and Beth wasn't at all happy when I got back.'

But Peter says he gives his support to the YHA because its concept is 'very similar to the theme of some of the presentations' he gives. 'Visitors cook together, eat together and sleep in dormitory accommodation, sharing ideas and companionship.' When they bought a new building in the Sydney CBD, Peter suggested they call the restaurant 'The Melting Pot', referring to it as a melting pot for ideas rather than the food reference. Partly as a result of this trip and for his long term support of the organisation, Peter was made a Vice President of the Youth Hostels Association of NSW later that year, a position he still holds.

Kimberley Anne Treseder was born on 5 July 1993 and, as with Marnie's birth three years earlier, Peter was with Beth for the occasion at the Sydney Adventist Hospital. 'We called her Kimberley,' Peter says, 'after the beautiful West Australian region of that name. And, after all,' he adds, 'she was conceived as soon as I got back from that trip!'

Suffering badly from asthma, Marnie had been difficult to look after for some time. Sleepless nights resulted from an incorrect diagnosis of her condition. This remained untreated until another doctor worked out the problem and prescribed medication that gave everyone some sleep. In the meantime Peter had been taking turns with Beth during the nights, but eventually Beth's Mum, Anne, took over from him.

The problem was only just being resolved when Kimberley was born and Beth was worn out. During her pregnancy, Beth had put on some weight and resolved to go to Weight Watchers with Peter's mum, Dorothy. In the end she had no need to go as she shed some 20 kilograms over the next few months through stress.

Kimberley was just a few months old when Peter left for his month-long expedition to Borneo where he would be out of touch with his family for a good part of that time. 'I wasn't happy about him going,' says Beth, 'but you can't stop Peter when he has an expedition planned.'

Before he left on that trip, however, Peter attempted a rather unusual skiing record. For some years he had harboured a desire to ski from Perisher to Kiandra, nude, at night. 'The trip grew out of all my previous trips,' he says. 'Both the runs and the snowshoe trips.'

It was a very serious trip, not unlike the nude canyon trip through Claustral, with high risks associated with potential accident, equipment failure and exposure.

Peter had been attending the Paddy Pallin Cross Country Ski Classic regularly as part of the support crew and, this year, he was as usual with his search and rescue colleagues, manning a drinks station for the event. The weather was exceptionally mild for mid-winter, with some rain that day that had brought the temperature up while there was still excellent snow cover. He felt the conditions were right and decided to make the run that night.

Following the events of the day Peter and some of his friends made their way to the bus depot at Perisher while others took his car around to Kiandra with his clothes. Inside the warmth of the bus depot, Peter stripped to his shoes, much to the amazement of those people inside. 'I drew quite a crowd,' he remembers, 'both inside the depot and outside as I fixed my lightweight cross country boots and skis.'

Checking his head torch, Peter skied off before any of the locals had the chance to call the police to stop him. Then, taking the usual route to North Perisher, Peter headed off on a unique record attempt.

It was a still night but the action of skiing made him feel cold almost immediately. 'I did think of pulling out,' he admits, 'but as I got numb I thought I would just carry on.'

Peter could feel that his arms and legs were working and that his fingers moved but his skin temperature dropped significantly, the blood retreating to protect the rest of his body in the extreme conditions.

You drop down past Mawson's Hut at one point and Peter could see a woman standing outside the hut with a glass of wine. He skied down quietly and saw her first in the light of the hut. She looked at Peter, then looked again in astonishment. 'Hey! There's a bloke out here skiing with no clothes on!' she called out to her friends Their reaction was to tell her she'd had too much wine, and to come back inside. Peter waved and was gone before they had a chance to come out.

The trip lasted for 9 hours 15 minutes, a long time to be naked in the snow. As soon as Peter reached the DMR depot at Kiandra he dressed and got into the car and drove off. Gradually the warmth and feeling came back into his limbs. Now, the feeling you get when your hands are freezing and the blood starts pumping again as they warm up can be agonising. Just imagine the pain and discomfort in his most private digit! 'It was the most powerful pain,' Peter remembers.

He had to get out of the car at one point but just staggered around, leaning over the bonnet, trying to control the pulsating agony. A car pulled up beside him and a couple got out to see if he was all right. The woman took a good look at Peter and asked what was going on. The man said, 'I think he's got an erection!' She leant over and had another good look. 'How come that doesn't happen to you?' she asked her companion before they got back in their car and drove off.

How well did Peter consider the potential risks? 'It's about making a critical decision to go at the right time,' Peter maintains. 'The weather has to be right, you have to feel right.'

On this trip Peter knew all the huts and had a series of escape routes planned in his head, should he need them. 'It was just the most extreme way to do it,' he says, 'although I don't think I would repeat the performance.'

When businessman and adventurer Dick Smith flew round the world, he came over the South China Sea, 100 kilometres south east of Brunei over Sarawak, on one leg of the trip and saw a spectacular white peak sticking out of the jungle. Altering course to have a better look, he photographed the peak and included the resulting picture in his book *Our Fantastic Planet*.

Dick included the longitude and latitude of Batu Lawi, hoping someone would take up the challenge of climbing it.

Peter saw the picture in the book and almost immediately decided to have a go—despite not really knowing where it was, having no knowledge of Borneo or any information about the peak. Nonetheless, he began to plan.

On the train one day, travelling to work, Peter saw over someone's shoulder an article in the newspaper about the death marches of Sandakan and knew this was near the area where he wanted to go. He tapped the man on the shoulder and asked if he could read the page.

Peter didn't know the story, and what he read saddened and horrified him. He saw parallels between the young men who, through no fault of their own, got caught and died in the jungles and his group going in to climb a mountain. The risks were similar but the reasons were worlds apart.

'I look at some of the things I've done,' he says now, 'and the risks attached. I have orchestrated them for myself. These soldiers were in a situation they could not control. To my mind that requires more bravery than anything I have ever done.'

Peter resolved to include a tribute run to the soldiers on the death march during his visit to Borneo and used the death march theme extensively in his emotion-packed presentation developed on his return. A series of photographs of long-dead soldiers appear on the screen as the narrator repeats their name and rank. These soldiers had been captured by the Japanese in Singapore and thousands moved to Borneo so they could not assist a re-invading enemy. Some British and Australian troops spent the war in Changi prison camp while thousands ended up on the Burma railway and in Sandakan.

By the last year of the war the Japanese wanted to move this group again, to the other side of the island. The local Malaysians were conscripted to construct a track and they routed it through really difficult terrain because they thought the Japanese soldiers would be walking it. But it turned out that the prisoners of war did, walking in groups of fifty.

Just 30 enlisted men made it to the other side of the island only to be executed by the Japanese two weeks after the war ended to prevent the Allies knowing what had really happened. Although they tried to wipe out the evidence, eventually the sad story trickled out through the six survivors who had managed to escape.

During his research after the trip, Peter was moved by the discovery that one of his outdoors heroes, the legendary Gordon Smith, who pioneered tiger walking with Dot Butler in the 1930s, had died as a POW in this region. 'In jungle like this,' he says, after his introduction, 'these men died. It was in this jungle we sought to climb Batu Lawi.'

'Who were these men?' Peter asks his audience. 'Ordinary fathers, brothers and sons,' he continues. 'This is what happens when there is no caring. Our trip shows what can happen when there is some caring.'

More soldier pictures flash on the screen towards the end of the presentation. During one evening address, Peter distinctly heard an anguished voice coming from one of the front rows of the audience. 'That's my brother!' Seeking the woman out after the show he talked with her for some time as, indeed, it was her brother who had been among those who had died during the death march.

Peter works his audience to gain their emotional involvement in the hope that his presentation will help inspire ordinary people to do more to improve society. He talks about making changes, making the audience think about how they can make a change themselves. Inspiring them, he refers to John Denver's song 'It's about time' and its concept of living together and sharing. 'And I try to build up a sad feeling,' he admits, 'to contrast it with the beauty of the Borneo jungle and to show that we can all achieve great things if we care enough about each other.'

For an attempt on a 2043-metre sandstone peak located somewhere in the middle of a jungle in the Kelabit Highlands of Sarawak, Malaysia, you would expect that Peter would assemble a team of expert climbers. But he admits he didn't pick the obvious people.

In the team were two very experienced climbers, Ian Brown and Tom Williams, plus Keith Williams and Peter himself. 'What distinguishes these guys from other modern climbers,' Peter says, 'is that they can climb something from the ground up. Good rock climbers climb in gyms and do acrobatic things but they need a row of bolts to protect themselves as they go up. Ian and Tom were from the old school and could climb anything without assistance—essential for this expedition.'

Morie Ward and David Robinson completed the party. Older than the other men in the group, neither had done a scrap of climbing. 'They were more mature than the rest of us,' Peter recalls. 'I thought their gentle characters and maturity might temper the more intense personalities in the group.'

Morie also had good contacts in Borneo through his previous travels and helped a lot in the organisation stage. At this point none of the group knew exactly where the peak was, how to get there or what they would find once they arrived. Since there were no detailed maps available, Morie pinpointed the peak as being on the edge of Sarawak's Kelabit Highlands, between the village of Bareo and the Sultanate of Brunei. It was known as Peak 200 during the Second World War and was used as a navigation beacon by Allied aircraft.

While Peter was scared of malaria, concerned about what natural hazards awaited them in the jungle and wondered whether the group could climb the peak safely, he also wondered whether Batu Lawi had been climbed before.

Morie had introduced Dave to Peter at a search and rescue training day. Dave asked if he could come on the trip and Peter agreed. 'I said yes on instinct,' Peter recalls. 'Dave is a big strong man, imposing, and looks like a weight lifter, with a long pony tail. Striding through the markets in Malaysia he towered over the locals looking like an Indian chief.'

Training started and included rock climbing instruction for Morie and Dave. 'You're never too old for training,' says Peter. 'The first time I took these guys up to Narrowneck they were jumping around saying it was fantastic!' Sadly however, Morie had trouble on an early training climb with his arm and was unable to complete the climb of the actual peak.

In the meantime though, Morie had found a guide, sending him $3000 as a retainer for his services. A short while later the guide wrote back demanding thousands of dollars more to complete the contract! This was completely unacceptable and the group was forced to write off the deposit and find another guide quickly through another source.

Before they left, they all soaked their clothing and tents in horrible smelling chemicals and took tablets to prevent malaria. Malaysia Airlines had become a sponsor and the party flew from Sydney to Kuala Lumpur where they disembarked in stinking hot heat. 'I found the combination of heat, cigarette smoke and incense in the airport overpowering,' Peter recalls with distaste.

With time to spare, the party perused the shelves of the airport bookshop, and came across *Mountains of Malaysia*. Finding Batu Lawi in the index, they opened it to find a picture of the peak and another of a British team claiming victory for the first ascent.

Devastated by this discovery, Peter called a conference in the hotel. They had so much wanted to be first and considered looking for another challenge. After discussion they decided to carry on as they would still be able to claim the first Australian ascent.

There was to be another member of the team. Major Tim Daniels, Commanding Officer of the Army Survival group in Darwin, had been invited to join the crew. Arriving separately the next day, he was to bring all the lightweight survival rations that they would take with them into the jungle. Peter had wanted to ensure that they had more than enough supplies for self sufficiency. Now, already disheartened by their discovery about the British team, Peter broke the news to the group that Beth had telephoned to say that Daniels was not coming and there were no survival rations. He had simply dropped out.

Keith, as quartermaster, then had to recheck the food they had brought with them and work out what to take. They put all the gear together in a hotel room in Kota Kinabalu.

The next day they negotiated with a bus driver who took them to a small airfield at Lawas. Travelling through manned, armed checkpoints, the group eventually arrived and transferred their gear to a twin engined Otter. Then, with no navigation aids, they flew to the village of Ba Kelalan in the central highlands of Sarawak, landing in the dirt and unloading the plane themselves.

There were no roads to the villages and they were invited to stay in a village longhouse to prepare for the trek into the jungle. This was quite a substantial timber building on stilts with a steel roof, 'a bit like an oversized Scout hall,' as Peter puts it.

Up in the highlands, the villagers are mostly Christians, having been converted after the Second World War by missionaries. They followed the Allied forces who made use of the villagers' head hunting skills to catch the Japanese! 'We saw a few skulls still stored in the huts,' Peter says. 'And incongruously there was also a TV satellite dish on one roof, although it was only able to receive very boring old black and white Muslim shows.'

Most of the porters came from this village of Ba Kelalan and were members of the Murut tribe. One of them proudly carried a shotgun which had been passed down from a missionary to father to son. Peter had arranged to bring modern packs for the porters, but they preferred their top heavy, hand made rattan packs, which looked like huge laundry baskets. They put the modern ones inside!

The villagers made Peter and his friends very welcome—including giving Keith permission to use one of the cooking areas in the longhouse.

The group's head porter, James Padan Mutang, spoke about six or seven languages and would be their communications source to the outside world. Just finding your way through the paddy fields out of the village is impossible without local knowledge, and so the party relied heavily on this porter as well as the other of their native guides.

Starting from Ba Kelalan, they passed briefly into Kalimantan, the Indonesian part of Borneo on their trek to the mountain. Morie Ward later described the journey in an article he wrote for Malaysia Airlines. With guide James Padan they walked into the jungle. The rain came and they only just made it across the Rapung River before it became too deep and swift to cross. Then James and the porters built a shelter in the rain, using giant bamboo to keep them out of the mud. With a few quick cuts from their parangs, they cut more bamboo and started a roaring fire with latex they had collected earlier in the day.

The second day was rain and the group continued to climb through the jungle, coming across an old Kelabit burial ground, littered with clay urns with dragons on the sides. After lunch they slithered down a hillside eventually reaching the small village of Pa Lungan. Following a well worn track to the village of Pa Ukat, and arriving in a very dirty state, they were greeted by a woman with oranges while the head man sent out fresh pineapple, later welcoming them into the village longhouse which was simply enormous.

Learning more about the culture of the Murut and Kelabit people, Keith again prepared the evening meal over a clay hearth set into the timber floor, a simple set-up that allows the villagers to cook indoors. They were made very welcome once more and Peter enjoyed the friendly atmosphere when all the families came in together. 'It was smoky and warm,' he recalls, 'with maybe 30 or 40 people together enjoying big communal meals.'

The next day they set out through a rocky pass and began the long climb into the Tamu Abu Range through spectacular rainforest, around steep mountain sides and criss-crossing rocky creeks. Bridges were constructed from huge bamboo or were simply fallen logs across ravines. They were the only way to cross and there was often a 10-15 metre drop into a rushing creek. It was wet and slippery, but the porters walked back and forth nonetheless. 'Different people are scared of different things,' says Peter. 'Ian had no problem but I had to get down on my bum to slide across! I wasn't taking the risk of falling off a log!'

It took the group less than a week to walk through the jungle to the peak. There were leeches everywhere. 'We would take off 20 at a time,' Peter says, 'in our gaiters, on our legs, everywhere!'

Walking into the slippery moss forest, they saw amazing jungle plants including the world's biggest pitcher plants and giant rhododendrons. Mosses of different colours and masses of orchids and beautiful ferns added to the primeval beauty of the jungle. 'The best I've ever seen,' recalls Peter.

They also thrilled to the sight of gibbons and giant hornbills. Hundreds of monkeys seemed to fly overhead through the high canopy. The porters would drop everything and charge after them. They were good food!

One day the porters came back with a big boar which they cut up with their parangs. Gorging themselves, they then smoked the rest in strips to carry with them.

The porters would have six or seven meals a day, based on rice wrapped in leaves. And they all wore cheap plastic soccer boots, some with studs and some without, presumably to give them some grip in the slippery mud of the jungle. As they walked they sang Christian hymns which would echo all around the jungle. At night they would sit on one side of the hut, very close together, their limbs intertwined, stroking each other, comforting each other after a hard day's work. 'It was a fascinating culture to observe,' Peter says, 'and one that emphasised sharing and caring.'

The group stopped overnight in a hut on the edge of the Limbang River, crossing it the next day over a fallen log. It had rained every day so far, but it was so hot they did not worry about it.

Reaching their planned base camp hut on a tributary of the Tabun River, Keith set about working out what supplies to take up the mountain. It was here that the question of the British climbing team arose again. The porters were adamant that no-one had successfully climbed Batu Lawi, which means 'fish-tailed rock' in the Kelabit Highland dialect. There was no dispute that six Kelabit men and a British soldier named Tom Harrison had climbed the lower peak in 1946. However, according to the head man, the British team had gone in and managed to climb half way when one of them had a fall. They apparently brought helicopters in from Brunei which landed them on the top of the peak and took them off again. 'This made us feel better,' Peter says, 'that we still had the chance to be the first to climb the whole thing.'

A few days later the group came up over a ridge and there it was—Batu Lawi. The white of the rocks stood out against the dark green of the jungle. They all took a step back lost in thought about the immensity of the job ahead. 'It looks a lot bigger than in the photo,' Ian had said nervously to Peter.

About half the height of the main peak, they figured the smaller peak would make an ideal observation post while the saddle between the two peaks was the best place for the safety crew. The expert climbers, Tom and Ian, started to work out a route using binoculars. They had to decide what equipment to take. Wildsports had provided all the ropes and gear but, because everything had to be carried in and out, they'd taken a minimal kit of gear with them.

Now, as they got closer, they were able to see the true scale of this impressive peak. Loaded down with ropes and climbing aids, Tom and Ian made their way slowly up a 70 degree slope, then up a series of cracks on the east face. The plan was for Ian and Tom to climb and put fixed ropes up, come back down, then the others would climb the next day. The fixed ropes would also be invaluable if the climbers got stuck or needed some sort of assistance.

Ian Brown recounted the climb in the July 1995 issue of *Australian Geographic* in an article called 'Blade Runners'. 'We started our climb on the east face at dawn', Ian reported, 'fixing ropes for the others to follow that we'd also use in our abseil descent. Nearly six hours into the climb, as Tom began the fourth pitch 170 metres up the rock, it started raining. I lost sight of him.'

On the climb up they found discarded army ration packets. Evidence of an attempt, but not necessarily of success. A rusted steel piton, karabiners still attached, was hammered into the rock, but there was nothing beyond that.

Peter remembers the rain obscured his vision of the face from his observation point on the smaller peak, and the climbers were lost to sight for several hours. Finally, the rain and mist cleared around 2pm, and the nervously waiting group could see the climbers were already two thirds of the way up. 'They looked like small specks on the rock face,' Peter recalls, 'but we were pretty sure they would make it by that point.'

Then, as Ian's article continued, 'Tom led the sixth and final pitch to the top, a 20-square-metre patch of flat springy heath supporting a single tree.'

They had made it, and all in one hard day. 'Better than our wildest expectations,' Peter says.

The porters were so excited when Tom and Ian got to the top they were calling out 'Australians best climbers!' and said they would name their grandchildren after them. Undoubtedly the story will become part of local legend!

The next day the other members of the party followed the route to the top using ascenders on the fixed ropes. Peter, always careful to ensure that his sponsors get a good return for their investment, arranged for the customary photographs wearing *Australian Geographic* T-shirts, with flags and symbols from the sponsors together with the Sandakan Society symbol.

Although Ian's brief search the day before had revealed nothing, Peter soon found a battered old British Regimental flag tied to the tree on the heath and some smoke canisters used to signal wind direction for helicopters when landing. They also found a line of piton marks in the vertical crack section down below, up to a big block which had been dislodged—although there was certainly no evidence of anyone climbing or descending from this point up on this side of the rock. It was still a mystery whether the British team had succeeded or used a helicopter.

On the third day all the climbers helped to go up again and de-rig the climb. It was a massive vertical face, and a high grade of climb, almost 1000 metres straight up. Then, packing up all the equipment, the group made their way out along the same route to Pa Ukat and flew from the small airstrip at Bareo via Miri.

Quite rightly, the expedition claimed the first Australian ascent of Batu Lawi. Peter, however, is reluctant to concede that their team was beaten by the British. 'At the end of the day we're not sure,' he says, 'but taking into consideration the head man, porters and evidence on the rock, we think we were the first to actually climb to the top.'

Ian Brown, however, has since spoken to a member of the British team and gives them the benefit of the doubt in his article. They claimed to have made the complete ascent on the other side—with six men from the 14th/20th King's Hussars, raising the Regimental flag on the summit.

In Issue 39, *Australian Geographic* published the following: 'The leader of the regiment involved in the British ascent confirmed that the team had made the summit via the north side. Their success came after several failed attempts and, to our relief, without fatality.' Peter however remains unconvinced.

Once back in Kota Kinabalu the group decided to walk to the top of Mount Kinabalu, a 4101 metre peak. They took the tourist bus as far as it goes then walked slowly to the tourist hotel and restaurant at about 3500 metres. Only accessible on foot, the hotel provided a big meal and beds. After a few hours' sleep, the group rose and walked to the top using head torches in time for sunrise.

Peter and his companions walked with a group of about twenty from the hotel and he remembers it was extremely cold. Guided up sloping rock shelves running with water, they were glad of the ropes set in place to haul themselves up to the top. Predictably the view was fantastic. As the sun rose behind tall spires of black rock Peter's thoughts were of the soldiers who had died in the country to the east where the sun was rising. They returned to the town and Tom, Dave and Morie went home, while Ian and Keith stayed to do some serious rock climbing on the peak, setting themselves up in a hut. Meanwhile, Peter prepared for his tribute run across Sabah. While the others sampled local food in Kota Kinabalu, Peter however ate only Kentucky Fried Chicken. He was the only one who didn't get sick!

Starting at the coast, Peter ran 334 kilometres in 38 hours, finishing in Sandakan, probably the first sea to summit run. He pounded up the steep road that the buses took, past the hotel and up to the peak. Then back down again, taking the road to Ranau and following the route the soldiers had taken back to Sandakan. 'I tried to follow their route as much as possible,' he says, 'as I knew they had marched to the north of the road.'

When he'd finished, he hitched back to Kota Kinabalu. Once there he went to see Datuk Harris bin Mohd Salleh, the retired Chief Minister of Sabah, who he had contacted by way of a connection through a friend of Beth's mum. Now a very rich and powerful man, Harris had been supported as an urchin kid during the war by the Australian man who had sponsored him to come to Australia to be educated.

Peter walked directly from the squalor and poverty of the markets to the Chief Minister's residence, an opulent house set amid quiet, manicured acres.

'I found the jump quite disturbing,' he recalls. 'One of the oddest things to me at the time was a huge jar of Kit-Kats near the pool area.' Nevertheless while there Peter took the opportunity to mention the guide who had ripped them off and Harris agreed to investigate. At the same time he confirmed that Peter's run across Sabah was a first.

All in all the expedition had been an outstanding success and although lots of expeditions end in conflict, this one didn't—they came back friends. Why? Peter believes it was the bond of caring and support they built. 'The difference,' Peter says, 'between coming back as friends and hostility is the careful selection of people for the trip. My instinct tells me that every trip needs a different combination. Some people could never achieve particular trips, however fit and physically capable they are.'

Ian Brown and Keith Williams had both been on this trip, as they had on many others with Peter. Not only was the trip well within their capabilities, it was on a different scale to the later South Pole expedition, and a different level of intensity. Peter's leadership style was different on this trip too. 'If I had led it from the front, instead of the back, it wouldn't have worked,' he reflects. 'I needed to push everyone along, not pull them.'

He makes the further observation that Tom is a very strong character, one who needed to be in the lead, adding that Keith may have felt he could have done more since he is also very capable and could have led from the front. And he recognises that Tom and Ian needed to put all their energy into their role on the expedition. No doubt Peter could have made the first ascent with either of them, but he stood back and let them do the hard work to get them all to the top. Similarly, Morie had done a lot to get them to Borneo. Things had often proved tough and his input was not generally recognised.

'If I had done it any other way we would have had tension,' Peter says. As it was, they all felt very satisfied with their part in the expedition.

It was very important for Peter to maintain the camaraderie—and ultimately to see the whole team rewarded for their efforts. He was delighted, therefore, when the entire team was awarded the Australian Geographic Society Silver Medal for their achievement.

Chapter 16

Pirates in the Timor Sea

'One doesn't discover new lands without consenting to lose sight of the shore for a very long time.'

André Gide

New Zealand offers exciting challenges for the outdoor person and Peter had fond memories of his first major trip just after he left school. His plan in late January 1994 was to traverse the length of New Zealand, including the water crossings, by his own efforts. 'I also wanted to climb the highest peak on each island,' he says, 'and make it a complete north–south solo traverse.'

Flying into Auckland, Peter headed straight for a youth hostel to recruit a support crew. He hired a car and bought a second-hand canoe, offering the use of the car to three young travellers in return for their support over the next few weeks. Part of the deal too was the loan of a bike from one of the travellers which Peter planned to use for the long road stretches down the islands.

Peter told the guys that they could do what they wanted, go wherever they liked in the hire car, as long as they met him at all the prearranged points. He had managed to secure the all-important support crew at minimal cost and, typically, had also managed to help someone else out at the same time. Peter even promised to give them the canoe when the trip was completed.

The trip started with a drive to the Bay of Islands, where Peter mounted the bike at the northernmost tip of the North Island, Cape Reinga, and pedalled south towards Wellington. On the way he stopped to climb Mount Ruapehu, the highest peak on the North Island. 'I was lucky to do it then,' Peter says, 'as the volcano erupted some years later!'

Swapping the bike for a canoe, Peter then crossed Cook Strait, paddling into Picton, a picturesque town located on Queen Charlotte Sound in the

South Island. 'It was a magnificent stretch of water to paddle up,' says Peter. 'But the pine forests on the sides had just been cut and it looked terrible.'

Back on the bike, he then rode to St Arnaud where the support crew picked up the bike as Peter traversed the Nelson Lakes and Arthurs Pass national parks on foot. The mountains were covered in snow, but Peter didn't have much time to take in the scenery!

An exhilarating ride followed as Peter wound his way down from Arthurs Pass to where Copland Valley meets the sea. Immediately turning around, he then made the first recorded sea-to-summit ascent of Mount Cook. This was the mountain so foolishly climbed by Peter many years before when his experience didn't match his ambition. This time you would think he was better prepared.

Most climbers wear boots with crampons—but Peter didn't want to carry heavy boots with him on the run up from the coast. Instead, he wore his favourite running shoes with a home-made contraption that allowed him to fit the crampons. 'I cut two sheets of plywood,' he remembers, 'roughly to the shape of my foot, but a bit bigger. I put these under the soles of my running shoes, then attached the crampons.'

It was hardly an ideal arrangement. Although they did give some stability, Peter risked frostbite of the toes as the running shoes offered little protection against the cold.

It was Peter's third time up Mount Cook and his route this time took him up the Grand Traverse. He climbed the low peak, continued over the middle peak and up to the high peak. The Linda Glacier was his route down as he made his way to the Ball Shelter in the valley via the Grand Plateau. Unable to carry much food, he ate whenever he could, the support crew meeting him with supplies. Then he'd have a 'big feed'.

The three islands traverse continued with a bike run down to Bluff, on the southern tip of the South Island. The next destination was Stewart Island across Foveaux Strait. Peter was lucky with the weather as he paddled the canoe across and the trip to Stewart Island progressed more smoothly than the last time, when Peter had thrown up over the side of the ferry. Landing at Halfmoon Bay, he continued on foot to the summit of Mount Anglem, the third and final peak of his trip. Satisfied that he had achieved his objective, Peter turned his mind immediately to the task of getting home. 'I felt fantastic at overcoming the difficulties,' he says, 'but felt the urgency of needing to get back to Sydney and work as my leave expired.'

As usual, Peter was attempting to pack as much as possible into the shortest time and had a plane to catch in order to return to work after his allotted leave. Unfortunately, the ferry timetable was not very accommodating and it looked as if Peter would miss the plane back to Sydney. So he decided to paddle back across Foveaux Strait.

The support crew were due to meet him from the ferry at The Bluff and were certainly not expecting him to canoe back. As the trip progressed however, the seas got bigger. The swell became impossible to paddle and eventually Peter was thrown out of the kayak. He couldn't get back in— the swell was just too big and the boat was swamped.

At this point Peter was a long way from land and had to make a difficult decision. 'I had to work out what to do to improve my chance of survival,' he says. 'Whether to stay with the canoe and drift wherever it took me on the chance that I might be rescued—or swim for shore.' By now no-one knew exactly where Peter was—only that he was supposed to be returning on the ferry.

With no life jacket, Peter swam about 10 kilometres to shore in huge seas. He could see Bluff every time he reached the peak of a wave, then lost it again in the troughs. 'I was pretty desperate,' he recalls, 'I thought there was a real possibility that I might not make it.'

After nine days of solid running, cycling, paddling and climbing, he was very tired and had every reason to be worried. The Foveaux Strait is notorious for huge seas and bad weather and any search would undoubtedly be launched far too late to save him.

'I felt really stupid,' Peter admits. 'I had done what I set out to do, completed the trip as planned and was just being impatient. I thought about the prospect of disappearing without the family knowing what had happened to me.'

Peter did not give up however and kept swimming, checking his direction every time he rode the top of the enormous swell. After several hours he dragged himself up onto a wharf at Bluff and made his way to the ferry terminal, cold, wet and physically exhausted.

'The guys in my support crew were pretty cut up because I didn't bring the kayak back!' Peter remembers. 'They didn't seem to recognise the significance of what had just happened.'

He was so tired he ignored the emotional outburst. The crew drove him to the airport at Christchurch where the car was returned and Peter flew home. 'I knew I was right and dismissed their complaints,' Peter says. 'I just turned off. By then all I wanted was to get home.'

A couple of months later, Peter took himself off to south-east Queensland for a few days, completing the Scenic Rim traverse in less than two days. This was one of many trips Peter has taken over the years, exploring new places and testing himself in different environments. Peter often likes to see how far he can 'push the limits' as he puts it, how fast he can get through the country. With this trip, and a solo ascent of the east face of 280-metre Mount Barney later in the year, Peter achieved his objectives of establishing new standards in this region.

In July 1994 Peter was on the water again, this time in a bold attempt to be the first person to cross the Timor Sea by canoe. 'I'd been on the water for about a week,' he recalls, 'when the water exploded in front of my canoe, sending the sea snakes and sharks which had been my companions for some hours, flying into the air.'

He must have been dozing at the time, because he had not been aware of the large timber vessel that was now moving menacingly towards him. On the prow of the boat stood a grizzled looking old man flanked on each side by several younger tough looking men. The old man had both hands on a small cannon, mounted on the prow, which was clearly the cause of the explosion in front of Peter's canoe. It was obvious that they were pirates who wanted him on board. 'In fact, I had no choice,' Peter recalls. 'They would have simply blown me out of the water or run me over if I had not cooperated.'

The pirates drew roughly alongside Peter's canoe and hauled him out.

At the time he couldn't walk as he had been in the canoe for so long his legs had gone to sleep. They dragged him across the deck and started to kick and beat him, all the time shouting in their language. The young men then bound Peter's hands behind his back and lashed him to the wall of the cabin down below. A guard was left behind while the others disappeared.

The pirates must have assumed that Peter couldn't walk at all because they didn't take much care in binding his hands. Within about twenty minutes he started to get the feeling back in his legs and wondered how he might escape. 'Otherwise I knew I was going to die, especially after being bashed,' Peter says.

He sat quietly, thinking furiously, while the armed guard nodded off in the corner. Peter thought about the trip so far. He had left Darwin Harbour about a week earlier and paddled almost non-stop for 600 kilometres to reach his present location just 5 kilometres off the East Timor coast.

Feeling ready to escape, Peter was, nonetheless, scared the pirates would kill him in the attempt. His plan was to get to the guard before he woke up, thinking that he might have the element of surprise as they did not know he could walk. The guard was a tough looking man whose most striking feature was his large gnarled and decaying looking hands. Peter watched as he fell asleep, finally giving him the chance to escape. The binding was neither tight nor well secured. 'Not Scout knots!' Peter thought as he wriggled free.

Creeping across the cabin floor, Peter had almost reached the guard when he woke up, reaching for his sawn-off shotgun which had dropped to the floor against his leg. 'I gathered all my strength and launched myself at him and we wrestled on the cabin floor,' Peter says. 'I had nothing to lose by trying to escape. I had to do something—get out or sit there and wait to die.'

Being shot at was a better risk than waiting, he considered. But while Peter was imprisoned below decks, the pirates had been trying to dismantle his canoe. Earlier he had seen them slash some of his water containers with their knives and now they had taken some of his gear and, for some reason, had apparently removed the rudder. As usual, when planning this journey, Peter had tried to think of all the risks associated with his adventure, but he hadn't given pirates a thought! The south-easterly winds had helped in the crossing. The seas had been small, giving Peter the opportunity to inflate his rubber raft and lash it to the side of the canoe. This created a platform for him to sleep on and stretch his tired legs, and he had been lucky as each rest blew him a little closer to his destination. Now his struggle ended suddenly when Peter clouted the guard hard over the head with a piece of timber he had picked up from the floor. With the guard unconscious he moved quietly to the door of the cabin only to find that another guard barred his way at the end of the passageway. 'Holding the timber firmly in one hand,' he recalls, 'I sprinted four or five steps down the dark and narrow passageway and shoulder charged the second guard in the back.'

The man staggered and they both fell heavily. Struggling briefly on the dirty floor Peter, in his desperation to escape and with the adrenalin pumping, managed to get on top, once again using the piece of wood to good effect. Leaving him groaning, Peter found his way up on deck. He had to keep low and quiet to avoid the other pirates. He thought there must be about six more somewhere and figured they would not be happy with his escape.

Luckily however the pirates must have been down the front of the boat as Peter made his way cautiously to the stern where he had last seen his canoe. Finding it in the water and still tied to the back of the pirate boat, he grabbed his paddle from the pile of stolen and wrecked gear, ran for the canoe and jumped in. After an anxious moment struggling with the mooring line, he cast off for Australia. He was lucky that it had been nearly dusk when he'd been captured. Now, hours later, it was still dark, helping his escape. Then, just as he pushed off, he could hear shouting from the boat. The pirates had discovered Peter's escape and were looking for him. 'I had to get as much distance between my small canoe and their big boat,' he says.

Fortunately for Peter they assumed that he would head for the closest land, East Timor, and searched in that direction. He could see their lights towards the coast while he paddled furiously in the opposite direction, 600 kilometres back towards Australia.

'The trip back was a nightmare!' Peter recalls. 'I didn't have enough water because the pirates had destroyed some of my containers.' Forced to ration himself, he was constantly thirsty and became increasingly dehydrated. It was very hot and there was nowhere to escape from the sun. The missing rudder made it difficult to paddle and steer, which made him very tired.

But Peter's 'fight or flight instinct' didn't stop until he had paddled for almost a whole day, well over the horizon. He knew that the pirates would surely come after him and kill him if they could. 'I had to go for it while they were looking in the opposite direction,' he said.

The south easterlies were still blowing strongly which meant Peter could not use his raft and get the rest he needed so desperately. If he stopped paddling he would drift back towards East Timor. He had no choice but to continue on his way to Australia as best he could, sometimes dozing until a breaking wave woke him up again.

Eventually, after six days, Peter was picked up by fishermen just off Bathurst Island, situated about 100 kilometres off the north Australian coast near Darwin. The fisherman gave him food and water and took him back to Mandorah Beach where he had started the crossing two weeks earlier. There were no welcoming crowds, just the grim and silent concrete gun emplacements from another conflict.

Peter's journey was over. He had overcome extraordinary odds to become the first person to cross the Timor Sea by canoe—both ways. Curiously, he told no-one of his encounter with the pirates for some time. Perhaps he kept it secret to spare his family the worry, or perhaps it is an example of Peter wanting to keep everything emotional packed away from sight. Certainly he did not tell Beth until he decided to use the story in an *Australian Geographic* presentation at which it would become public knowledge.

Two weeks after completing the Timor Sea trip, Peter set off with his friend, Ron Moon, in an attempt to set a new east–west driving record across Australia. Denis Bartell had set the original record in the 1970s as a solo driver in about six days and Ron expected to cut that in half using a company sponsored Land Rover Discovery Tdi. 'Ron is a fantastic driver,' Peter enthuses, 'with enormous stamina. He can drive off-road tracks quickly and safely for long periods.'

Peter had spent time with Ron and his wife, Viv, in the Cape country, and they operated well together. At the back of his mind, Peter also wanted to find out more about the deserts. This was a way of having a great adventure, setting a record in an area of expertise totally foreign to him, and opening up a new part of the world with an expert. Originally planned as a double traverse, a record held by Hans Tholstrup, the expedition would set a new record, but not without a few problems.

Ron came through from Melbourne, picked up Peter and they drove straight to Cape Byron. Peter had the symptoms of flu, his resistance lowered by the Timor trip and the bashing he had sustained at the hands of the pirates. Meeting Dave Moon and staying in a caravan that night, the pair slept poorly. Next morning Dave drove with them to the lighthouse at 6am and flagged them off, taking a few photographs as they left.

The pair drove without a break to Birdsville, swapping drivers regularly and reaching the outback town at 4am the next morning. The local service station opened up to provide them with fuel.

There were a few accepted rules that applied to record attempts. You must keep to the speed limit, cross the Simpson Desert on the French Line (just a line in the sand) and cross the Gibson Desert.

Leaving Birdsville and deflating their tyres to the right pressure for sand dunes, Ron gunned the vehicle up and over the first big red dune, headlights piercing the night sky. Up and over they went and headed west. As Ron taught Peter to drive across sand dunes, he became more proficient, gaining experience and confidence. Some he couldn't get over, particularly when a dogleg approach was required at speed. 'I would chicken out, lose momentum,' he recalls. 'I would try several times then Ron would take the wheel and get us over.'

Peter became sick in the Simpson, partly from the flu, partly as a result of lack of sleep. He threw up frequently out the passenger window while Ron took more of the burden of driving.

Crossing the Simpson in a day along the French Line, they pulled into Dalhousie Springs at 9pm that night, had a swim in the hot spring, and kept going to Mount Dare Station. 'Then we'd had it,' says Peter. 'We stopped for two hours' sleep in our swags.'

Feeling a bit refreshed, the two drove on to Uluru. They stopped again—

for a sandwich—and then drove all the way across the Gibson Desert through the night without any sleep. 'The theory was that one of us would sleep while the other drove,' says Peter. But by now he felt so sick he couldn't sleep.

Rover Australia had set up the trip as a fuel economy run to test their latest diesel Discovery. And ultimately they were pleased with the result of 27 miles per gallon (10.46 litres per 100 kilometres)—notwithstanding various problems along the way.

Arriving at Carnegie Station at 2am that night for instance, Peter and Ron needed to fill up with fuel. But the people at the station refused to help, despite Ron having called them beforehand. They drove on in disgust and luckily had enough fuel to get to Wiluna where they'd fill up. Even though the car had a 120-litre long range tank they still had to be careful. Fuel was only available at certain places, and they had to arrange in advance for people to open at odd times. Peter remembers asking the service station attendant at Wiluna how much fuel he put in. 'A hundred and twenty-one litres,' he'd replied. The tank had been dry!

Later, when they pulled into Meekatharra, they realised one of the welds on the long range tank had fractured, dripping diesel everywhere. Making the decision that they would not attempt the repeat trip with a leaking fuel tank, they nursed the vehicle carefully on a slightly less tortuous track across to the west.

Neither Peter nor Ron had been out to Steep Point, the westernmost point of the continent. They followed the track for hours, wondering if they were even going in the right direction. After about 70 kilometres of sand dunes, they arrived at Steep Point early in the morning, got the swags out and had a good sleep.

Later that morning they drove down to Perth and stayed with friends of Ron for a day then drove back to Melbourne in just a couple of days. The new record for a team drive east–west across Australia had been set—at just three and a half days.

More than that however, the trip built up Peter's proficiency with 4WDs and made him more comfortable about the desert country. It also led directly to his attempt in the following year to run across Australia from west to east. Once again Rover Australia would supply a support vehicle, needed to put out all the food and clothing dumps for the run.

While preparations for this major expedition went on in the background, Peter continued his solo trips, heading for Tasmania again in the summer of 1995. He had in mind a traverse of the core wilderness area, taking in several key regions from north to south.

The result was a four day run from Penguine on the north coast of Tasmania to Cockle Creek on the south coast. The route included the Cradle Mountain Track and a climb of Mount Ossa, a traverse of the King William Range and a climb of Mount Anne, the Arthurs Plain Track, a traverse of the Western Arthurs and Federation Peak, finishing along the South Coast Track.

Peter planned the run across Australia to start almost a year after the drive with Ron, in June 1995. Starting again at Cape Byron, he was put up in a hotel by friends Tracey Dare and Malcolm McKenzie. The back of the vehicle was full of food, clothing and sleeping bags for the dumps. Peter's meticulous planning had resulted in a decision to place water dumps every 50 kilometres and food dumps every 150 kilometres, right across the entire continent.

'I took off reasonably slowly,' Peter recalls, 'with my main focus on placing the dumps. However, I realised during the first day I could have a go at Denis Bartell's solo drive record at the same time.'

There are a lot of wrecked cars in the outback, particularly in Aboriginal areas. Once the vehicles stop the owners never bother to move them again. Peter would arrive at a wrecked car, open up the boot and put his cache inside, closing the boot again. 'It was safe from the weather and animals,' he says. He recorded the location of each dump on a chart and sometimes took a photograph, because he had to be able to find the dumps exactly. While many of the dumps contained only water, others had spare shoes, maps, food and perhaps a camera and film.

Even stopping every 50 kilometres to put out a water dump, Peter managed to cross the entire continent from east to west in four and half days, thereby breaking Denis Bartell's longstanding record. A critical element of this solo drive was that Peter did not have a radio, unlike on the drive with Ron when they had used a cell phone to keep in touch with their families. 'I could call Beth,' Peter remembers, 'and tell her we were just going over the tenth sand dune from a particular crossing. But this time I wanted to get psychologically used to being out of touch for the solo run.'

It was a considerable risk as some parts of the drive were in very remote country with no backup and Peter was not the best 4WD driver. At Warburton he stopped for fuel. As the attendant unlocked the steel mesh cage protecting the fuel pumps, he told Peter that a huge storm had just come through and the road to the Heather Highway and across to the Gunbarrel Highway was all mud and slush. 'I didn't even know if I could get out of the garage,' he remembers. 'All I could do was take off from the bowser and head off in low range, slipping and sliding in half a metre of mud, struggling to keep to the middle of the road and keep the momentum going. Once you stop you won't get going again.'

Stopping at a large puddle to check the depth, Peter walked into it—up to his chest. If he had driven on the vehicle would never have got out of the hole again.

At Giles Weather Station Peter had spoken to the police and asked if they thought anyone could get across the Gunbarrel Highway. They weren't sure, so he drove across anyway, coping with a lot of water on the track, and knowing all the while that he could get bogged 'in a big way'. With no contact possible with the outside world, he would then just have to sit and wait for the next people to come through.

The journey was completed in safety however and Peter's time of 4 days, 16 hours and 5 minutes established a new record. He left the vehicle in Perth, planning to return there with his family after the run for a slow holiday trip back to Sydney.

Getting a lift back up to Steep Point, Peter started running, replenishing his water supply at the dumps as he went. Then, some 300 kilometres into the run, west of Meekatharra, he slipped into a hole, breaking a bone on the outside of his left foot. 'The second I was doing this I was thinking about the South Pole,' he recalls ruefully, speaking of the unpromising meetings with Howard Whelan of *Australian Geographic* and mountaineer Greg Mortimer which had taken place just before the trip. Clearly Peter was focusing more on that than the run. 'I should have been concentrating more,' he admits, blaming himself for the accident.

Hobbling 150 kilometres back to the road, Peter hitched a ride back to Perth to see a doctor. He told Peter that he had done so much damage to his foot running back the 150 kilometres, he wouldn't be able to set it. To complete the run was now out of the question.

Peter took the next plane back to Sydney and went straight back to work, thinking as always about keeping his leave entitlement up and not wanting to waste it. Then, when the family holiday was due, he went on leave again taking Beth and the girls and his mum, Dorothy, to Perth. They picked up the Land Rover and drove out, picking up a few dumps in the west as they went. This led into a six or seven week family holiday as Peter brought the vehicle back to Sydney the long way around. They went up through Darwin, Tennant Creek, Mount Isa and Carnarvon Gorge. It was the first time Dot had experienced that sort of camping and she slept in the annexe of the family tent. And it was also the first time Peter had taken so much time to be with his family—something which would remain a rare experience for them all.

Arriving in Sydney, Peter returned the vehicle to Rover Australia with thanks. There were still some dumps on the eastern side of Australia and he asked Dave Moon and his wife to pick up some as they had more expensive gear in them that he did not want to lose. 'From Cape Byron to Tenterfield, Dave found all of them from my instructions,' Peter says, 'including three or four sleeping bags and some cameras and so on. I eventually got it all back.'

On the final leg of the journey, Peter called on Denis Bartell in Noosa. Peter already knew about Denis' lengthy trek with a cart from the north of Queensland to Adelaide and was interested to hear more. They sat together in the garage and Denis told him about his attempt to cross the Simpson unsupported. He also gave Peter a copy of the video 'The Desert Walker' which tells the story of his Gulf to Gulf trip. 'As soon as I saw that video,' Peter says, 'I knew immediately I was going to give it a go.'

Back home in Sydney, refreshed by the holiday, Peter immediately threw himself into the organisation of the South Pole expedition, writing letters and contacting his old friends, Ian Brown and Keith Williams. Both expressed an interest in joining Peter on what would prove to be an exciting expedition.

Although rock climbing had been a passion for Peter in his teens and early twenties, he hadn't climbed seriously for a long time. One day he returned to his old training ground, Lindfield Rocks, to discover that things had changed. 'In the old days,' he recalls, 'there were Scouts and a few hard nosed climbers. Now I could see men and women who looked as if they had fallen out of a fashion magazine, with bright pink leotards, trendy gear and the ability to climb all over the place. Actually, it made me feel a bit old.'

Feeling old of course was not what Peter wanted and he decided he had to make 'a bit of a statement'. He planned to climb 100 classic climbs in the Blue Mountains, solo and in one continuous circuit. He'd climbed most of these areas over the last 30 years, and so was familiar with them. He asked Ian Brown to help him select the 100 classic climbs. 'Ian is a fantastic climber,' Peter says, 'with a very detailed knowledge.'

Between them they discussed all the possibilities, eventually coming up with a list. Now, to Peter, a classic climb is not necessarily the hardest. 'I look at it more in terms of the proud route it follows up the cliff, the classic moves you have to make or just the great feeling you get when you're climbing it,' he says.

The solo nature of these climbs however meant that, with a few exceptions, there would be no ropes. One fall and you're dead. This sort of challenge is undertaken quite regularly by far better climbers than Peter, but till then no-one had strung so many together in one continuous climbing marathon.

As usual, the planning was very precise. Peter got himself climbing fit as well as psychologically fit for the attempt. And he had some reconnoitring to do. Most of the climbs he'd attempted at some time before, but there were a few that were new to him. Some climbs too were harder and more risky. Eternity, the climb Peter had been pulled off by Linc Madden many years earlier, was just one of the climbs, and Peter was worried about

"Fuddy Duddy", a grade 15 at Narrowneck. 'Psychologically the grade 15s at Narrowneck are harder than elsewhere,' Peter says. 'It's something to do with the exposure and height. This climb has a particularly fine part of the crack in the middle and I actually took a rope and did a self-belay, which means going up then down again then up again. That meant I couldn't fall to the valley floor at that point.'

Using that technique a few times on some of the climbs, Peter made his way around the circuit. By the time he reached the penultimate climb he was very tired and he picked the wrong climb. The grade 18 Controversy Corner face was therefore climbed by accident. 'It was a serious error of judgment,' he admits. 'With no sleep for more than 60 hours it was a shock to the system when I realised it was much harder. I just managed to scrape through.'

Peter completed the final climb and got out. He had climbed from one end of the mountains to the other, continuously for three days. 'It was my statement against age,' he confirms. 'I could still do it, at the great old age of 38.'

CHAPTER 17

WALKING THE SIMPSON DESERT

'A winner is not necessarily one who wins . . . A winner is someone who gives it a go.'

Denis Bartell, *The Desert Walker*

By the end of 1995 it had become obvious to Peter that the South Pole trip wasn't going to come off in 1996, so instead he brought forward his planned expedition to cross the Simpson Desert. All the planning for the crossing had been done in tandem with the preparation for the South Pole trip, and Peter had already worked out in his mind how he was going to do it.

In fact, he saw the desert crossing as good training for the Antarctic challenge. Both were vast empty wilderness areas where the team would have to haul large loads for survival. And the desert trip would also impact on Peter's long term relationship with his friend, Keith Williams, who would accompany him to the South Pole.

The Simpson is 143 000 square kilometres of arid, uninhabited country in central Australia, bordered by the McDonnell Ranges in the north, Lake Eyre in the south, the Finke River in the west and the Mulligan River in the east. Till then no-one had ever traversed it on the north to south route on foot, unsupported.

But one of those who had attempted it was Denis Bartell, whom Peter had long admired and by now met. Denis had tried to do a longitudinal crossing of the Simpson, through remote areas with a cart, some 20 years earlier. Running out of water, he realised his cart just wasn't big enough to carry the right amount and had to call for help.

Before that, in the 1960s, Warren Bonython and Charles McCubbin had also made an attempt. They too failed through lack of water and had to call for the Royal Flying Doctor Service to drop them emergency supplies. Clearly the longitudinal crossing from north to south was harder—the route was longer than the east–west crossing, and through more remote country.

Once again Peter was on for a challenge. 'I'm really stirred that you can do something for the first time in the 1990s, right here in Australia,' he told a reporter from the *Sun Herald* after the trip.

And here was a challenge that no-one had yet achieved, and Peter intended to write his name in the record books once more. 'It wasn't for money or glory,' he continued in the *Sun Herald* interview. As with his previous adventures, success brought no media glare or victory dais. 'What it's all about,' he says, 'is pushing the limits.'

The world's largest parallel sand ridge desert, the Simpson is mostly steep dunes, spinifex and cane grass with a few salt lakes and clay pans. The rivers disappear into the sand. The sand colour ranges from white to pale golden to red, the oldest sand being darker, having oxidised over many years. Rivers like Coopers Creek bring the white sand down from the north, deposit it in the southern part of the desert and the wind blows it north where you can see pale yellow river sand contrasting with the orange to red sand on the river banks.

Denis was very helpful with information and advice, as was Warren Bonython who sent Peter a copy of his book *Walking the Simpson Desert*, complete with plans for his cart and detailed logistics. As Peter read and then watched Denis' video again, he saw that there were weaknesses with both trips. One was having the starting point at Atula Station in the north, which meant following a series of bores down the line of sand dunes, which run south-east to the end of the desert. While this natural route avoids crossing the dunes, the northern part of the desert seemed the roughest part. Why not reverse the direction, Peter thought, tackling the easier part of the desert while your cart is less heavy as the water supply was used up.

The second problem was the cart design. Bonython hauled the 'Comalco Camel', a design based on sleds used in the Antarctic, partly propelled by using ski stocks. However, while a sled sits on the ground, the cart had a higher centre of gravity and two wheels instead of skids. It had to be balanced by using a steel bar braced against the walker's back—potentially an uncomfortable and dangerous position. In fact, the shaft eventually broke on Bonython's trip. Denis' cart was completely different. Much smaller and lower, it was balanced on his arms.

Peter's cart design combined the best features of both. The basic design is like Warren's cart, with big wheels while the balancing mechanism is like Denis' using a steel bar controlled by the arms. Peter also designed—and got Scott McPherson to make—a better harness system so the force is derived from the hips, the strongest part of the body for pulling, more like a traditional sled harness. And, whereas Warren's wheel track was too narrow and his cart fell in and out of ruts, the wheel track on Peter's was designed to be the same as a motor vehicle, quite wide, so that the walkers would be able to make best use of any 4WD tracks they came across.

With Paul Fardouly's help, Peter built a prototype from his plans. Constructed from square section steel bars, the frame was painted white. At Stockton Beach, near Newcastle, Peter and Simon Buckpitt, an army surveyor who had been invited to join the expedition with Keith Williams and Ian Brown, tested the cart. Loaded with the expected amount of water however, the cart would not budge a single centimetre on the soft sand. Disheartened, Peter returned to Sydney. As he told the *Sun Herald*, he had a vain hope that the sand in the desert would be a little more compact. And they decided to add slightly larger wheels.

At this point, Simon pulled out. And then Ian pulled out too, although he claimed later he had other reasons for doing so. Keith however decided to stay in and take the test to the desert with Peter.

There had been a long lead-in time for this trip—and a lot of research. Peter had by now undertaken two drives across the Simpson which, although fast, had made him more comfortable with the environment. And, after his unsuccessful attempt at running across Australia and the uncertainty about the South Pole expedition, he was determined to give it a go.

Enlisting the help of Ron Moon, Peter was introduced to Neil and Helen Cocks, a retired Victorian couple who had spent a lot of time in the desert and were very experienced. Ron asked the Cocks to write a story for *4×4 Magazine* and back up the expedition. They agreed and set about their own planning.

Rover Australia had once again come to the party and provided a support vehicle, while Track Trailers provided the all-important off-road trailer to carry the carts and water in and out of the desert. Colin French provided the maps while Simon the navigation advice. Other sponsors included Rebel Sport and *Australian Geographic.*

After making all the arrangements on the telephone, Peter and Keith set off from Sydney, driving the Discovery to meet Neil and Helen at Mount Gason Bore on the Birdsville Track, 40 kilometres south of Clifton Hill Station. After a quick lunch the four drove through wet and muddy country to the start point in the desert. Arriving in the late afternoon, they had only an hour or so before the light went to set up the radio and the carts before Neil and Helen headed back. By this time the Warburton River was flooding, making it hard to get in and out and they would have to travel during daylight to find the safe corridors through the mud. The Cocks' role now was to take the vehicle away, drive it around the desert and then meet Peter and Keith out at the top.

Communication was crucial, and Peter carried a 25 watt QMAC HF. Neil selected 4010 VNZ, Port Augusta's main Royal Flying Doctor Service (RFDS) frequency and arranged to make contact at 4.30pm every day. After Peter gave Neil their GPS reading VNZ would enter this on their Safety Log. Neil had also secured a Codan 9323 with Telstra's Radphone Direct Dial (RDD) to stay in touch with Beth and the outside world. This would be a first, as until now she was not used to knowing where Peter was during an expedition.

At this point the carts were still untested and Peter and Keith were by no means certain they would be able to get them going. Setting themselves up on the clay pan, they loaded the carts and settled down for a restless night. Neither slept well and they rose at 4am to make use of the cool of the night. Strapping themselves into the carts, they adjusted their head torches and pulled. The carts actually moved and they were off!

They were heavy. Each cart weighed 260 kilograms when they started, including 140 litres of water—5 litres a day for 28 days—plus food, the radio and a solar panel to provide power. They also took small solar panels for the head torches. 'But they didn't work so well,' Peter says.

Keith takes up the story in an article he wrote for *Australian Geographic*

(Issue 47, July–September 1996) as part of the sponsorship arrangement Peter had organised. 'We'd set out from the northern boundary of Cowarie Station on Warburton Creek, west of the Birdsville Track. Because the dunes run roughly north–south, the idea was to walk northwards parallel to them as much as possible. Our first week would take us up the K1 Line, a seismic exploration track, past huge dry salt lakes. Beyond Poeppel Lake we would cut east across the dunes before turning north-north-west again at the Hay River.'

Meanwhile, Neil and Helen headed north along the K1 Line, catching up with the walkers. Peter refused a drink of cold water as that would spoil the 'unsupported' nature of their trip. Neil then completed a brief reconnaissance about 100 kilometres north, before returning to confirm that the track was mostly good to Beachcomber, a capped bore, where they would turn east-north-east across the dunes on the old shotline.

'For much of that week,' Keith's article continues, 'our days started at 4.30am. Hauling our carts at first under a magnificent starry sky, we continued until 8am before stopping for breakfast. The bird life on this morning was astounding, magpies, wedge tailed eagles and millions of budgerigars seemed happy in this dry salty environment.'

Making a creditable 24 kilometres on the first day, the pair averaged about 30 kilometres a day up the K1 Line, achieved only through strict discipline. In the afternoon the temperature would rise into the high twenties and the men's sweat attracted swarms of bush flies. In anticipation, Keith had made himself what looked like a beekeeper's veil attached to a large sunhat to protect his face from their constant buzzing. But he had made only one. 'After all the work I had done on the carts and the research,' Peter complains, 'I was pissed off that Keith didn't make me a veil too.' It was a small thing—but one that added to the unspoken tension between the pair as the trek continued.

After about ten hours walking, they would make camp at 4.30pm and establish radio contact with Neil and Helen. On the eighth day they turned east-north-east along the shotline as planned, crossing huge dunes. Through Ron, they had obtained a rough map from someone who knew the old mining tracks and this made the going easier as the sand was more compacted for the carts to run on. It was about 80 kilometres to go to the Hay and the hardest day—they made just 8.5 kilometres. To get over each dune one of them would drop their cart at the bottom of the dune, help push the other one up, then both would go back and get the second cart. Rolling down the other side was potentially very dangerous as the carts were heavy and would knock you over if you slipped.

As Keith was eating some fruit cake one afternoon, he saw an orange cloud approaching across the horizon. Neither had ever been in a sandstorm before. 'I realised it was a sandstorm as what looked like a pollution cloud in the distance enveloped trees as it approached,' Peter says. The pair dived into their Gore-Tex bivvy bags and did them up over their heads. 'The sand blizzard struck with such ferocity,' Keith wrote, 'that dust penetrated the seams of our bags. The storm raged till midnight after which we slept where we lay, half buried in our own personal sand dunes.'

Peter remembers that he could 'feel the sand getting through like lots of needles. I couldn't open my eyes, there was sand everywhere, blasting through the material.' He regarded the storm almost like an initiation test from the desert. 'You may proceed with caution,' it seemed to say.

The forces of nature were to continue to test the walkers over the next few days. Woken at about 3am, a lightning storm surrounded them on three quarters, and was approaching fast. They started to walk. The storm caught them around 9am in a really big way, flashing all about them and blowing up small trees close by.

'Suddenly lightning struck the ground about 20 metres away,' Keith recorded, 'splitting the air with sound and light.' Kaboom, they would go in a flash of flame, small branches being hurled through the air. Attached to the only metal for 1000 kilometres they decided to stop, unhitch their carts and sit it out in the open. Taking the radio with them they sat in the middle of a clay pan, under a tent fly, eating breakfast.

'It was bucketing down with rain,' Peter recalls. 'You could hear the trees going off, but there was no point being scared because, if the lightning was going to get us, we wouldn't know anything about it!'

After an hour, the lightning passed. 'Here we were,' Peter mused, 'carrying the precise amount of water we needed in the carts, surrounded by water. We were told later it hadn't rained in July in the desert since 1966.'

The ground was so flat the water collected everywhere. Peter and Keith were very cold, soaked even through their Gore-Tex jackets. That night they tried to find somewhere dry to camp. Putting a tent fly up against the prevailing rain they tried to sleep but the rain changed direction. 'It was like someone putting a jet hose on us as we slept,' Peter says. 'We were soaked—even through the Gore-Tex bivvy bags we'd put over the sleeping bags.'

Nearly three days of rain followed, during which 80 millimetres fell. The desert responded by turning into a sea of white, purple and yellow wildflowers and, as the sky cleared, their spirits lifted. Long term it probably helped as it consolidated some of the sand making it easier to cross with the carts. But this massive storm cut off the whole of central Australia, worrying Neil and Helen who still had to get to the meeting point at the north end of the desert.

Two weeks into the expedition, the pair reached Madigan's Tree, blazed by Cecil Madigan in 1939. Sixty years earlier, Madigan had used a camel team and this tree was the furthest extent that diehard 4WD explorers venture to. Given that the rough country was very hard to get through, when Peter and Keith reached Madigan's Tree they were probably the first to make it on foot.

By this time, both men had problems with their feet. Terrible blisters formed on their insoles from walking in the soft sand. Keith also experienced difficulties with his hips and ankles, surprising Peter with the first physical breakdown he had observed in his long term companion. Keith needed to stretch and take care of himself at every opportunity. Peter continued to push him, wanting to keep the daily distances up.

They navigated mainly by Silva GPS and compass. Colin French had provided basic plot line maps and put grids on them. 'We always knew where we were,' says Peter. Indeed his planning had examined every aspect of the previously unsuccessful trips. Even simple things can ruin your chances. Small burrs can damage tyres, deflating them regularly, so Peter had put 'Slime' inside them so they would self-seal if punctured.

Walking for an hour or so in the dark each morning, it was usually cold enough to have to wear gloves. Keith hated getting up early but Peter insisted. Water management was critical with a measured 5 litres a day for each person for everything including cleaning your teeth! They wrote down every drop they used in a book and used a plastic pump to get water out of the jerry cans so not to waste any. A half litre plastic container was the measure. 'We left it to each other to decide how we used the water,' Peter says. 'After a while we had a very good feel for how much we were using and what we would need.'

As it turned out, they were not using quite what they expected and later took a decision to dump about 40 litres each. The difficulty is knowing when and how much. Dump early and risk shortage or later when you know you are nearly there? As usual Peter had been cautious.

Camping was basic. They'd back up the carts and spread a bright blue tent fly over the top. One would sleep at one end, the other between the carts.

Hygiene was also critical. Illness in the desert would spell disaster. There was no water to wash their hands after going to the toilet. To ensure no germs spread, they used a latex glove and toilet paper, disposing of the latex glove by using it the next morning to light the fire. 'We also used a plastic bag in the billies for cooking food and put that on the fire when we'd finished. That way there was no washing up.' Simple techniques—but ones that would help to make the trip successful.

Meanwhile the flies were terrible and at one time Peter even suffered from maggots in his ears. His ill feeling towards Keith over the veil was compounded by Keith's physical breakdown. Peter never said anything about the flies, just pushed Keith hard, not allowing rest days. In hindsight this was a response that was a pointer to what would happen later on the South Pole expedition.

Neil and Helen in the meantime had endured their own problems with flooded roads, finally making it to their base camp under a lovely ghost gum in the dry riverbed. The plan was to retrieve the carts after the trek was finished, but now Neil was concerned that the daily distances were dropping from 21 to 19 to 17 kilometres and decided to go in to meet Peter and Keith a bit earlier.

Writing in *4×4 Magazine,* Neil reported that they made progress along the track with the trailer, making camp 25 kilometres from the walkers' plotted position. Telling them on the radio that day where they were, Peter was at first totally surprised, then elated. He said they would try to reach Neil the next evening.

By 4.30pm the next day they were just 2.5 kilometres away when they made radio contact and Neil and Helen walked out to lead them in. Peter walked towards them, hand outstretched, big grin on his face, saying, 'It is really good to see you.'

Unloading the carts and securing them on the trailer, Peter and Keith then set off with backpacks containing three days rations and enough water to complete the final leg. Neil and Helen returned with the trailer to their base camp at Mount Winnecke, 80 kilometres away on the desert's northern rim.

Peter and Keith, with about twelve litres of water each and without the carts, walked the last stretch in a day. It was quite difficult because by now their legs were used to walking with the carts. Walking with a pack made it even harder. When they reached the end Helen had strung a ribbon across the track and awarded them a gold medal each. They had completely missed the Olympic Games while walking through the desert!

Camping under the few trees they enjoyed good food, showers and a great evening. In the morning they drove back out through some remote country, calling into Tobermorey Station to thank them for looking after Neil and Helen during the big storm. One of the young blokes came and saw them and pointed out that they had cracked the rear differential. He helped them remove the petrol tank and weld it up so they could continue.

When they got back into the car an approaching storm caught them and they had a really difficult time getting back to the tar in the Land Rover with the trailer. They drove in low range, sliding about at 60–80 kilometres per hour. Unknown to Peter, the road was already officially closed and they could neither get off it nor stop or they would bog. Eventually they reached the tar and kept going most of the night in the pouring rain to find somewhere to camp.

Although they had completed the trip successfully, Peter thought the final time was too slow. 'I could have knocked a week off,' he explains, 'if Keith had been able to go faster.'

But their success, in the end, was due to the combined talents of everyone involved. Interestingly, not one of the sponsors pulled out, even when Peter explained before they left that the chance of success was slim.

All along there had been a contingency plan if the carts were unusable, but it would have led to a much longer trip and no guarantee of success. 'And we could perhaps have relayed water loads into the desert,' Peter suggests. This would still count as 'unsupported'—but fortunately was a theory that did not have to be tested.

Peter's presentation on this trip starts with slides of a mighty electric storm and soaring music that evokes the feeling of an Arabian desert. He describes the desert as a place of magnificent contrasts. The harshness of the environment, the amazing desert wildlife including lizards and snakes, birds and insects. He shows the beauty of the Sturt desert pea with its glorious pink flowers, and a big salt pan full of millions of bleached shells. There are other splashes of colour, low tough looking vegetation on the bare ground, dry salt lakes. 'This is the home to the fierce snakes, with the world's most deadly venom,' he says. 'In this harsh and lonely country we saw camel prints and were followed by a dingo for several days.'

His presentations certainly provide inspiration. A phone call to his office at the bank one day was from a woman on a property out near Longreach. Her husband had given up and was ready to walk off the property until he read the newspaper reports of Peter and Keith's successful trip. 'If those southern softies can walk across the desert,' he said, 'I can get this property working.'

CHAPTER 18

OPERATION CHILLOUT

'The only return and privilege an explorer has in the way of acknowledgement for the help accorded him is to record on the discovered lands the names of those to whom the Expedition owes its being.'

Sir Ernest Shackleton, South, 1919

'My earliest memories of being involved in search and rescue,' Peter says, 'are when I was in Venturers.' But when the New South Wales government was awarding him the highest service award for his contribution, Peter had to ask Robert Pallin if he remembered exactly when he started. Robert produced a photograph of Peter as a young lad in search and rescue uniform.

The New South Wales government had instituted the awards because Search and Rescue was a State-based volunteer organisation and thus members were not able to receive the appropriate national civil award. Over the years this had caused some irritation to members and supporters, who felt that their contribution should be recognised in much the same way as that of the Rural Fire Service is.

While Peter's involvement stretched over 25 years, an informal group of experienced bushwalkers had been assembled by the legendary Paddy Pallin over 60 years previously. Going out whenever someone was reported lost, this group eventually became the Search and Rescue Sub Committee of the Federation of Australian Bushwalking Clubs.

As a youngster, Peter would participate in the searches and practice days. Later, he became a member of the committee, a small group of 10 people with specific jobs such as Equipment Officer or Radio Officer. Peter trained as a Field Officer, responsible for managing rescues, then became Assistant Director and is now Patron.

When a rescue became necessary, and the authorities called in the volunteer group, a Field Officer was appointed to run the search. Peter would liaise with the police and come up with a scenario of what he thought might have happened, together with a plan of where to send people in the field. 'Over the years you learnt particular areas in the mountains where people would most likely get lost,' Peter recalls, 'and send your searchers to those places.'

It might be a particular creek junction where people tend to take the wrong track, getting completely disoriented and lost—for example, where Kanangra Creek comes into the Cox River. 'People would walk up Kanangra Creek thinking they were on the Cox,' explains Peter, 'and get lost in Wallania Creek instead of being on Breakfast Creek.'

Equipped with a base trailer, the search and rescue team would have radio and first aid equipment, ropes and so on. The Field Officer would divide volunteers into groups, and part of his responsibility would be to know the capabilities of the people in those groups. 'You can send an experienced group into a difficult area,' Peter says, 'knowing they will look after themselves. A less experienced or older group might be sent along fire roads.' Ultimately the primary responsibility of the Field Officer is the safety of the searchers. 'You don't want to lose anyone else or get them into trouble,' Peter adds.

A major search may involve police, ambulance, a fire service plus State Emergency Service and National Parks and Wildlife Service personnel— and television crews and helicopters buzzing everywhere. 'There is a tremendous feeling of camaraderie on a big search when someone is missing,' Peter says. 'Despite the problem, everyone is really cheery and helping each other.'

Each group of four or five people would have a radio, with perhaps 15 groups searching along ridges, along creeks, down canyons, wherever was necessary. 'We can coordinate with the helicopters, get them to pick our people off one ridge and put them down on another to do another sweep,' Peter explains.

Turning up with 48 hours' worth of gear, Peter's team can look after themselves in the bush. The big advantage of his group is that they know what they are doing—and they are fit. And their HF radio set is a good band so they can communicate into really deep gorges. Members of the other groups tend to wear overalls, totally inappropriate in the scrub when they get wet, and need to be pulled out at the end of the day.

Over his 15 years on the committee Peter has run hundreds of searches. Understandably, there have been mixed outcomes.

A man with two broken femurs was found alive after a day of searching at Claustral Canyon. He and two companions had become lost as a result of taking the exit route to the canyon and mistaking it for the way in. The man was injured trying to climb out and his companions could not tell rescuers where they left him. As was usual when Peter's team was called out, in this difficult rescue the weather conditions were atrocious.

While Peter did not usually go into the field himself when managing a rescue, sometimes he would need to accompany forensic teams in those cases when a body was found. 'A young man had blown the top of his head off,' Peter recalls of one such instance. 'He was found sitting under a rock overhang in Marramarra National Park.'

Often it would be Peter's role to tell waiting relatives or the police of the outcome of the search. The searcher would ask for radio silence and, using headphones, then inform Peter what had been found.

Peter remembers another sad case when a young woman was found in the Blue Mountains near Katoomba. She had hanged herself with a dog leash, Peter recalls thinking it was such a lonely place to die.

When a light plane went missing in the Blue Mountains near Kanangra, a massive search was launched, although Peter's team was not called in for several days. They found the two young men about 4 kilometres away from the wreck. They had survived the crash but died of exposure. 'They had walked down to the river, not up to the ridge where they might have been found,' comments Peter.

But perhaps the most unusual search was for Wade Butler. On Wednesday 29 November 1995 a team of 10 from Bushwalkers Wilderness Rescue flew to Tasmania to assist in the private search. Wade Butler had not been seen since he left for a six day solo round trip to Precipitous Bluff via the exposed Southern Ranges. Dot Butler, Wade's mother, had called Peter, Patron of Bushwalkers Wilderness Rescue and an old friend.

'When I heard the search was going to be called off after two weeks,' Peter says, 'I formed the view that Wade was probably injured and alive somewhere but they just hadn't found him.' Peter called Dick Smith, who also knew Wade and Dot, and Dick agreed to meet the costs of a private search.

Assisted by Greg Hodge, a dedicated Tasmanian volunteer search coordinator, Peter proceeded to run the search from his desk at the Commonwealth Bank in Sydney, as he couldn't get away personally. The search of bluffs, ridges and false leads was extensive and thorough, aided by effective radio communication and helicopters.

Wade was 'as tough as nails' according to Peter. A very hard man who knew exactly what he was doing. If he had been injured near a main trail Peter felt confident they'd find him eventually.

On 2 December however, the team was pulled out. Peter again contacted Dick who agreed to extend the search for another week, funding helicopter transport. This time Tasmanian volunteers were used, searching until 8 December. Nevertheless, the only trace of Wade that was ever found was a footprint located by the official search team at Precipitous Bluff low camp.

Tragically, Dot had already lost her daughter Wendy in a cascading accident, and Wade's twin brother Norman had died after being bitten by a tiger snake. She was deeply affected by Wade's disappearance and Peter was later involved in the sale of her house to provide money to her daughter-in-law to look after her and Wade's five children.

'Wade was a very adventurous character,' Peter says sadly. 'He must have wandered off, got hurt or fallen down a hole. Most people involved in the search felt guilty about giving up, even though they'd busted a gut for two to three weeks.'

There have been, of course, hundreds of successful rescues—both of individuals and groups. And Peter maintains that everyone involved can claim part of the success. But Peter's team is so successful they claim they can find a missing person by lunchtime on the first day of the search! They just have 'better knowledge and skills and know where to look' as Peter puts it. 'We can usually work out what happened.'

Unfortunately however, in times past, they were rarely brought in at the first call—a case of rescue politics between official agencies as well as between professionals and volunteers getting in the way of common sense. And nowadays rescues that used to be coordinated through the Police Rescue Squad in Sydney are regionalised. The regional prime response group, which may be a professional or a volunteer group, may not know what other resources are available to them, particularly if they are out of area. 'If they don't know we exist,' Peter says, 'they can't ask us to help.' Subsequently the number of rescues the team has been involved in has decreased.

However, members of the Rock Squad, formed by Peter, have performed a number of rescues without attracting the attention of any authorities just because they have been on the spot when needed. Peter says he knows who he would rather have come and rescue him. 'It would be the volunteers any day,' he says matter-of-factly. 'They just have so much more skill and knowledge.'

Knowing the Rock Squad's reputation, outdoors people continue to use the organisation as a resource base or to ask advice about contacting police. Peter can readily refer to his huge collection of maps and offer suggestions about how people can help themselves.

But all rescues, both successful and unsuccessful, emphasise the potential dangers of the Australian outdoors. They also put into clearer perspective Peter's own skills and abilities in remote wilderness areas.

Some time after completing the Simpson trip Peter felt he wanted to cross another desert. The Gibson was the most logical because he had driven across it several times and was friendly with Len Beadell, who had built the Gunbarrel Highway and had helped him with his planned run across Australia.

The Gibson followed on from these drives and Peter's attempted run as well as his successful crossing of the Simpson. The major difference however was the size. And although the Gibson is about 500 kilometres across Peter—still feeling rather dissatisfied with his time across the Simpson and wanting to do something different—decided to attempt it without the cart.

'You have to balance the risks,' he says. The choice was either fill the pack up with water and run, leaving the cart behind to get it over quickly. Or take a longer time with the cart. The disadvantage of the quick method is you are very isolated. And with no radio, Peter would be a long way from support if anything went wrong.

He calculated he needed five days' water at 4 litres a day. With 20 kilograms of water in his pack there was room for a few chocolate bars but no sleeping gear. Neil Cocks and Ron Moon would provide backup, but if Peter had failed to arrive at his destination any resulting search would be of epic proportions.

Cutting down from the south-east of the Rollaston Range, Peter crossed the highway and followed the lay of the desert, taking bearings off the highway. 'I wasn't following the Gunbarrel,' he says. 'I thought that was too easy.'

The Gibson desert is mainly sand dunes, but the consistency of the sand is more clay based. With some roughly parallel dunes, it is rather a mixed up terrain with a variety of features. Peter would run up and over the dunes and through the valleys, checking his position at junctions of roads built by Len.

He completed the crossing in four and a half days, arriving west of Carnegie Station. It was, in Peter's words, a 'bloody fast and extremely risky trip'. Its success, by being the longest solo run so far, not only set yet another standard but laid the foundations for subsequent trips Peter would do, including the next five deserts he would tackle. And he carried out a rescue during the drive home to Sydney!

It may seem that Peter Treseder spends every waking hour preparing for and undertaking one adventure after another. The truth is that, like most of us, Peter works for a living and has family responsibilities. Given that he has worked for the Commonwealth Bank since leaving university, some journalists have referred to this part of his life as boring, contrasting it with the excitement of his expeditions.

Peter sees it a little differently. 'You're not trapped in one job all the time,' he says. 'There's a great variety of things you can get involved in and lots of first-class personalities.' In his opinion the bank is a collection of ordinary people like him, 'trying to make the best decisions by society'.

While this may not ring true to the average bank customer in these days of closing branches, reduced personal services and increased fees, Peter is clearly proud to be associated with the Commonwealth Bank and is sensitive about satisfying the expectations of not only a major sponsor of his expeditions but his employer.

He has undoubtedly enjoyed his work experiences, deriving satisfaction from the intellectual challenges put his way. At North Sydney, he headed up a team of corporate lenders involved in major projects ranging from the Sydney Harbour Tunnel to small business—a time he regards as an opportunity to be involved in society, helping customers build their dreams. The Manager, John Martin, had built the branch to the third largest lending institution the bank had, with 50 loans staff. 'He was phenomenal,' Peter enthuses.

Having learnt on the way home from one of his Cape York trips of his promotion to Group Credit Policy and Control under John Edwards, Peter became the Branch representative, important to balance the majority of head office staff. In the late 1980s banks, collectively, had major credit problems brought on by relaxed lending policies and were now focusing their activities on this area. Group Credit set the standards for credit, making staff accountable for the loans they were recommending and approving. The decisions made affected thousands of people, particularly when loans went bad. There were moral as well as financial obligations and judgments when private schools were struggling, when a politician's personal financial downfall could affect a government or when a business closure would put hundreds of people out of work. Group Credit took a proactive role, analysing risks and heading off disaster. There were, however, entertainers, construction companies and property developers who went bad, icon names in business and high profile corporate failures who sometimes escaped the net.

Proud of his contribution in Group Credit, Peter considers the bank lived up to its responsibilities. 'We should be proud,' he says, 'of a team of individuals like Les Taylor, Steve Nelson, Bryan Fitzgerald and a whole range of solid characters who have made the bank work over the years.'

Involved in many sensitive cases, Peter clearly cannot divulge confidential information about his role in the bank at that time but does tell of one unusual deposit from a loan defaulter. 'This man walked into my office,' he recalls, 'and dumped a bucket on the desk. "That's full of bull semen," the man exclaimed, "and you can do what you like with it!"'

One of Peter's long time colleagues and friends is Phill Evenden, a Vietnam veteran, who shares Peter's lunchtime runs. 'He's a tough guy to go out with on a call regarding a credit problem,' Peter says. 'Not scared of anything or anyone!' On one occasion the pair travelled to far north Queensland and were standing in the middle of a dustbowl, in business suits, while the two massive sons of the defaulting farmer circled them threateningly on horseback. 'Phill dealt with it,' Peter says.

It was 27 February 1997 and Peter laid out the wonderful *Australian Geographic* map of Antarctica on the coffee table. Lachlan Murdoch knelt on the floor and peered over the map, looking at it intently, talking about the revered Antarctic adventurers of the heroic age. Tracing the routes of Amundsen, Scott and Shackleton, he asked Peter who was his favourite Antarctic explorer. No-one spoke for a moment then Peter broke the suspense. 'Shackleton,' he said. 'Mine too,' replied Lachlan, continuing to discuss the risks and hardships and how Peter and the rest of the team were mentally training for such a difficult journey.

Clearly a leader in the making, Lachlan was decisive when he'd been approached for support. His interest and knowledge about Antarctica, obviously from personal research, was almost breathtaking. Arranging for the team to meet with his marketing and editorial staff, he also generously offered funds as well as newspaper coverage of the expedition.

Up till then the South Pole Expedition had no commitment of funds from any major sponsor. It was February 1997 and the trip had to be paid for by July.

A few months earlier at Peter's house a mood of uncertainty filled the air as the evening finished without an outright commitment. John Leece, in his new role as expedition manager, offered to leave the room so the adventurers could discuss the decision but Peter said it was not necessary. Peter addressed Keith Williams and Ian Brown directly. 'Are we going?'

It seemed an age before Keith took the initiative and said almost half heartedly he would be in it. Peter obviously was already committed and the question did not need to be asked of him.

But still there was an air of reluctance as they considered the enormity of the project. 'I need to speak to Marianne (his wife),' Ian said. 'I will talk to her tonight and let you know in the morning.'

Although sponsorship was not in place at this time and transport to and from Antarctica was yet to be confirmed, much had been going on in the background. Paul Kelly, then Editor-in-Chief of *The Australian*, had previously hosted a meeting with John, Peter, Ann Chang, Kerry James and Professor Bob Graham to discuss sponsorship and fund raising for the Victor Chang Cardiac Research Institute. Grasping the concept immediately, he offered support through a schools supplement on Antarctica. And he provided the introduction to Lachlan. To reinforce his approach, Peter was able to tell him that a letter had just arrived from the Prime Minister's office, saying that John Howard had agreed to be Patron-in-Chief of the expedition. And Kim Beazley, Cheryl Kernot and Bob Carr had also offered their support.

The year before, on Sunday 1 September 1996, chartered accountant John Leece had read an article in the *Sun Herald* about Peter and Keith and their Simpson Desert trip. 'It captured my interest and imagination,' John says, 'although I'm still not sure what made me pick up the telephone on Monday morning, call the Commonwealth Bank and ask for Peter Treseder.'

It was however to be the start of a long journey of self discovery for John as well as the three who walked to the Pole. Although John ostensibly had phoned Peter to offer some small financial support towards the South Pole trip, Peter was reluctant to take the money, saying he did not have any other sponsors.

Inviting him round for lunch, John listened to Peter's plans and formed the opinion that he would never raise the sponsorship money he needed with his current approach. Peter handed John a brief information sheet which outlined the reasons for the proposed expedition. It included two features which drew John's attention. The first was the aim to raise funds for worthwhile charities; and the second the hope of inspiring fellow Australians to achieve their dreams. 'I quickly became convinced that this was no ego trip,' recalls John. 'I could see that the post-expedition goals were critical to obtaining funding.'

Although busy, John agreed to make a few calls on Peter's behalf to obtain support and wished Peter well in his endeavours. Within a few days Peter had called to check progress, an example of his tenacity and singular focus. Before long there were meetings with Ann Chang, widow of the late Dr Victor Chang, and Dr Brian Pezzutti, a New South Wales Liberal Senator. And these led to the meeting with Lachlan Murdoch. John Leece was hooked!

Adventure Network International, based in the UK and run by globe trotting Managing Director Anne Kershaw, was approached by Peter for transport into and out of the Antarctic. Operating out of Punta Arenas on the southern tip of South America, ANI was the standard way for most private expeditions to get into Antarctica. ANI's support came, however, at a cost of several hundred thousand US dollars, so John Leece determined to find a cheaper alternative.

Knowing that US aircraft fly out of Christchurch, New Zealand to McMurdo Sound in Antarctica, John tried several approaches to secure seats for the three expeditioners. But he continued to run into obstacles. 'If such seats had been attainable they would have reduced the budget by $280 000,' says John.

Then, finding out that President Clinton was to make a private visit to Australia, John talked to a number of people who might get the President's ear. Since the Americans are all powerful in Antarctica, support at the highest level was important. John also asked his brother, David, to use his connections as a Brigadier in the Army Reserve to enlist the help of the Australian defence forces by conducting a joint services exercise that would land at McMurdo Sound, taking the expedition team as baggage.

David tried to arrange for the team to carry out medical or scientific research that would gain them seats on official flights, but all to no avail. One of the problems was that scientists view Antarctica as their domain and not that of adventurers, whom they view as threatening to the ecosystem. An interesting concept considering the mess down there has been caused almost entirely by scientists. So much so that the US is undertaking a massive cleanup program of their own.

All the while, part of Peter's drive to get the expedition underway had been the rumour that another Australian team was preparing for an expedition in the December 1998 season. Peter naturally wanted to be first—there was no room for second in his mind.

So John Leece now tried his American colleague, Charles Thornburg, who worked for Lawrence Livermore National Laboratory on a Zinc Air Fuel Cell project in which Leece had invested, as well as with the scientists at the National Science Foundation.

'Just get me three seats on a US C130 Hercules transport out of Christchurch mid October 1997,' Leece said to him.

'I can get you three,' Thornburg replied, 'but not this year. Maybe next year but more likely the year after, if you're lucky.'

Next John tried an approach through New Zealand, which also had C130s flying into McMurdo Sound. 'Antarctica NZ were fantastic,' John recalls, 'positive from day one.' The aircraft and seats were committed. Then ANI told Peter that if they went in via McMurdo Sound their cost of support and rescue would be much higher than if the team was supported from Patriot Hills. The New Zealand support seemed doomed to failure.

By this stage the chance of getting sponsorship looked desperate. Then Leece met Brian Paterson, who runs an event management company in Sydney. In his role as National Treasurer of Scouts Australia, Leece sought sponsorship through Paterson for a children's television program, originally conceived by Scout Leader, Jon Willis, a Director of Commercial Video Productions in Melbourne. Tentatively titled 'Don't Try This at Home', the program would have wide appeal to primary school children.

Paterson had already proposed to his client, Arnott's, a concept store in Darling Harbour to attract children. Now he was looking for a 'big adventure' to promote the concept—and they don't come much bigger than the South Pole Expedition. His marketing strategy was to enthuse kids, but also to subtly encourage them to be loyal to Arnott's as a brand, just as their parents had been. All this was going on while Arnott's was in a recovery stage after suffering from a very public and expensive extortion threat. The upshot was that Chris Roberts, the Managing Director of Arnott's, loved the idea.

The previous week John Leece had met with David Kinchin, Chief Commissioner of Scouts for New South Wales and his CEO, Hilton Bloomfield. They agreed to support the expedition and help with fundraising through Scouts.

Sources of support now included *The Australian* newspaper and News

Ltd. Arnott's were on board, using their Arnott's Adventures branding to tie in with a new marketing initiative. And the Commonwealth Bank was in, together with Scouts Australia as the fourth major sponsor. Contracts and amounts of money were however yet to be confirmed.

Peter then, through the Commonwealth Bank and its associate company, Commonwealth Connect Insurance, arranged a rescue insurance policy, the first ever to be written by an Australian company and one of very few worldwide. Such a policy became necessary once the decision had been made for the expedition to be totally self-sufficient, relying on no-one for assistance should anything go wrong. Peter, in particular, did not want to end up on the front page of the tabloids if a government had to direct resources to their rescue.

Finally, the Expedition was launched publicly at The Bunyas, a rambling Federation house and the New South Wales Headquarters of Scouts Australia. Stuart Leece, John's nephew, arranged for the boardroom to be made over to look like the inside of an Antarctic hut, complete with memorabilia, packing cases and an audio-visual presentation put together by Peter. This meeting was to bring together a number of parties, including the major sponsors, so everyone knew what their responsibilities were—all just three months from the expedition start.

Keith couldn't make it as he lived in Orange and wasn't able to get the day off work. And Stuart ran late for this important meeting, bringing some of the essential props with him. But with so many bodies crowded into the boardroom it actually did feel a bit like an expedition hut. Peter made his passionate presentation. Ian Brown talked about equipment. And everyone received an Antarctic ration box before getting together in small groups to discuss the next steps.

In the months following, John Leece continued to use his own extensive network, together with that of his identical twin brother Bob, to secure support for the expedition. By the time they were ready to leave there was a ground team of at least 30 or 40 people working on different aspects—a huge commitment of both personal and corporate time. 'It was easier to get support,' John Leece comments, 'when the people attending meetings had creativity in their own thinking and grasped the inspiration and passion we shared. It was not just the mission that was important, it was the message that followed.'

Meanwhile, involving the Scouts to assist in fundraising was proving difficult. As a voluntary organisation, its communication system is based on word of mouth through meetings and there simply wasn't enough time to mobilise them. The marketing committee set up under Paterson's management considered many fundraising schemes, most of which were rejected by Scouts on the basis of time and organisational demands. And, as a voluntary organisation without government funding, Scouts had its own funding priorities. Eventually however, a national Trekathon was planned for November 30 when the expedition was well under way and generating publicity.

Peter made the suggestion that the expeditioners all be reinvested as Scouts and undertake the expedition in the name of Scouts Australia. Thus, Peter rejoined the movement along with Ian and John Leece who had each been awarded Queen's Scouts as Venturers, and Keith who had been a Scout and earned his Duke of Edinburgh's Gold Award. The ceremony took place at Government House in Sydney, where they were reinvested by the Chief Scout of New South Wales, The Hon Gordon Samuels, AC.

Much to the frustration of John Leece, other promotional opportunities such as displays at Westfield shopping centres and sales of Antarctic kits at Coles Supermarkets failed through lack of proper organisation and support. Leece was also frustrated by the cost of a television community service announcement made by advertising agency Leo Burnett, Conaghan & May. Winning industry creative awards for the way it showed a tent pumping like a heart, even so it raised little money as the TV stations gave it scant airtime. More successful in generating public interest was a 50-minute documentary, narrated by John Laws and shown shortly before the expedition left for South America.

The quest for sponsorship continued. Dick Smith was a great personal supporter and finally *Australian Geographic* offered more money than they had ever offered before, and sent their logos in anticipation. News Ltd however were very reluctant to allow *Australian Geographic* in, as it was at the time owned by Fairfax. Fortunately, media politics were eventually put aside.

223

Stuart Leece was also able to secure some last minute sub-sponsors and agreements with these were signed in Punta Arenas after the expedition left Australia. Les Taylor, the Solicitor for Commonwealth Bank, had assigned one of his support staff, solicitor Marion Hetherington, to prepare the sponsorship contracts, another valuable contribution. Marion had another important role—to ensure the cheque was issued for ANI while the three were in Punta Arenas. Without it the expedition would not even start.

At departure time they were still short of money. Then an anonymous businessman donor personally underwrote the expedition to the tune of $140 000—without any guarantee of being repaid. It was a supremely generous gesture. The funds were telegraphically transferred to ANI in October 1997. A few days later the Asian crisis hit and the Australian dollar plummeted. Had the money been delayed the expedition would have been off as the ANI fee was payable in US dollars and there was no more money.

When John reached Punta Arenas there was one last contract to sign. Peter, Ian, Keith and John signed over all individual rights that might arise out of the expedition to the company, Operation Chillout Pty Ltd, owned jointly by the four. That would assist in repaying some of their debts on their return.

CHAPTER 19

TRAVERSING SILENCE

'We had discovered an accursed country. We had found the Home of the Blizzard.'

Sir Douglas Mawson, *The Home of the Blizzard*, Hodder & Stoughton 1930

Ian Brown suggests that Keith Williams was keen to have him along on the South Pole Expedition to temper Peter's inevitable pressure on his fellow trekkers. They had both taken part in Peter's expeditions before and Keith had probably been his companion more often than anyone else. The three were good friends and respected each other's abilities. And, perhaps not surprisingly, they each had a complex character with the underlying toughness necessary to accomplish such punishing physical challenges as the South Pole trip.

Keith is deeply religious. He usually takes a Bible with him on trips, but never pushes it at anyone. Occasionally he will 'speak in tongues' and in an interview after the expedition stated that he had 'communed with his creator' while hauling his sled. His stubbornness is both one of the difficulties of dealing with him and one of his greatest strengths, because he simply does not give up and is really tough. Diagnosed a haemophiliac, Keith ignores his doctor's advice to not take risks and embarks on expeditions in the knowledge that a serious injury could result in his death where another may survive. 'We had to accept that risk, too,' says Peter, 'and understand why Keith is so particular about his diet and fitness.'

It is perhaps ironic that Keith had tried for years to get into the Antarctic Service, only to be knocked back on medical grounds. Apart from previous expeditions with Peter, his credentials for this trip included an ascent and descent of Mount McKinley, North America's highest peak, extensive mountaineering in New Zealand's Southern Alps, canoeing many wild rivers and climbing the remote spire of Balls Pyramid, off Lord Howe

Island. A teacher and Program Director with the NSW Department of Sport and Recreation he is also a qualified ski and canoe instructor.

Ian, a much published outdoors writer and photographer, has a strong character which also doesn't allow for giving up. A District Operations Manager with the NSW National Parks and Wildlife Service, and a qualified rock climbing instructor, Ian has traversed California's Sierra Nevada Mountains on skis, trekked for eight weeks through the wilderness of Cape York and scaled mountains in the New Zealand Alps and Balls Pyramid.

With three such strong-minded people relying on each other for 60 days it is unsurprising that tensions would find their way into the open when times were tough. Peter for instance seemed to feel the responsibility for the trip far more than the others did. 'Keith and Ian were not the ones who made the promises to sponsors,' he says. 'And sponsors don't put the money in your pocket unless they expect you to succeed.'

To ensure success, Peter arranged for specialised help before they left. They went to podiatrist Alan Donnelly, who told them how to look after their feet, especially critical for Peter who has a problem with the bones of his heels which have grown out to cover his expanded Achilles tendon. 'It started when I was at school,' Peter remembers, 'and makes it difficult for me to wear boots.'

For this reason, the expedition used Norwegian style soft boots. Donnelly showed them how to care for their feet using methylated spirits and foot powder and warned of the dangers of trench foot through constant moisture. As a result, after all the gear was shared out, Keith made a beautiful pair of vapour barrier socks for himself but not for Ian or Peter. 'Nothing was said,' Peter remembers, 'but it was annoying considering the trouble and expense we had gone to.'

Peter's self-control in these situations is interesting. He can always see why it is better to say nothing, although the emotional hurt may stay with him.

Peter, Ian and Keith were booked on Qantas flights from Sydney to Papeete, then were flying with Lanchile airlines to Sandiego de Chile. A media conference was arranged for their departure on 20 October 1997.

Ian and Peter fielded a barrage of questions. 'Right now I'm feeling scared,' answered Peter. 'Not just about the journey but because of the huge infrastructure behind us. I'm scared of failure.' Keith didn't turn up for the Press Conference; 'He doesn't seem to understand that you have to repay the sponsors' faith in you', is Peter's explanation.

Sometime before, when being interviewed by the *Sun Herald* in September 1996 after the desert trip, Peter had said that he saw the expedition as being 'a significant endeavour for Australians leading up to the turn of the century'. But while he had every intention of all three expeditioners reaching the Pole, he also had a strong conviction that, even if only one were capable, they should carry on to achieve what they had promised their sponsors. This attitude was to continue to cause great tension as the trip progressed.

They arrived in Punta Arenas and, in a farm shed on the edge of town, unpacked their gear, some of which had come directly from London. Ian called John Leece to explain that some vital sled parts were missing and asked if John could take them off the display sleds, which John had ordered in anticipation of Westfield involvement, and bring them with him. John would take up the fourth seat on the aircraft to Patriot Hills, acting as official photographer and supporter when they reached Berkner Island.

'I called Beth and went round straight away,' says John. 'But I had to call my brother, Bob, to help me get the parts off.'

Meanwhile, waiting in Punta Arenas, the equipment was checked and double checked. Ian was responsible for navigation and checked the GPS and the chest mounted, fluid-filled, Silva marine compass, which had been adjusted for use close to the magnetic Pole. Their supplies would include 40 litres of white spirit stove fuel, purchased from the ANI base at Patriot Hills. There would be 69 days' supply of food, some 285 kg in total, loaded onto kevlar sleds with HDPE runners and both rope and rigid harnesses. The expeditioners would wear Paddy Pallin thermal clothing in layers, balaclavas and goggles, nose shields and carry Black Diamond adjustable stocks which could also be assembled into 2-metre probes to find hidden crevasses. Paddy Pallin 'expedition grade' sleeping bags would keep them warm while a single skin Bibler dome tent would provide just one millimetre of protection from the elements. The parkas were custom made in Gore-Tex and Black Diamond heavy touring skis were covered in synthetic skins and attached to Alfa polar sledging ski boots by Rottefella cross-country, three pin bindings. They would take crampons but use them only for three days on the ice. While snow fell gently outside everything was checked to the last buckle.

Delayed by this bad weather, the three fixed sponsors' logos on their sleds. But someone in Sydney had forgotten to sew the logos on their jackets—a regrettable oversight, and one not appreciated by some of the sponsors after the event.

Originally the funds were committed only for a Hercules Inlet start. Setting out from Berkner Island added about $US185 000 to the funding needs, but Hercules Inlet was not as desirable because, as the ANI base was about 400 kilometres closer to the Pole, it would have been less of an achievement and one potentially beaten in later years. So this expedition started where the summer sea breaks at the northern tip of Berkner Island on the Weddell Sea at latitude 78 degrees south. The route was to traverse 300 kilometres across Berkner Island, cross the ice shelf for 150 kilometres, trek into the Pensacola Mountains and from there traverse the Polar Plateau to the South Pole, another 950 kilometres, rising to about 3000 metres at their final destination.

A Hercules transport took them from South America to the ANI base at Patriot Hills. After six and a half hours the heavy plane landed on a natural ice runway. 'You can't use brakes in these conditions,' Peter says, 'the pilot has to steer with the props and hope the plane stops in time.' The four unloaded their gear and John Leece took a photograph of Peter and Ian with the Australian flag. Keith however refused to take part, saying he was too busy organising the stores. Even so, the resultant photograph in *The Australian* irritated his wife.

From Patriot Hills they waited for the right weather and then flew across the edge of the continent to Berkner Island, knowing they wouldn't see darkness again for two months. The sleds were unloaded from the Twin Otter and the three put on their harnesses, not saying much. The only noise was of them shuffling about in the snow. They had been blessed with fine weather for the start—but it was 31 degrees below zero when they landed. 'Bloody freezing,' recalls Peter.

Occasional requests for assistance came from one to another. Ian attached the compass harness to his chest. 'Everyone knew what they had to do and just got on with it,' says John. He filmed them as they put their gear on and loaded up the sleds. They were ready. In the anticipation John almost forgot to take the important still photograph of them leaving and had to call for them to stop. Wearing red jackets with red covers on the white sleds and yellow harness ropes, the scene almost looked like a designer television commercial as they made ready next to the red and white plane.

It was 8pm on 2 November 1997 and everything seemed in order. There was no ceremony as it seemed during the last half hour they were all lost in their own thoughts. This is what they had come for. It was a long, long way and the word remote took on a new meaning. The breathtaking grandeur and beauty of the frozen continent was balanced by the knowledge that it was a cruel, hostile and isolated environment.

'There's no adrenalin rush,' Peter says, 'none of this "heroes down in the wilderness" business. Most of the time you're just damn scared.'

On the first day they made just 7 kilometres in difficult conditions. 'Dragging tyres for an hour is not the same as a sled for eight,' as Keith puts it. By the third day it was snowing constantly, producing a total white-out in which it was very difficult to navigate. When they stopped, they quickly put up their small green tent, trying to improve on the outside temperature of minus 20°C. It could be as warm as minus 5°C in the tent, quite pleasant and the same as the average household freezer! Planning to walk eight hours a day for the next week, they gradually increased the distance covered and the hours they walked to 10 a day when there was slightly better snow. But frostbite started on Keith's fingers within a few days, which made it hard to do even ordinary things.

'It was an extremely slow process working in the cold,' Peter remembers. 'It would take two hours to melt enough snow to make a meal. By the time we wrote our diaries, checked where we were and sorted ourselves out to sleep it was 10pm and we would be up again at 4.30am.'

A typical day would start by boiling snow for lunchtime soups while they ate a muesli breakfast, supplemented by olive oil and a mug of Milo. This was necessary to get the total calorie intake up to an average 6021 calories a day, four times the normal intake. They knew of course that Scott had died in the Antarctic; his party consumed more than 4000 calories a day and still got sick. Two thermoses each containing a litre of soup plus more olive oil were prepared from packet mixes. The remaining olive oil would be stored in a nalgene container and used for dinner that night. They each also had two packs of Arnott's biscuits per day. Specially baked with minimum water to avoid freezing, these special expedition biscuits provided 1900 calories on their own. One hundred grams of standard Cadbury fruit and nut chocolate was also rationed for each day.

'Tea', as Peter calls it, would be one of three gourmet offerings planned by Keith for the whole 60 days. Soup would start them off and this would be followed by a main course of either 100 grams of macaroni with parmesan cheese and some dehydrated vegies, or rice with a powdered curry sauce, or powdered Deb potato with soya grits for vegetarian Keith or about 100 grams of salami for Ian and Peter. A cup of Milo and a fruit bar would finish the meal.

Each night Keith would try to use some different spices to make the meals a bit more interesting. 'Meals were very important,' says Peter, 'not just for the nutritional value but because they were something you looked forward to for hours as you trudged through the snow.'

As the snow fell while they slept it would gradually build up around the sides of the tent, sliding down the dome. It was essential to dig the tent out to prevent the weight of the snow breaking a pole and they took it in turns to complete this task.

The sun shone 24 hours a day. So, because it was psychologically important for the walkers to have an organised day and to maintain a set biological rhythm, their schedule was set by watches.

Needless to say, some daily habits were hard to maintain. 'It's very difficult to use toilet paper,' Peter says, 'and your hands get too cold to do up your trousers again.' The solution was to dig a hole and use a pointed piece of ice from the hole you dug, then bury it. 'That way you could keep your gloves on,' Peter says. They used paper underpants some of the time, burning them after a few days when they got putrid, but they used to ball up and were uncomfortable. And infection and dampness were always a problem, causing chafing.

On day nine they made 11 kilometres and Peter knew they had to increase their pace substantially. 'We needed to get it up to 20 to 25 kilometres a day,' he says as he describes the effort required to trudge for eight hours in two hour stints with 15 minute breaks.

Ian's diary for 9 November records his feelings: 'It was my day to lead two of the four legs, first and last. I was tired and there were many low, icy ridges that had to be "winched" over. This is an extremely uncomfortable business. You plod along, with a number of little requirements bothering you. A boot needs adjusting, your goggles are iced up, you need to urinate and replace the cream on your lips. But you know you can only stop for long enough to do one of these or you will cool down too much.'

By 13 November they were travelling faster and Peter exclaimed, while checking their position on the GPS, that they had made 21 kilometres that day. For the most part however the walking was tedious and plain hard work. Once you got warmed up, Keith says, you could think about nicer things like a lush green forest. Peter visualised where he would put all his outdoor gear in his rearranged garage, or where he could be on holiday with the family. Ian, plodding along in the tracks behind, found it monotonous, almost falling asleep. Out in front with the compass, trying to maintain a bearing and the pace, it was all hard work and full-on attention.

As the days passed, so did birthdays—for both Ian, 43 and Peter, 40. Both were celebrated with hand carved ice cakes and a song.

Meanwhile the ice shelf took a week to cross. The walkers kept their faces covered against ultraviolet rays striking through the hole in the ozone layer. 'We could feel our faces burning in the first few days,' says Peter.

The sun's rays were however put to one good use. Sony digital handycams had been adapted for use in the Antarctic and solar panels were mounted on one of the sleds to recharge the batteries. The resulting video of the expedition, released by Showboat and entitled 'Walking on Ice', reveals a totally flat environment on Berkner Island. When it was clear you could see so far you could even make out the curvature of the horizon.

An unusual phenomenon worried the group at first. The top layer of snow has an air layer under it. By skiing across it you can set off a snowquake and the ground would seem to fall away several centimetres, followed by a booming sound. 'It was really scary at first,' says Ian. 'You could hear them reverberating for 20 to 30 seconds. It's amazing to think that just our body weight could set it off.'

The closer to the polar coast they walked, the worse the weather became. Day 23 was 'horrific' according to Peter. With bumpy terrain like a frozen ocean and sticky snow it was hard to pull skis and sleds through. Peter had problems with his glasses icing up too but still they managed 20 kilometres, a good effort in the conditions.

As they progressed the snow itself seemed different. Indeed to Keith it was unlike any he had seen anywhere in the world. 'Falling gently, it had huge 3–4 centimetre crystals. Full of air and dry,' he says, 'like textbook snow.'

All the while Peter was totally focused on what he wanted to achieve. He wouldn't—and didn't—bend from that aim one iota, an attitude that got on the nerves of the other two who would have preferred him to lighten up a bit.

Leece Pass, named out of respect for John Leece, was traversed on day 27. 'It's steep, a real grunt,' says Peter. 'By far the hardest thing I've ever done,' remarks Ian who, when his leg was temporarily stuck in a crevasse, was grateful for the short rest. They pulled their sleds up huge slopes as the snow blew horizontally. Keith's ankle was playing up and for the next week 'gave him hell'.

Throughout the expedition Ian was responsible for photography but he found it very difficult—especially when he was lashed to a sled. And the constraint of the cold made it possible to shoot only one frame at a time with his gloves off. On day 29 Peter used the video camera and filmed himself. 'After 2 hours 20 minutes the other guys are well behind,' he recorded.

Two days later they began a series of climbs. It was minus 15 degrees with a 20 knot wind. Two thousand metres up in the Pensacola mountains, with Peter in the lead, they encountered a major crevasse field. 'I expected the other two to support me,' says Peter, 'But I saw them wandering off to a pile of rocks and had to find my own way. It was damn dangerous.' Ian and Keith had been excited to find the first rock outcrop, mainly quartzite, but Peter was 'as annoyed as I have ever been'. They picked their own way through the field while Peter sat at the top 'freezing my butt off.'

A lot of the time Peter felt that it was him against the other two. Keith acknowledged that Peter was the leader but disagreed quietly with the pressure he put on Ian. But there were other basic differences. Ian and Keith were inspired by the mountains, 'the wonderful sensory stimulation' as Ian described it, while Peter saw them only as an obstacle to be overcome as quickly as possible.

Now, leaving the mountains behind, the snow looked shiny and crystalline and they hoped it would soon change. As they passed the halfway mark, their average distance had reached 26 kilometres a day. 'We worked hard for our 26 kilometres today,' Peter says to the video camera. 'The snow was very crusty and you tend to fall through it. I want to keep an average of 25 kilometres a day to achieve our 60 day target.'

As they walked they'd sweat, their beards iced up, and their feet were wrapped in plastic bags to prevent the sweat freezing in their socks and boots. At one point Ian had dropped back, frostbite taking hold on the front of his thighs. Starting with a burning sensation—frost nip—it turned into stabbing pains, initially only at night, then during the day.

Every night each of them treated his feet with methylated spirits as advised. 'With your foot in water most of the day from your own sweat,' Peter says, 'You need to be careful of trench foot.' The metho would clean and sterilise the skin, then they'd add foot powder.

On the coldest days the stove would be hard to start and they'd have to warm it up in a sleeping bag. Peter kept the gas lighter, along with a camera battery, in a special pocket close to his skin, for the same reason.

Meanwhile, back in Sydney the Scout Trekathon was planned for 30 November 1997. The plan was for 140 Scout teams to walk a sponsored

10 kilometres each to equal the total distance being walked by the expeditioners to the South Pole. Scouts rose to the challenge but the late delivery of promotion material hindered them. Notwithstanding, several hundred Groups took part around Australia, raising around $50 000.

At the same time, NSW Scouts Australia CEO, Hilton Bloomfield, was providing the energy, drive and organisational skills to develop the Scout EXPO at Darling Harbour which would coincide with the Trekathon, thereby publicising the expedition. Mobilising a select team of senior and experienced volunteers, Scouts Australia put on the largest outdoor event ever held at that location, showcasing the organisation to the public. Hugely successful, it attracted about 6000 Scouts and supporters.

Other fundraising ideas were considered but not carried through as the time frame was too tight. On behalf of the major sponsors, professional publicity services for the Trekathon and the Expedition were contracted, but these people did not live up to expectations. Their efforts achieved little that Scouts and *The Australian* had not already organised and much of the media failed to mention the four major sponsors as was the intention.

'Aussies, Aussies, Aussies. This is Patriot Hills,' called the radio operator at Patriot Hills, before announcing to Peter that the Trekathon had been a great success and had received strong media coverage. Peter broke out in a big smile. 'That's great, isn't it? I hope they make a lot of money, make this grunt worthwhile.'

'The media are watching very closely,' the operator continued, 'and you're getting a great response back home.' By now all three looked pleased—the news had given them even more incentive to succeed.

Continued white-outs, however, hampered navigation. Taking turns to lead and working on a bearing between the mountains, there was no horizon, nothing to sight on. Camped below the marshmallow mountains, their next stage was the Polar Plateau. Peter once again stressed that the only way they could achieve the time they'd set was to keep up the pace. 'One factor you haven't considered,' Keith replied in the tent over tea, 'is whether our bodies will sustain the punishment of your schedule?'

Then came the hardest terrain of all. Sastrugi is formed by the erosion of the winter blizzards which carve out ridges and fantastic shapes. It looks like a snap frozen ocean with breaking waves up to a metre high. Difficult to traverse with the sleds, the three changed from rope harnesses to shafts to prevent the push and pull reaction of a dog on a chain, but they were struggling for breath on the 3000 metre plateau.

Around this time, Peter had to use the dentistry skills he had learnt, but on himself. 'It was so cold,' he says, 'that my fillings simply fell out.' The extreme cold coupled with a diet of very hard food had dislodged several fillings and Peter took out the dentistry kit. The small mirrors continually fogged up and the cold made it difficult to work. 'I had to redo some fillings a few times,' Peter says, 'because the ones I put in fell out again.'

They still had 406 kilometres to go and continued to battle the sastrugi. On the 44th day, 15 December, Ian finally admitted to the frostbite on the videotape. His blisters were very painful and quite large, like burns, on the tops of his thighs. After the first session of two and a half hours the group stopped that day and Peter agreed to have a rest day. It was difficult for all three. Ian was in great pain and frustrated. He became very emotional and Peter admits that he did not know how to handle that and chose to ignore it. He did, however, put immense pressure on Ian by activating the rescue procedure to advise Patriot Hills that they may need to evacuate one person.

As Ian wrote in his diary that day, 'Pete is obviously focused on the success of the trip overall and therefore I am expendable if I cost too much time. I told Peter it was best to stop and camp and he went off to get Keith. He stopped and said "what about two slow shifts?" I said "no it's better to stop" and I was right.'

The group had a locating device, the Argos, which could also activate an emergency evacuation by sending a signal from Antarctica via satellite to Paris to Melbourne to Punta Arenas to London where the ANI headquarters was situated. But at this stage Peter used the HF radio to call Patriot Hills. The operator then, by satellite phone, contacted Anne Kershaw who was in Punta Arenas, not London, as there had been four fatalities already that season, three parachutists and one on foot. Another trekker, Helen Thayer, had already been rescued after an accident and now there was a call from Peter. 'Prepare for the evacuation of Ian, owing to frostbite. Don't tell his family yet.' The message was relayed to John Leece in his Sydney office. 'Ian's got severe frostbite and a decision is to be made imminently whether to evacuate him or not.'

Leece called Chris Ortlepp at Commonwealth Connect Insurance. Chris told him replacement cover for a further rescue would be OK and John should let him know if an evacuation were necessary.

Meanwhile the rest day in the tent continued to be the most intense time. Peter, teetering on the brink of calling for an evacuation, Ian in pain and Keith disagreeing with the pressure Peter was exerting. 'As far as I was concerned,' Keith says, 'all three of us would make it to the Pole. The frostbite could be managed in the field.'

Then Peter put further pressure on Ian by not giving him the time to sit in the tent. He got on the radio and started to organise a plane to pull Ian out if necessary. It was never his intention to actually activate the rescue, he claims. 'If Ian needed a week to rest he would have had it,' Peter explains, adding that it was prudent at that stage to warn that an evacuation may be necessary simply because it would take a couple of days at least to get a plane in.

Ian however thought Peter was being unreasonable, saying that they could easily wait a day or two then pull him out if necessary. 'I didn't find his attitude very supportive,' he says. And Keith supported Ian. 'You could cut the air with a knife,' he remembers.

Peter then explained that he did not want to walk into the South Pole with only one day's food left. 'It was tough,' he says. 'I wanted us to finish and had to apply pressure that I wasn't comfortable with.' Nevertheless, Keith was of the view that the pressure 'was a bit more than should have been applied', while Ian maintains that he was putting pressure on himself so any added pressure didn't affect him although he did feel disappointed with Peter. On the other hand Peter says that he only applied the pressure because it was Ian and he knew he could take it.

The next day Ian wrote in his diary. 'Pete kept saying "We've got to be at full speed tomorrow." Not once did he say it's important for us all to reach the Pole. I am clearly expendable and he has not been supportive.'

After a day they headed off again. The decision was made reluctantly, but as a group, and they got going. Each of them had up till now been taking a lead, two and a half hours on, therefore each person got two leads a day in rotation. But they decided to put Ian between the others, with Keith and Peter sharing the lead.

The video camera was not used for another ten days. 'The weather was so bad,' Peter says, 'it was just far too dangerous to take your gloves off to film.'

After a week they changed the pace again. They had to increase the distance covered each day. The danger of waiting for a slower walker was that they would get too cold. 'You only stay warm while you're working,' comments Peter, who during all this time was suffering in silence from a frostbitten cheek and severe heel blisters.

Since Peter was faster than the other two he took the last lead of each day, pushing out as far and hard as he wanted. Putting the tent up, he controlled the distance for the day. Ian would turn up an hour and a half later by which time Peter would be warm in the tent. It worked quite well because by the time Ian arrived, the camp work was done, the stove was on and he could come in and relax and get into his sleeping bag. He was trying to manage his own pain and keep going.

'Sometimes Ian was a long way back,' remembers Peter. 'This was dangerous.' If the weather was bad they would have to wait for him. 'At times he just looked like a tiny little dot, a flea on the horizon,' Peter says.

Christmas Day was day 54 of the expedition. Tea was the normal menu followed by a packet of cashews that Keith had packed as a special treat. The night before they had enjoyed an extra special treat when the men's wives rang via satellite phone, patched in through the radio, to wish them a garbled 'Happy Christmas'.

By then there were only six or seven days to go. 'We're all really keen to finish it,' Peter said to the video camera. 'The last few days have been a real drag.'

At that stage they had been averaging 22 kilometres a day through heavy sastrugi, and were now back to 26, the average they had to achieve.

On day 59 they walked about 28 kilometres, a pretty good effort, and found themselves just 7 kilometres from the South Pole base. 'We are going to continue for another two to three hours to see if we can complete it,' Peter recorded.

Ian was, by now, running an hour or so behind Peter and Keith. They decided not to put the tent up but to prepare tea for when Ian arrived. By the time he arrived, Peter and Keith were both very cold. Stuffing some food down, they all carried on, although Ian was not impressed that he was not getting a rest in the tent. Peter took off like a rabbit, keen to get to their ultimate destination and travelling much faster than the other two to get warm. He stopped a kilometre outside the base and someone skied out to say hello. Filming on a long lens Peter made a wide sweep of a motley collection of huts and structures in a flat featureless land—the Pole!

He had nearly an hour to wait, so he dropped his sled and skied back to Ian and Keith who were ambling along, reminiscing a bit. They all knew they were going to make it and Peter didn't want to go in on his own. 'Wow, three years of work and we're almost there,' Peter exclaimed just before 9pm on 31 December 1997.

They were met at the Base by a huge crowd of around 100 people including the National Science Foundation representative, Hilleary De Everist, and the Base manager, both of whom congratulated the trekkers with a bottle of champagne.

Then the Base Manager took Peter aside and spelled out the rules of the Base. No use of the radio, no showers, only one meal and they must sleep outside. Otherwise they could have the run of the facility inside, together with as much tea and coffee and snacks as they wanted.

'We did it,' Ian wrote in his diary. 'We reached the Pole today in a fabulous reception from the US base. It was an emotional moment for me as we congratulated each other and shook hands with our welcomers. Immense satisfaction and relief that the strain was over, a release of pent up stress of the past three weeks.'

From film and photographs, you might think that the shiny chrome ball on a red and white striped barber pole about 1.5 metres high marks the South Pole. But it's not, it's only the representational position. The pole itself moves a metre or so every year on the ice and has to be replotted. A series of wooden poles, each with a 1 kilogram brass plate about the size of a large paperweight, mark the actual spot every year. Peter bought one from a US tradesman who had produced a couple of spares in the machine shop. It depicts a map and is inscribed '90 degrees South—Geographic Pole—US Geological Survey—1 January 1998'. Quite an unusual holiday souvenir! Governments generally don't support private expeditions in Antarctica and the politics are horrendous. But Peter's team got a great reaction from the people at the Base who quickly invited them inside the dome to the recreation area. In spite of what had been said the reality was that during the few days they spent time lying around, enjoying the luxury of showers and all they could eat.

The canteen was clearly the focal point of social life. This communal area was always full and served lots of delicious food. 'I had roast chicken, turkey, the lot!' says Peter. 'It was just fantastic.'

However, they weren't given permission to use the base radios and their own would not work, so the base contacted Patriot Hills on their behalf to arrange transport out. And they would have to wait until they reached the ANI base, and could use the satellite phone, before they could make contact with their families.

During the last days of their trek, Peter had been maintaining contact with a group of three Icelandic walkers who had been trekking from Hercules Inlet. They arrived the next day and the two teams agreed to combine their exit request to ANI to get the twin engined Otter to come in to get them out with their gear. Previously both groups had arranged for single engined Cessnas at $US85 000 each but the Otter at $US170 000 would be big enough to take their gear which otherwise would have to be left behind.

Curiously Peter admits that he felt dissatisfied with their achievement when they arrived at the South Pole. 'When I actually got there it was a bit of a disappointment,' he says. 'It had taken too long—and the trip was too slow.'

Ian and Keith would argue that it doesn't matter, they made it within their time frame. But in some ways Peter is never satisfied, it could always be better, faster. In the long run the trip was a compromise, faster than they wanted for Keith and Ian, slower for Peter, who claims he could have done the trip in a week less. 'You add up 20 minutes for every three hour stretch of walking and that adds up to a week over a month,' he says. He did however feel a sense of relief, even though he was already thinking of the next trip. 'I made the first arrangements when I got to Patriot Hills,' he admits.

Once at Patriot Hills they had to wait almost two weeks for the weather to clear enough for the Hercules to take off with both teams and a group of 20 Belgians. Back in Punta, they felt very tired but boarded a flight almost immediately to Santiago only to find their connections had been messed up. After a day in a hotel they flew to Los Angeles for interviews with a News Corporation journalist. The diary extracts handed over by Ian were to be the cause of some friction when they were published in *The Australian* the day they arrived back in Australia since this was the first Peter knew of Ian's dissatisfaction with his leadership.

A plan for the expeditioners to appear at the closing ceremony of the Springfield Scout Jamboree was ruled out by the weather delays but the 3 January edition of the *JAM*, the daily Jamboree newspaper, announced their safe arrival at the Pole with the headline 'They made a difference'. Since the theme of the Jamboree was 'You can make a difference' it fitted well with Peter's own ideals.

Other media coverage followed, including an editorial in *The Australian* on 2 January, 1998,

'The success of the three-man team in reaching the South Pole on New Year's Day, the first Australians to walk to the Pole unassisted, is a valuable and inspiring present to the nation on the first day of 1998.

'Their success reminds us that extraordinary achievements are not the domain of mysterious, historical figures whose names conjure images of super-human feats. Brown, Treseder and Williams are ordinary people, although obviously possessed of talents of resilience, endurance and skill.

'Now, with their South Pole walk completed, the three men have surely achieved their goal of inspiring a nation.'

Belinda Hickman reported the expedition in an irregular column as part of the sponsorship arrangement and, on 28 February the newspaper included an eight page colour liftout: 'Antarctica, The Great Australian Trek'.

The expedition was covered in other newspapers and magazines, although some of the main media opportunities were lost as the public relations firm withdrew its support.

Arriving at Sydney airport, Peter, with a funny smile, told his brother, Neil, that he had promised Beth that he would give her and the family all his attention for the next twelve months. Full of good intentions, but focusing on his duty to the sponsors, Peter didn't miss a step as he moved straight into a demanding lecture tour around Australia to repay their faith in the expedition.

The tour started with an address to the Prime Minister's conference at Thredbo in February 1998. It was the first time the Howard government had met this way and the more than 400 delegates in the audience gave Peter a standing ovation. 'A mind blowing reaction,' he recalls with pride.

Sponsor Paddy Pallin underwrote a national tour called Traversing Silence, which travelled from Sydney to Melbourne, Brisbane, Adelaide, Canberra, Hobart and Launceston. It played to packed houses all the way through.

'I tried to inspire audiences through my presentations,' Peter says. And it worked. By the end of July 1999, he had made 132 presentations to more than 40 000 people and received standing ovations at more than half of these. There were presentations to Scout Groups and charitable groups, to commercial organisations, hospitals, police forces, the SAS, industry and professional organisations and at many Commonwealth Bank events. The call on Peter's family time has been significant but in the meantime he has raised over $300 000 for charity.

'I have to relive this trip hundreds of times for the presentations and, on one level, I can feel and share the emotion I create in the audience,' Peter says, 'But on another level I have dismissed it completely. I've never watched the video for example. I don't want to go back.'

Peter has also had to relive the expedition reading Ian's book. He was involved in the editing and admits he has felt 'uncomfortable dealing with Ian's account of the emotional trauma of the trip, the relationship between the three of us and the tension between myself and the other two, how I pushed them'.

Nevertheless the Thredbo presentation had been a high point and there have been others. In April 1999, when he presented to the cast of Hornsby Gang Show, Peter thought someone had turned up the volume on his audio system. Then he realised the Scouts were singing along with it. '"I am

Australian" just built and built as they sang louder,' Peter says. 'They had such good voices. It sounded great and reflected the tremendous emotions of the trip.'

'Kids need to have these positive images,' he adds. 'So many are struggling to get jobs, a lot of them give up.' In fact at heart he likes the idea of the positive imagery he can provide of ordinary people who have pulled off such challenges as the South Pole. 'If we can live our dream you can live your dream, too,' he says.

At the conclusion to his presentations, Peter hands around Mawson's balaclava, the one Mawson himself took to Antarctica and which Peter carried on his own journey as a talisman. Given to him by Alun Thomas, Mawson's grandson, it really fires up the kids' imaginations.

But what sets this trip apart is the organisation. There are many people in Australia who would have the physical capacity to complete such an expedition, but few who can handle the difficulties of securing sponsorship and repaying the sponsors on their return. 'I have a strong belief that when you commit yourself to something it all works out,' Peter says, 'and that the most extraordinary things come into play that you never dreamed about. I believe that all the goodness in people comes out at the toughest times. People can still say thank you in adversity.'

CHAPTER 20

DESERT RUNNER

'Capacity for survival may be the ability to be changed by environment.'

Robyn Davidson, *Tracks* Johnathan Cape 1980

Much of Australia's wilderness area is difficult to access at certain times of the year on account of extreme weather conditions. This applies as much to deserts as any other terrain. Peter's next opportunity to consider desert crossings came when he was setting himself up for the second attempt at the double traverse, driving east-west across Australia, this time in a Land Rover Freelander. Rover Australia had provided the vehicle as part of its sponsorship of the South Pole trip, with a request that Peter try it out for the traverse. The Freelander does not have low ratio gears or the clearance of a traditional 4WD like the Discovery and Peter and Ron were concerned it might not get through the sand dune country on the eastern side of the Simpson. Nevertheless, they took it out there, driving from Sydney to Broken Hill to Birdsville, along the Strzelecki Track to Cameron Corner. 'When we ran it out into the Simpson Desert,' Peter recounts, 'it flew over the sand dunes.' Ron directed operations, tutoring Peter as they drove. 'Hit the bottom of the dune flat out in third,' he'd instruct, 'as fast as you can go!' The trick was to gather as much momentum as possible before changing down into second gear to drag the vehicle over the dune.

Peter had decided before leaving Sydney in May 1998 that on this trip he would have a crack at running across the Strzelecki Desert. 'It's quite an easy desert, short and sweet' as he puts it. Ron had other priorities and left Peter to his run. Starting at Mulka Station, Peter consulted the maps provided by Colin French and started running. 'I took a pack full of water and ran across,' he says. An expert cartographer, Colin's maps were detailed and provided information without which it would have been difficult to identify exactly where the boundaries of each desert lie. Peter completed his run at Waka Station in just over 34 hours and then hitched his way back to the vehicle which he had left near the Birdsville track. The track makes an artificial boundary for the Tirari Desert, which runs between it and Lake Eyre. 'It's only about 100 kilometres across,' says Peter. 'So I ran across that one too and then drove home.'

For his attempted drive across Australia, Peter had enlisted support from the TJM 4WD Warehouse to kit out and detail the Freelander the way he wanted it. 'We stripped out the back seats,' Peter says, 'and added driving lights and three spare wheels. The panels were covered in sponsors' stickers.'

On a wet and miserable Friday night, suffering from a cold, Peter left work and drove to Hawks Nest, staying in the family holiday house. Next day he continued to Byron Bay where his friends, Tracey Dare and Malcolm McKenzie, put him up in a hotel. 'I felt lousy,' he says, 'and stayed there a day or two.' It had poured with rain all the way there and Peter sat in Byron, waiting to go. Impatient, and with a limited amount of leave, he telephoned the police at Birdsville who told him there was a lot of water in central Australia, making it impossible for anyone to get through.

After several days, Peter finally decided to go on police advice that, if there was no further rain, the roads would be opened. Although psychologically he would rather start in the day, Peter set off in the early evening wanting to time his arrival at a particular fuel dump during daylight hours. Mount Dare station would be closed at other times.

It bucketed down with rain all the way to Charleville. There, the police said the roads would be closed for another two weeks. Peter's hopes were dashed and, particularly as the trip was sponsored, he was not prepared to go against that advice. He rang Ron and told him he'd had to pull out. Then he almost thought of going back to Cape Byron and starting again, but didn't. As he always likes 'to salvage something from an abandoned trip' he went off to run the Sturt Stony Desert.

Preplanning for the driving trip had been as efficient as ever, and Peter had the desert maps in his vehicle. The furthest he could drive was to the end of the tar so he started his run from Mooraberree on the northern edge of the desert. Running south he finished at Cordillo Downs on the southern boundary. This property is part of a large landholding owned by a grazier who had attended Peter's South Pole presentation in Birdsville and he received a warm welcome. Then, to get back to his car, Peter curved off towards the west.

Running towards the Birdsville Track Peter came across a man walking resolutely in the opposite direction. It seemed that he had been driving out from Birdsville and got his 4WD vehicle bogged. Leaving his wife with the vehicle, he walked off to get help—but in the wrong direction! 'The sad thing is,' Peter relates, 'he didn't know he was lost. He thought he was going in the right direction instead of heading north into the desert.' To begin with, the man did not believe Peter, but eventually he accepted Peter's advice and walked back to his car with him. With at least three days' food in the car, the couple was quite safe to wait until the rains stopped. Peter told some locals at the end of the road and they agreed to pick the couple up when the rain stopped.

'This was one of the easier desert crossings,' Peter recalls. 'Almost ideal with so much water around.' He carried only a half litre of water, moved very quickly and got water from the claypan whenever he wanted it.

During the 1998 Paddy Pallin national tour, Traversing Silence, Peter completed presentations in Brisbane and Melbourne before returning to Brisbane for a Scout presentation. He was driving himself, Lucas and the audio-visual equipment in the Freelander. Lucas Trihey, who had organised the Paddy Pallin tour, was then going to drive the vehicle from Melbourne to Adelaide where Peter would pick it up again. Then Lucas received a call to say his wife was ill and he had to return to Sydney. He left the vehicle in Melbourne where Peter picked it up to drive to Adelaide himself. This entailed going past the Little Desert and Greater Big Desert in Victoria. 'Stopping on the way to run these deserts was opportunistic,' he says.

The Little Desert runs from Wimmera River to the South Australian border. About 100 kilometres long, it is skinny in shape and tightly packed with small trees on a sand base. 'It was a simple job to follow the length of the 4WD tracks,' Peter says, and he completed the run in 12 hours, finishing on the western side of the desert.

Apparently the Ranger didn't quite trust Peter's intentions, and followed him in by 4WD. 'I only found out,' Peter says, 'because I ran into him some time later and he told me.'

Incorporating Ngarkat Conservation Park, Big Desert Wilderness and Wyperfield National Park, the Greater Big Desert has three management areas, with a wilderness area in the middle. Peter contacted the local Ranger for advice about the best tracks to use and headed off. Starting at Coonalpyn in South Australia, Peter ran to Emu Springs then across to and along the Milmed Rock Track to Lake Albacutya on the eastern edge of the desert in Victoria. The densely packed vegetation of some of this desert made the going slow and Peter took more than 28 hours to complete his run.

Peter has now completed unsupported traverses of all the smaller deserts in Australia except the Painted Desert which he intends to tackle when he has time. And he also has plans for the Great Victoria, Great Sandy, Little Sandy and Tanami—all huge deserts. They will take some time to cross and, as Peter explains, 'They're too big to run so I'll need to use my Simpson cart.'

Planning solo trips through these major areas for the years after his second Antarctic trip, Peter has enlisted Neil and Helen Cocks to help, already asking them to check out sections of the Great Sandy Desert for him. And while the challenge to cross up to 1400 kilometres of desert without support is awesome, just as challenging is Peter's long term plan to run across Lake Eyre. Researching again with Neil, he plans to use a cart and skis to cross the north and south lakes. There is an area called the slush zone which is 'quite risky'. Warren Bonython has been into this muddy quagmire and Donald Campbell ran his Bluebird trials on the salt pan at Madigan Gulf. 'I'll have to wait until the water level is right,' Peter says.

The Treseder family had spent a number of years holidaying at Hawks Nest and Beth's mum, Anne Ferguson, eventually bought a house there. Peter is always training and would do lots of runs from the house. In July 1998 he managed to get away from the South Pole presentations for a short time and while at Hawks Nest with his family, Peter took the opportunity to run the Tops to Myall Heritage Trail.

An idea conceived by Dr Hans Pacey, who lived at Tea Gardens, the trail ran from Barrington House in the Barrington Tops to Hawks Nest Surf Club.

Along the way it went through the Craven State Forest and along the Mungo Track. Unique in that it goes through a range of ecosystems, it had long been Peter's intention to run its whole length. Stuart Gales, the President of the surf club, met Peter at Bombah Point, taking his clothes on the ferry so he could swim across. Pam Allen, the NSW Environment Minister then, was due to open a section of the boardwalk that day and Peter's run was timed to coincide with her official visit. 'When I arrived early,' Peter says, 'I discovered she had been delayed, so I kept on running.'

In October the Paddy Pallin tour took Peter to Tasmania where he delivered lectures in Hobart and Launceston. With a day spare, he decided on a quick trip. Staying with Lars and Jenny, the people who owned the Paddy Pallin shop in Launceston, he heard them describe a trip called the Frenchmans Cap Circuit. Peter had done part of it before with Steve Trémont and had walked in another time with Mark Foster but became ill from a tick. Peter's friends now lent him a vehicle and he was off! He climbed up Frenchmans Cap and down the steep ridge to the Chasm of Peace, the Irenabyss—a flat water area on the Franklin River with vertical rock walls either side. Peter then swam across the cold river, walked up the other side and followed the ridge systems around to the Lyell Highway. It was a good break in the tour.

Peter's biggest strength, perhaps, is his ability to see something through to the end. With very few exceptions, he has always completed the task he has set himself. 'I don't like to give up,' he says. When he has, for whatever reason, abandoned a planned course of action, he has replaced it with another. On leaving university without graduating and joining the bank he saw the potential and quickly threw himself into the system, progressing throughout his career. The bank, however, has not always been his main priority in life and, at times in the early stages, he almost deliberately slowed his career path by maintaining a slight distance from his colleagues. 'I never joined the unofficial drinking and socialising clubs,' he recalls, 'and was told by several managers that this would harm my career.' Nevertheless, the bank clearly values Peter, supporting his expeditions financially and leveraging his outdoor activities commercially and in the community to their benefit.

Indeed, commenting on the bank versus outdoors activities in the *Sun Herald* on 1 September 1996, Peter said, 'It isn't that much different. Both involve risk analysis. The difference is that if I get the risk analysis wrong on an expedition I'm likely to die. But I'm extremely cautious—and that's the only reason I've survived.'

As a child, Peter experienced strictness in the family home that was more than a reflection of the standards of the time. As the oldest child, he was aware of tension in the family and learned to control his own emotions. To this day he keeps his feelings under tight rein. But what are those feelings? Even to those who know him well—his family, his fellow expeditioners—Peter can be emotionally remote. 'Peter is very private with his emotions,' Beth admits, although this should not be mistaken for a lack of emotion. He can, in fact, get quite passionate, and this is best seen in his public talks. The slide shows take the audience from a low to a high and occasionally Peter gets a bit overwhelmed, even after doing one a hundred times or more. 'I sometimes stumble over some of the words,' he says, 'because I can release some of my emotion through them.' Tim Lamble understands the value of this real passion and, in his role as production adviser, encourages Peter to use the images and music to develop an emotional connection with his audience.

Appropriate, given that music has always been important to Peter. From his teenage years of listening to Credence Clearwater to the operatic arias he sometimes listens to now, Peter uses the emotion of music to help him train, to psyche himself up for forthcoming trips, and for these public talks afterwards.

Peter's emotions are a bit like a steam engine. He builds up a big head of steam, only to let it out to power what he wants to do. 'I'm not the sort of person you'll see crying at a funeral,' Peter says. 'I'll hold that in, won't let it out.' And Peter says that, as he gets older, he exercises even more control over his own emotions. As a child, he found it necessary to hide his emotions and was wary of showing anything in front of his parents. 'Mum would show physical emotion and comfort us,' remembers Peter, 'but Dad always appeared to be detached emotionally, although underneath he was quite soft.' To a large extent that same emotional base drives Peter through everything he does. 'When I feel a swelling of emotion I don't let it out,' he states. 'While I feel proud of my achievements such as records or rescues, I have always kept it fairly quiet.' In his current role at the bank, he is inundated with sponsorship requests, for example a child who needs money for an operation. 'I read it and get quite emotional,' he confesses, 'but no-one will ever know.'

No-one knew what he was feeling a lot of the time in the Antarctic, either. Trudging across the ice, Peter found himself getting quite emotional at times but would never tell the others. 'I knew where the emotion was coming from,' he says, 'and I would just get over it and trudge on!' Mentally alert, and his thoughts crystal clear, he would start thinking about kids in hospital or something similar. 'I would rationalise,' he reveals, 'that I had to get this thing finished for those kids—or my own.' For him, this provided the emotional drive.

Ian Brown was critical of the apparent lack of compassion Peter had for his companions during the South Pole trip, but Peter says he had no compassion for himself either. 'I had frostbite on my face and was in the same sort of pain as Ian but I just didn't talk about it,' says Peter. A photograph at that time shows Peter, almost expressionless, his eyes showing internal anguish and pain.

'When we stopped to put up the tent once, Ian cried for 25 minutes,' Peter recalls uncomfortably. 'It caught me by surprise.' The three just sat in the small tent while Ian cried in pain and frustration. 'I felt awkward,' Peter says, 'because I knew I was about to apply more pressure on him. He was also very emotional when we reached the Pole and I didn't know how to handle that either.' Keith, on the other hand, is also fairly cool, with guarded emotions. 'The way in which your emotions are channelled is part of your driving force,' Peter says. 'It's a critical part of what drives you to complete things, not so much start them,' he states matter of factly. 'The power has to come from somewhere to enable you to break records. Being fit and motivated is part of it,' he says, 'but something else has to be there to finish it off.'

Being fit is part of Peter's way of life. He has always done his 'training' since high school. Even when an expedition is not imminent he trains every day, running, dragging the tyre, the rowing machine or weights in the garage. Peter uses words like 'discipline' and 'control' to describe his regimen. For the last eight years since being based in the city he has run at lunchtime, every day he can. 'I run 4–15 kilometres with my colleagues at a leisurely pace. I use the time for social interaction and I don't try to race.' His lunchtime runs are for up to 45 minutes but he does an extended run on Fridays, which used to be the traditional bankers' drinking lunchtime! Then he has a shower and eats a home-made sandwich provided by Beth at his desk.

Food and nutrition is important for an athlete, yet Peter's attitude to it is very casual. On major expeditions someone, often Keith, will organise the food and Peter eats whatever there is. But on his solo trips he carries and eats very little. 'You can push the body to extreme limits and it will repair itself quite quickly when you rest,' he says. 'The reality is I can't carry enough. The reality is I often don't get enough. The reality is I push on anyway.' Ultimately the body will break down, however, if not supplied with what it needs, and Peter has found that if he has a really intense four days he has used every scrap of energy and couldn't go on at that pace for any further length of time. Asked by *Out There* magazine to comment on his favourite diet for walking, Peter promptly described a particular trip where he enjoyed sausages and onions and a 2 litre bottle of Coke. 'It kept me going,' he said, which was hardly the scientific answer they were expecting.

Developing his wide range of outdoor skills over the years, Peter acknowledges that he owes a lot to Scouts. In *Scouting—The Way to Success* (Scouts Australia, 1997) Peter wrote: 'Scouting introduced me to independent thought and initiative, responsible risk taking, the concept that once you commit yourself to a project anything is possible, and a spiritual connection to the land. It also provided me with inspirational people who I could emulate and the tools I needed to do the things I do today. Scouting taught me that you must take responsibility for yourself and for others but, most importantly, it showed me the worth of people caring for each other.'

Curiously, although individuals have benefited from his experience in different ways, the Scout movement has taken little advantage of his high profile to improve their image. 'I have had all sorts of involvement with Scouts,' Peter recalls. 'Leaders would call me and ask me to inspire a group of kids or take them walking up the mountains for their first experience of hiking.' Peter has presented numerous Queen's Scout awards and made many presentations at a Group level. Scouts sometimes contact Peter direct to talk about their Green Cord hike. Now somewhat tougher than when he completed his First Class hike, it is symptomatic of standards shifting upwards. 'I still get a buzz out of helping kids, that's what it's all about,' he says. 'Those kids are the ones who will go out to keep society running, they are the self starters, the self motivators.'

Self motivated himself, Peter knows what he is talking about, though he finds it hard to express. In an interview for *Australian Geographic* Lincoln Hall asked him what inspired him. Peter said he didn't know. But clearly, being at the cutting edge of a number of skills is important to him. 'I like to go from really difficult rock climbing to walking across a desert,' he says, 'where different skills are required and different risks taken.'

While Peter approaches trips in a significantly different way to most people, his plans are very sensible and not as outlandish as they first appear. He says there is a lot of heartache, bad weather and many abandoned trips, plus numerous planning and survey trips before breaking a record. 'It's not the instant achievement the public perceive. If you look at the history,' he says, 'it is the build up of knowledge. The big trips are the end result of many years of experience.'

In *Wild* magazine, Summer 1994, Quentin Chester examined Peter's career from his first trip to New Zealand to his long distance runs through Australia, finding a paradox in the way Peter puts himself forward as an example to others while decrying his hero status. 'I don't have a heroic image of myself,' Peter says, 'because I can see my frailties and all the times I've been standing there feeling really scared, thinking "well, you're no hero".'

Chester also remarks on the dilemma that, for someone so actively involved in search and rescue missions, the solo trips Peter undertakes surely must make him 'one of the nation's most energetic risk takers'. He concludes by saying: 'In Australia, Peter Treseder is, well, an extraordinary ordinary bloke.' In response, Peter adds, 'What motivates me to adventure is to explore in the traditional style of the early explorers, to be the first or to do it faster.' Peter's record times are the result of a combination of factors. He has the mindset of an outdoors person combined with the unique attitude of a professional athlete. Navigation needs and the real risk to his personal safety make his expeditions and tiger walks a more impressive feat than an organised marathon run, with drink stops and helpers, could ever be.

Not everyone is convinced of the value of Peter's achievements however, and Dorothy Treseder says Peter hates dealing with criticism, choosing to walk away rather than argue. Ignoring letters that question his achievements, Peter has long adopted a 'No comment' technique with magazines to avoid drawn out disputes. Lincoln Hall reported in *Australian Geographic* in 1988 that 'A few conservative bushwalkers have gone as far as to suggest that his records are fabrications'. But a lifetime of recorded achievement would be difficult to invent and most outdoors people like to read of his exploits. Explaining why he keeps outdoor magazines well informed about his plans and achievements, Peter claims that 'an average sort of person like me has no other access to the media', and points to his success in the outdoors as a point of leverage to push his twin themes of conservation and inspiring young people.

To build such an impressive outdoor record, Peter has encountered a number of dangerous and potentially life-threatening situations. While he dismisses these events and claims to put every trip behind him as it is completed, you would expect that being attacked by pirates or crocodiles would leave some permanent emotional scar, but Peter seems not to be affected. 'I rarely think about it,' he says, 'or any other traumatic experiences. My focus is always on the next trip.' Where other people tend to react emotionally, Peter seems to be able to separate potential emotional trauma from actual physical events. Whether it is crocodiles, a man overboard or stuck half way up a mountain, Peter is very matter of fact and shows almost no emotion. The strongest response seems to be irritation. He says he does, on such occasions, think about his family—and about the possibility of not coming back—but then 'concentrates on what I have to do to survive the situation'. Once safely home, the trip is quickly forgotten. 'I never go back and dwell on a trip,' he says. 'I will only think about it when I'm returning to an environment that created those fears, like the crocodiles in Cape York.' Claiming that he is trying to protect them, Peter often neglects to tell his family all the details. This refusal to let his emotions come to the surface is further demonstration of his personal control mechanism.

Unlike some of his colleagues in search and rescue, Peter has never felt the need for counselling either. 'We've been involved in some horrific situations,' he recalls, 'and I don't like it—but I don't get nightmares and don't need counselling.' His distrust of such processes extended to a course facilitator, who introduced psychological testing for some bank employees. 'This guy walked into the room,' Peter remembers, 'and said "I'm going to tell you what your personality type is". He got my back up immediately.' As he gave each of them a written test to complete, Peter stood up and walked out, refusing to do it. 'I was criticised by the bank for being uncooperative,' he adds. It's as if Peter was wary of the potential for his emotions to overwhelm him completely.

Perhaps not unexpectedly, the pressure on family life can reach ignition point while Peter is planning a major trip. His singular focus on the expedition goals, his determination to ensure good value for his sponsors, his desire to use the trip to inspire others and raise money for causes leave little time and energy for anything else. 'Daddy spends a lot of time on the phone and dragging his tyre,' says eight year old daughter Marnie as he prepares for the second Antarctic expedition. And yet, 'Being a Dad is the best thing I've ever done,' he says. 'The kids mean more to me than anything else.' While undemonstrative, Peter has great compassion for members of his family and would always be there if needed or asked with no questions. 'Taking responsibility for the family you have created has been instilled in me,' he says simply.

'It is always difficult to keep up with news of Peter's exploits,' says Neil. 'You have to call him and ask.' The brothers live very different lives but have great mutual respect and closeness. Proud of Peter's achievements, Neil is 'his best fan'. but wouldn't want the public profile. With a sporting potential set to surpass Peter in the early days, Neil chose family and career as his lifetime priorities, balancing his sporting activities with his other commitments.

Beth switches off when Peter goes away on a trip and the all-female household lives another life. 'I develop my own routine,' Beth says, 'and it's very hard to adjust when he returns, particularly from a long trip.' Peter expects normal service to be resumed as soon as he arrives and adjusts immediately to his concept of family life. This includes Peter's long term idea that Beth's mum, Anne, would live with them. To accommodate her when her husband died in 1986, a self-contained flat was built to extend the house, handily extending the upstairs living area at the same time. Beth is a teacher/librarian and Anne helps her with childminding, often cooking for the family and eating with them, too. The value of this extended family is clear when Peter is away.

Peter has always 'controlled his own destiny' as his brother, Neil, puts it, right from the time he bought his first block of land, which Neil now owns and lives on. With the Wahroonga home and properties elsewhere, the Treseders are now financially secure. 'Managing these investments is another task to ensure security for my family,' he says. And this financial base together with his job at the bank provides a secure platform for Peter's outdoor adventures, though financial resources for major expeditions require sponsorship funding.

In attempting to understand what drives Peter Treseder it would be all too convenient to point to some event in his childhood, some aspect of his personality, that provides the key. Life, of course, is far more complex than that. Numerous journalists have asked Peter 'Why?' but his answers and explanations are at best incomplete and, in some cases, quite deliberately focused on a cause Peter wishes to promote.

Clearly, Peter has been able to combine natural talent with opportunity. His athletic abilities and his clear self determination were nurtured through school sport and the techniques and attitudes he learnt through Scouts. The Westleigh bush environment, combined with the adults who inspired and guided him, made it possible for him to develop a unique set of skills.

His passion leads him to follow up any opportunity that could further charity or conservation causes, and inspire young people. In 1988, Peter applied for the position of Director of the recently established Australian Geographic Society. While unsuccessful, Peter received a handwritten reply from Ike Bain, Chief Executive of the Society, who said, 'I'm impressed by your achievements. ... Your adventuring activities were far superior than anyone I'd interviewed.'

As his friend, John Leece, says, 'Peter's motivation is altruism and he believes each one of us can truly make a difference to society.' Leece claims that adventurers like Peter have an added dimension to their characters—courage and a belief in themselves—that enables them to challenge the unknown and go beyond the accepted limits of human endeavour.

Peter's appearance belies his physical strength and endurance and masks a strong and resolute character. Of average height, he has the spare frame of an endurance athlete, reddish hair and a neat beard. His glasses and slightly protruding teeth give him an air that is anything but macho. In his business suit he looks every centimetre the bank employee. Peter Treseder remains something of an enigma, a complex man with a world perspective that sometimes obscures his view of his immediate surroundings.

CHAPTER 21

BEYOND THE SOUTH POLE 1999–2000

PLANNING FOR THE ANTARCTIC TRAVERSE EXPEDITION

'The attainment of the Pole was the culmination of days and weeks of forced marches, physical discomfort, insufficient sleep and racking anxiety. It is a wise provision of nature that the human consciousness can grasp only such degree of intense feeling as the brain can endure, and the grim guardians of earth's remotest spot will accept no man as guest until he has been tried and tested by the severest ordeal.'

Robert E. Peary, The North Pole, 1910

In his foreword to *This Everlasting Silence*, the collection of Mawson's love letters compiled by Nancy Flannery, Peter wrote, 'As I plan our next expedition, to traverse 3,000 kilometres of the Antarctic Continent from Berkner Island in the Weddell Sea to McMurdo Sound in the Ross Sea, again unsupported, my family and I renew our attempt to deal with "This Everlasting Silence".'

This expedition will be the first traverse to be made on foot, unsupported, all the way across the official continent, including the ice shelves that mark the edge of the summer boundary when the sea melts. People have traversed the continent from sea to sea in various ways, but they have used dogs, tractors or sails. Walking it is as different as comparing swimming with sailboarding.

Organising the trip in October 1998, Peter estimated, 'In round figures I need a million dollars. And this time the trip will only be for two people.' During this trip, the International Trans-Antarctic Expedition 1999-2000, Peter and his companion, Tim Jarvis, intend to haul their sleds from the edge of the summer ice shelf on Berkner Island to McMurdo Sound via the South Pole. At 193cm tall and weighing 102 kg, Tim, an Environmental Consultant based in Melbourne, is a big man! Outstandingly fit, younger than Peter and with valuable Arctic experience, Tim is more than physically capable of making the perilous journey. 'I'm hoping Tim will push me this time,' says Peter, remembering his dissatisfaction after the first South Pole expedition.

At the time of writing, Peter is finalising the last arrangements for the expedition, due to leave Australia in October 1999. John Leece was not surprised when Peter's plans really began to take shape. 'Soon after his return from the first trip I felt that Peter had already been formulating other ideas. After all he wouldn't be Peter if he didn't think of the next expedition while he trekked wearily and steadfastly over the frozen ice cap. Deep down there was always a plan.'

While some of the organisation has been made easier through the experience of the first Antarctic trip, Peter has again had to put enormous energy into arranging sponsor finance and support, insurance and transport. The success of the first expedition meant that Peter was able to secure sponsorship without John's extraordinary efforts, though he remains an important member of the overall team. 'You take one pace forward and two back,' Peter says of the stumbling blocks he has encountered along the way. 'First a sponsor pulls out, then the insurance is difficult to arrange, next there are difficulties with transport back from the polar ice.'

In his foreword to the Mawson book, Peter emphasised just how hard some of the organisation is. 'The huge struggle to make this trip happen, as with those that have gone before like Mawson, is the difficulty of making it happen,' he wrote. Peter explains that he too has experienced years of uncertainty, with organisation and fund raising pressure, and the even longer years of repaying expedition debts. And there are inevitable emotional strains too. 'Too often in polar literature the explorer is pictured as facing the wilds without fear,' he writes. 'Loneliness was never mentioned, nor were the feelings of loved ones left behind who suffered just as much. Nor was the ever present questioning as to whether you were doing the right thing or just being selfish.'

Peter's relationship with Beth took a long time to be restored after the first South Pole Expedition. For whatever reason, his promise to focus on the family was never really met, and while he did take quite a time off work in those early months he was still giving presentations all around Australia, and fitting in shorter runs through wilderness areas wherever he could. It is true that he took Beth with him to the Thredbo presentation and to another in Brisbane for the Coalition Convention. But Beth started full-time work soon after, limiting her ability to travel with Peter. 'Work and the girls became my priority,' she points out. Inevitably, Beth became resentful of the time Peter spent away, particularly when so many of the presentations were not connected with his job at the bank and took place at weekends and during precious evenings. This has shaped her feelings about the next Antarctic trip. 'I don't want him to go, the kids don't want it,' she says, concerned about the length of the trip itself and the inevitable round of presentations on Peter's return.

By April 1999 the pressure was really building up. Peter did a run over a weekend, returning Sunday afternoon feeling emotionally and physically flat. 'I came back to a whole pile of things that needed to be done, and couldn't be bothered to do anything.' Later that Sunday night he received a call from Chris Roberts, Managing Director of Arnott's during the first South Pole expedition and a Director of Telstra. Chris had taken the voluntary role of Joint Expedition Manager with John Leece, Lachlan Murdoch and Lucy Curlewis, and was negotiating sponsorship. The deal with Telstra, the last link in the money chain needed to make this expedition happen, had fallen through. Having received a really good reception from a General Manager a few months ago, and positive feedback ever since, it was a great and sudden blow.

Peter was left to battle his conflicting feelings, one minute wanting to throw it in, the next wanting to forge on. Calling Chris the next day, he said that he wanted to push ahead—he had decided it was too important to abandon. 'The importance was continually reinforced in me,' Peter says, 'like the recent evening when I did a presentation to the cast of the Hornsby Gang Show. It was fantastic. We got a standing ovation and it was a really nice feeling. That's what makes all this worthwhile.' Within days Chris was reporting back to Peter that more sponsors were coming on board. This left Peter free to work on the organisation of food, navigation, equipment, transport and insurance. With still so much to do, the deadline for a decision was almost upon them.

Meanwhile, Peter continued to make presentations, maintain a training regime and pursue new records in the outdoors. He completed some new tiger walks which included return trips from Katoomba to Black Coola and Bimlow Peak and another to Mount Cloudmaker. In April 1999 he managed to break his own longstanding record for the 3 Peaks traverse. The fifth time he has broken the record, it now stands at 14 hours and 19 minutes.

He even found time to participate in the 1999 Pollie Pedal, a charity bike ride that raised money for a children's charity, Youth Insearch. Also on the 1999 run in May were; Jackie Kelly, the Federal Minister for Sport and Tourism, Ross Cameron, the Federal Member for Parramatta, Charlie Lynn, the State Member of the Legislative Council and Peter's friend, Tony Abbott, the Federal Minister for Employment Services.

Driving to Lithgow on the Saturday morning, Peter had two speaking engagements during the weekend, including one at the start of the ride in Dubbo. 'We rode 120 kilometres on the Sunday,' Peter says, 'then I was driven from Gulgong to Lithgow where I picked up my car and headed back to Sydney along Bell's Line of Road.' Peter was tired, feeling unwell with a head cold and just wanted to get home.

Near Pierces Pass, at around 8pm, he and some other cars were flagged down by a young woman who introduced herself as Susie. She told the motorists that two of her friends were stuck after an abseiling accident. Peter hiked in with Susie about 5 kilometres down a fire trail to the site at the Gordon Smith Chimney, one of the access routes through the cliffs on Mount Banks. One friend, Sue, had fallen on a rock slope, tumbling headlong down the chimney and out the other end, saved only by the knot she had tied on the end of her abseil rope. She was dangling unconscious hundreds of metres from the ground. A second woman, Wendy, had tried to reach her, climbing down the rock slope alongside the taut rope. Because of the weight on it she could not attach her abseil gear. Finding herself in the dark and the rain, at the end of her physical endurance she panicked and could move neither up nor down, frozen in fear. Neither could hear

Sue, work out what had happened to her or determine if she was injured. Susie then went for help.

Peter was familiar with the climb and went down the slope using the rope as a guide until he reached the stranded Wendy. It was raining and blustery and he was soon wet through. Attaching her to the rope and her abseil harness with another spare piece of rope, Peter used a prussic knot, which allows you to move up but not down, and helped her up the slope to safety.

Just before climbing out he went down to the lip of the chimney, without ropes, to check on the first woman. 'I could see that she was hanging out past the end of the chimney and had obviously been knocked out or stunned by the fall, but by then she was able to tell me she was all right.' Peter promised to get her out, and continued up the taut rope with the rescued Wendy.

When he reached the top there was no spare abseil rope, so he rigged up a 'Z' pulley arrangement with three or four karabiners and the end of their rope to gain some mechanical advantage. Then, all three pulled Sue up through the chimney until she reached the sloping rock she had fallen from. Peter went back down and repeated the procedure he had used for the previous woman, bringing her up to the top and safety.

By the time they then walked out along the fire trail and Peter drove home, it was nearly morning and he had had no sleep. Showered and dressed, he went to work, feeling pretty awful. This particular rescue did not make the media and until now, only the participants and a few close people knew of it. But it illustrates the need for capable and experienced teams who can deal intuitively with these highly specific rescue situations. 'It is exactly the reason we formed the Rock Squad,' says Peter, 'to save lives with a minimum of fuss.'

Since 1997, Peter has shown a renewed interest in Scouts recognising the potential for inspiring young people through the organisation. His appointment, together with Keith Williams and Ian Brown, as a Branch Adviser to the NSW Branch of Scouts Australia (as part of the arrangements for the first South Pole trip) had no clearly defined role, and Peter was not called on to perform any particular duties. He did, however, maintain contact at a local level, particularly through presentations. Not long after returning from the Pole, Peter saw in *Australian Scout* magazine an advertisement for the position of Chief Commissioner of Australia. After discussions with John Leece, he applied for the job. In his application he suggested that, in order to attain a thriving and dynamic movement, Scouts Australia needed a grassroots focused leader who could participate, motivate and activate at all levels of the movement. Making the point in his interviews that he would not fit the traditional description of a Chief Commissioner, Peter offered visionary leadership but was not prepared to sit on a dozen committees, feeling that this responsibility should be delegated to those with the knowledge and experience. He was unsuccessful in his application and the incumbent Chief Commissioner was re-elected for a further twelve months.

In May 1999, Peter once again applied for the position, restating his case in similar terms. The advertisement had asked for someone who could 'formulate a vision for the Scouting Movement in the 21st century, identify goals and lead a team of volunteers in the achievement of those goals'. Asked what he might contribute over the first six months of the appointment from November, he calmly told the interviewing panel that he planned to spend five of those months in the Antarctic! Peter was once again unsuccessful, but his application and vision left a permanent impression on the management (in both paid and voluntary positions) of Scouts Australia. The new Chief Commissioner, Dr Bruce Munro AM, then asked Peter to work with him, a task Peter looks forward to. He anticipates that this will be in some sort of ambassadorial role, and hopes he can use it 'to inspire people to join Scouts and to help make Scouts Australia a stronger youth focused organisation'.

Meanwhile, preparations for the Trans-Antarctic Expedition continue, the pace not slackening. Peter's responsibilities include negotiations with Adventure Network International, sponsorship negotiations, communications including cameras, insurance and the link with a children's charity. 'And I want to make sure I've got some help for Beth because I will be away for so long,' he says.

Lucy Curlewis has been appointed to devise the menu and accumulate the food supplies. 'I have to provide 7000 calories a day,' she says, 'which is even more than for the last trip.' Her target is 120 bags of food, weighing 2 kilograms each, for 120 days. Lucy has just a few months to do it. Equipment, navigation, environmental permissions, freight and travel are Tim's responsibilities while John Leece looks after administration and contract negotiation and Chris Roberts tackles sponsorship and management. Both Peter and Tim will carry a diary. Their records will provide the basis for a book which will be written on their return.

As with any athlete, Peter will eventually find that he has reached and passed his peak. That the records he attempts no longer fall. The second Antarctic expedition is long, physically demanding and extremely hazardous. Some other polar explorers who have returned have endured permanent physical damage, limiting their future abilities. John Leece gives Peter until he is about forty-five years old, not far off, before his body refuses to keep up with his mental ambitions. What then? Peter says he will continue to find new challenges. Until then, expect the unexpected.

Fortitudine Vincimus

By endurance we conquer

Appendix

Highlights and Milestones of an Adventure Career

'I have no more difficulty believing Peter's achievements than I have believing the performance of the Olympic gymnasts I witness on television. Both show that amazing feats are possible when ability is combined with almost fanatical dedication. Peter Treseder's achievements are all the more inspiring because he performs without the encouragement of an adulating crowd, without the proximity of medical help, without the certainty that he will survive. Ultimately, he runs for himself, in the wilderness.'

Lincoln Hall, *Australian Geographic*

Born in 1957, Peter Treseder began his outdoor activities as a Scout in 1965, undertaking thousands of trips over the next 30 years, building his confidence, skills and experience in many diverse areas. He has set many speed and endurance records on foot, bicycle, and on water using canoes and sea kayaks. Wherever Peter has claimed a first or a record it is on the basis that he has been unable to establish that any other person has achieved the trip or the time before him. Much time has been spent researching and verifying these records and all have been reported in either *Wild* or *Australian Geographic* magazines.

Many of these informal records have been established under the watchful eye of his support crews, including people from wilderness search and rescue teams. Others have been observed and recorded by independent witnesses. However, the wilderness nature of some of Peter's more remote expeditions has made it difficult to document them more vigorously.

Tiger walking is a term used to describe speed and endurance wilderness bushwalking. The term was first used in the 1930s by a group from the

Sydney Bushwalkers including Dot Butler and Gordon Smith. Peter, however, has redefined the meaning of the term tiger walking, as his trips are completed almost entirely at running speed.

Many of the records have been set and reset several times by Peter. Numbers in brackets, for example, Record (2), indicate the number of times the record has been reset. While every care has been taken to ensure that these records are accurate, Peter has maintained a low public profile during much of his impressive outdoor career and this publication provides a complete listing of his most significant trips for the first time. These include the first time a route has been traversed and occasions where he has set a record time.

Peter planned and led all the trips described, including group expeditions. On some of the longer solo trips Peter relies on food caches, which he and his support crew place in specific places before the trip starts. Unsupported trips are those in which Peter has received no outside assistance, including food and water supply, once the trip has started.

While these records have been edited for brevity and clarity for the general reader, the complete details of the routes and times of all Peter's trips have been carefully recorded over the years.

Highlights and Milestones

Year	Awards and Other Achievements
1969	Community Service Award, Summer Hill Primary School.
1969	Prefect, Summer Hill Primary School.
1969	House Captain, Summer Hill Primary School.
1974	Awarded Bronze Medallion by Royal Australian Life Saving Association.
1975	Awarded Bronze Cross by Royal Australian Life Saving Association.
1975	Prefect, Normanhurst Boys' High School.
1975	Queen's Scout Award.
1975	Honorary Park Ranger, Hornsby Shire Council.
1982	Founded 3 Peaks Outdoor Society.
1985	Rediscovered what is believed to be General Macarthur's World War II control bunker under Bankstown, NSW.
1988	One of 200 people selected for each year of white settlement of Australia, for inclusion in the Bicentennial publication, Unsung Heroes and Heroines of Australia.
1988	Presented with the Bicentennial Medal by the Governor of NSW.
1990	Awarded Vertical Rescue Operator qualification, Australian Lightweight Vertical Rescue Instructors (re-accredited 1993, '96 & '99).
1991	Awarded Australian Geographic Society's Spirit of Adventure Silver Medallion for a continuing commitment to promoting the spirit of adventure in Australia and for work in search and rescue.
1992	Awarded the Order of Australia for inspiration to the community.
1993	Awarded Australian Geographic Society's Spirit of Adventure Silver Medallion for the 1992 Batu Lawi expedition, which made the second overall and first Australian ascent of this remarkable Borneo peak.
1993	Elected Vice President, Youth Hostels Association of NSW.
1996	Senior First Aid Certificate, St John Ambulance Australia.
1996	Awarded highest service award from NSW Government and NSW Volunteer Rescue Association for 25 years continuous service in search and rescue.
1997	NSW Branch Adviser, Scout Association of Australia.
1997–98	Leader of the first Australian expedition to walk unsupported, across the Antarctic continent, to the South Pole.

1998	Awarded Australian Geographic Society's Spirit of Adventure Silver Medallion for a third (record) time for continuing commitment to promoting the spirit of adventure, in particular via the South Pole expedition.		
1999	Recognised for outstanding community service by Hornsby Shire Council.		
1999	Accredited by the NSW State Rescue Board—V3 Vertical Rescue.		

YEAR	GROUP EXPEDITIONS	TIME	RECORD ACHIEVED
1989 June	First complete descent of Jardine River, Cape York Peninsula, Queensland (with Warwick Blayden, Steve Irwin, Ron Moon).	6 days	First
1990 June	First complete descent of Elliot River, Cape York Peninsula, Queensland (with Ron Moon, Dave Dickford, Steve Irwin).	1.5 days	First
1990 June	First complete descent of Dulhunty River, Cape York Peninsula, Queensland (with Ron Moon, Dave Dickford, Steve Irwin).	2.5 days	First
1991 June	First complete skyline traverse of Hinchinbrook Island, Queensland (with Keith Williams, Ian Brown, Greg Randell).	9 days	First
1992 August	First complete traverses of the Isdell, Charnley and Manning rivers, Kimberley WA—rafting and walking (with Keith Williams, Ken Wilson, Tony Gavranich)	c.30 days	First
1993 September	First Australian ascent (and 2nd overall) of Batu Lawi, Kelabit highlands of Sarawak, Malaysian Borneo (with Keith Williams, Tom Williams, Ian Brown, David Robinson, Morie Ward).	12 days	First Australian New Route
1997–98 October– January	First Australian overland journey from the north-western edge of Berkner Island to the geographic South Pole on foot and unsupported (with Ian Brown, Keith Williams, John Leece/Manager).	59 days	First Australian

YEAR	OCEAN KAYAKING	TIME	RECORD ACHIEVED
1977 May	Kayak from Cairns to Lizard Island and return, Queensland. 500 km.	c.4 days	First
1977 June	Kayak circumnavigation of Fraser Island, Queensland.	c.4 days	First
1980 January	Kayak circumnavigation of Maria Island, Tasmania.	1.5 days	First

Highlights and Milestones

Year		Time	Record Achieved
1992 January	Double crossing of Bass Strait by sea kayak. Direct route from Wilsons Promontory, Victoria, to Cape Portland, Tasmania, non-stop in 38 hours and returned in two stages via Flinders Island.	< 4 days	Record
1994 July	First crossing and double crossing of the Timor Sea by sea kayak. Darwin Harbour (Mandorah) to Timor coast at Longitude 126° E and return after being caught by and escaping from pirates in the Timor Sea.	9 days	First & Record
YEAR	DESERT TRAVERSES	TIME	RECORD ACHIEVED
1996 August	First longitudinal unsupported traverse of the Simpson Desert, SA/NT. Cowarie Station to Mt Winnecke (with Keith Williams).	21 days	First & Record
1997 April	First unsupported and solo crossing of the Gibson Desert on foot, WA. Giles Weather Station to Carnegie Station. Performed a rescue in Claustral Canyon, Blue Mountains during the drive home.	4.5 days	First & Record
1998 May	First unsupported and solo crossing of the Strzelecki Desert, SA/NSW. Mulka Station to Fort Grey.	34:22 hrs	First & Record
1998 May	Second unsupported and solo crossing of the Tirari Desert, SA. Mulka Station to Lake Eyre.	12:58 hrs	Second & Record
1998 July	First unsupported and solo crossing of the Sturt Stony Desert, Queensland (Double traverse). Mooraberree to Cordillo Downs and return along the Birdsville Track to Mooraberree. Rescued man on way out—returned him to his wife and bogged car on Birdsville Track.	22:05 hrs	First & Record
1998 September	Possibly first unsupported and solo crossing of the Little Desert, Victoria. Wimmera River to South Australian Border.	12:07 hrs	Possibly the First & Record
1998 September	First unsupported and solo crossing of The Greater Big Desert, SA/Victoria. Coonalpyn to Lake Albacutya. Incorporating Ngarkat Conservation Park, Big Desert Wilderness, and Wyperfeld National Park.	28:15 hrs	First & Record

YEAR	DRIVING	TIME	RECORD ACHIEVED
1994 August	Record east–west driving traverse of Australia, Cape Byron, NSW, to Steep Point, WA (with Ron Moon). Land Rover TDI Discovery, achieved 27 miles per gallon. Cape Bryon to Simpson Desert (French Line) and Gibson Desert (Gunbarrel Highway) to Steep Point.	3.5 days	Record
1995 June	Record solo east–west driving traverse of Australia, Cape Byron, NSW, to Steep Point, WA. Land Rover TDI Discovery. Cape Bryon to Simpson Desert (French Line) and Gibson Desert (Gunbarrel Highway) to Steep Point. Record was set while placing food dumps for attempted run across Australia.	4 days 16:05 hrs	Record

YEAR	MOUNTAINEERING AND ROCKCLIMBING	TIME	RECORD ACHIEVED
1975 December	First Australian solo traverse of Arthurs Pass Circuit, New Zealand. Included Mt O'Malley – Mt Aicken – Blimit – Mt Temple – Phipps Peak – Mt Rolleston – Avalanche Peak – Lyell Peak – Mt Bealey.	2 days	First Australian
1976 January	First Australian solo ascent of West Ridge of Malte Brun, New Zealand.	1 day	First Australian
1976 January	First Australian solo ascent of the 2000 m Caroline Face of Mt Cook, New Zealand.	1 day	First Australian
1976 January	The Hermitage Hotel (Mt Cook Village) to Mt Cook and return in one day, New Zealand.	1 day	First & Record
1977 December	First Australian (possibly first overall) solo ascent of the 400 m South-east Face (Sydney Route) of Frenchmans Cap, Tasmania. From car park on Lyell Hwy and return.	1 day	First Australian
1988 March	Climbed West Wall of the Three Sisters, Blue Mountains, NSW—22 times in 12 hours.	12:00 hrs	Record (2)
1994 October	First solo ascent of the 280 m East Face of Mt Barney, Queensland.	1 day	First
1995 December	Climbed 100 classic Blue Mountains, NSW. Rockclimbs solo 6259 m total ascent Average grade 12.3 Included the Wolgan Valley, Cosmic County, Mt York, Zig Zag, Mt Piddington, Mt Boyce, Rhum Dhu, Narrow Neck, Dog Face–Jamison Valley, Three Sisters, Sublime Point, Glenbrook Gorge.	3 days	First & Record

HIGHLIGHTS AND MILESTONES

YEAR	CANYONING, CAVING AND ABSEILING	TIME	RECORD ACHIEVED
1976 March	First descent of Anembo (Crikey) and Fortitude Canyons, Blue Mountains, NSW. Approximately another 30 previously unknown canyons descended over the next 2 years, possibly the first time.	2 days	First
1977 June	Descended every major cave (33) in Bungonia Reserve, NSW. All caves were descended to the known sumps at that time, except for Grill Cave, which had unacceptable levels of carbon dioxide. All ground between the caves was covered on foot and all gear was carried.	2 days	First
1978 June	First abseil Wallaman Falls (278 m—biggest single drop in Australia), Queensland. Main abseil was achieved in one drop. Descended the main falls and the three following falls down to Herbert River junction.	1 day	First
1986 January	Continuous descent of 6 major canyons, Kanangra Walls, Blue Mountains, NSW. Davies Canyon – Carra Beanga Canyon – Thurat Rift Canyon – Danae Brook Canyon – Kanangra Canyon – Kalang Falls Canyon.	37:30 hrs	First & Record
1986 December	Claustral Canyon, Blue Mountains, NSW, at night. One of many attempts leading to this record time.	1:50 hrs	Record
1987 January	Claustral Canyon, Blue Mountains, NSW, by day. Claustral Canyon car park (Mt Tomah) – Claustral Canyon – Rainbow Ravine – Claustral Canyon car park (Mt Tomah).	1:23 hrs	Record
1987 January	Williams River Canyon, NSW. Barrington House – Selby Alley Hut – Williams River Canyon – Barrington House.	4:14 hrs	Record
1987 August	Claustral Canyon, Blue Mountains, NSW. Midwinter, naked, at night. The most difficult way to do it!	2:00 hrs	First
1989 December	First bicycle descent, Kalang Falls Canyon, Blue Mountains, NSW. Using abseiling techniques.	1 day	First
1989 April	Continuous descent of 26 major canyons, Blue Mountains, NSW. All the ground between the canyons was covered on foot and all gear was carried.	83:15 hrs	First & Record

	Galah – Thunderstorm – Contradiction – Heart Attack, Surefire – Rocky Creek – Anembo (Crikey Creek) – Bungleboori Creek – Dumbano Creek – Cesspit – Wollongambe – Bowens Creek (North Branch) – Bowens Creek (South Branch) – Claustral – Thunder – King George – Mt Hay – Fortress Creek – Arethusa – Alphius – Davies Creek – Kanangra Falls (Direct) – Danae Brook – Carra Beanga – Thurat Rift – Kanangra Walls.		
1990 February	First sailboarding descent into Blue Gum Forest, Blue Mountains, NSW.	1 day	First
1995 December	Descent of Danae Brook Canyon, Blue Mountains. NSW. Then ran Kanangra to Katoomba return (car park to car park).	3:58 hrs 12:47 hrs	Record
YEAR	RIVER CANOEING AND RAFTING	TIME	RECORD ACHIEVED
1977 August	First complete descent of the Normanby River, Cape York, Queensland.	2.5 days	First & Record
1977 August	First complete descent of the Coleman River, Cape York, Queensland.	3 days	First & Record
1988 January	Descent of Franklin River, Tasmania, by raft.	26:04 hrs	Record
1989 February	First complete descent of Macleay River, NSW. Dumaresq drain centre of Armidale: on foot until Georges Creek; by canoe Macleay River to Kempsey; by bicycle to South West Rocks.	31:15 hrs	First & Record
1991 February	First complete continuous descent of Nymboida River, NSW, New England Tableland to Yamba. Barren Mountain on foot to Platypus Flat; by canoe to Yamba breakwater.	3 days 14 hrs	First & Record
1991 June	First complete descent of Mitchell River, Cape York Peninsula, Queensland. 650 km.	5 days	First & Record
1991 June	First descent of Stewart River, Cape York Peninsula Queensland. 85 km. Coen – Stewart River – Port Stewart.	1 day	First & Record
1991 June	First descent of Archer River, Cape York Peninsula, Queensland. 300 km.	2.5 days	First & Record

Highlights and Milestones

YEAR	TIGER WALKS AND BICYCLING OTHER AREAS	TIME	RECORD ACHIEVED
1975 December	Ran seven major New Zealand tramping tracks: the Heaphy, Waikaremoana, Hollyford, Copeland, Routeburn, Milford and Tongariro tracks.	c.19 days	First Australian
1979 June	Bicycle Sydney to Cameron Corner and return, NSW.	c.6 days	First & Record
1981 March	Ascent of Pigeon House Mountain, Budawangs. Car park to summit.	15 mins	Record
1981 June	Royal National Park Coast Track, NSW Otford to Bundeena.	2:05 hrs	Record
1981 October	Benowie Track, NSW, Berowra to Pennant Hills.	1:57 hrs	First & Record
1982 March	Bungonia Caves to Long Point Lookout and return. Drum Cave entrance – Mt Ayre – Shoalhaven River – Long Point Lookout car park – return via Bungonia Gorge.	2:25 hrs	First & Record
1983 May	Length of Bouddi National Park, NSW, and return. Southern end of Kilcare Beach to Little Beach and return, including twice ascending Mt Bouddi.	1:23 hrs	Record
1984 May	The Budawangs Circuit, NSW. Tanderra Camp – Folly Point – Hollands Creek – Darri Pass – Meakins Pass – The Castle (logbook) – Nibelung Pass – Monolith Valley – Mt Owen (logbook) – Mt Cole (top) – Corang Peak – Mt Tarn – Styles Creek – The Vines – Tanderra Camp.	6:45 hrs	First & Record
1984 August	Royal National Park Coast Track, NSW. Otford to Bundeena, completed four times continuously.	14 hrs	First & Record
1986 November	Barrington Tops (Mt McKenzie), NSW, to Walhalla, Victoria. Stage 1—Australian Trilogy. 1500 km.	10 days	First & Record
1988 July	Cape York, Queensland to Barrington Tops, NSW Stage 2—Australian Trilogy. 4000 km.	30 days	First & Record
1988 August	Walhalla to Wilsons Promontory, Victoria. Stage 3—Australian Trilogy. 150 km. A remarkable 3-stage journey completed solo on foot. Peter navigated through the bush, joining up with traditional bushwalking routes. Minimal equipment carried (no tent). Food caches located every 500 km.	1 day	First & Record

	During the Australian Trilogy, Peter achieved the following: Total number of national parks crossed 58 Average distance per day 135 km Total rise during trips 120 574m Total fall during trips 120 574m		
1990 May	Great North Walk, NSW, Newcastle to Sydney. Running, swimming and canoeing. Newcastle (Fort Scratchley) – Patonga by foot; swim to Brooklyn; run to Hunters Hill (Alexander St wharf); canoe across Sydney Harbour to Sydney Opera House; by foot to Macquarie Place.	32:38 hrs	First & Record
1991 June	First run across Cape York Peninsula, Queensland. Gulf of Carpentaria (Archer River mouth) to Port Stewart (250 km) after losing canoe to crocodile.	2.5 days	First & Record
1991 September	Binna Burra to O'Reilly's Mountain Resort and return, Lamington National Park, Queensland. Via Coomera Crevice and Coomera Falls.	3:58 hrs	First & Record
1991 November	First run of Hume and Hovell Walking Track, NSW. Murray River to Yass (Lake Burrendong by canoe).	2 days 23 hrs	First & Record
1993 January	The Mirage, NSW. Robertson to Warrumbungle National Park. Robertson (local store) — rafted and canoed entire length of Nepean–Hawkesbury rivers; Broken Bay — sea kayaked to Newcastle; bicycled to Warrumbungle Mountains; solo climb of Crater Bluff.	105 hrs	First & Record
1993 March	First circumnavigation of the clifftops of Norfolk Island, South Pacific, including ascents of Mt Pitt and Mt Bates.	3:18 hrs	First & Record
1993 April	Continuous ascent of 50 major peaks in NSW, starting with Mt Gower, Lord Howe Island, finishing with the Three Sisters, Blue Mountains National Park. The following approximate statistics apply to this trip: Distance by foot 600 km Distance driven 5 000 km Vertical distance climbed 22 533 m Vertical distance descended 22 533 m	197 hrs	First & Record
1993 September	First run across Malaysian State of Sabah. From Kota Kinabalu to Sandakan, including ascent of Mt Kinabalu (4,101 m). A tribute to the Australian soldiers who died during the infamous Sandakan Death March of World War 2.	38 hrs	First & Record

Highlights and Milestones

1993 December	Climbed every peak of the Glasshouse Mountains, Queensland.	7:32 hrs	Record
1994 January–February	Traversed the three islands of New Zealand by foot and bicycle, including ascent of the highest peak on each island—Mt Ruapehu, Mt Cook, Mt Anglem—and canoeing between the islands. From Cape Reinga to Wellington by bicycle; climbed Mt Ruapehu; kayaked across Cook Strait to Picton; bicycled to St Arnaud; by foot to Arthurs Pass; by bicycle to Copland Valley; by foot to Ball Shelter (completed a sea to summit grand traverse ascent of Mt Cook); by bicycle to Bluff; by kayak across Foveaux Strait to Stewart Island; by foot to the summit of Mt Anglem; lost kayak in big seas re-crossing Foveaux Strait and had to swim about 10 km to Bluff.	10 days	First & Record
1994 March	Scenic Rim traverse, south-east Queensland. A major traverse from Point Danger to Laidley, including Mt Barney's West and East Peaks as well as many other mountains.	40:50 hrs	Record
1995 June	Attempt to run across the continent. Ran from Steep Point, WA, towards Meekatharra. 300 km. Broke foot in very remote country. Hobbled back approximately 120 km to the Overlander Road House (North West Coastal Highway, WA).		Attempt
1998 July	Ran from Barrington Tops to Myalls Heritage Trail, NSW. Barrington House to Bombah Point (swam across), then to Hawks Nest (Surf Club).	30:26 hrs	First & Record
YEAR	TIGER WALKS — TASMANIA	TIME	RECORD ACHIEVED
1981 December	Overland Track (Cradle Mountain to Lake St Clair) including Three Peaks. Cradle Mountain – Barn Bluff – Mt Ossa.	11:05 hrs	First & Record
1981 December	Mt Anne Circuit.	5:05 hrs	Record
1988 January	Scotts Peak Dam to Federation Peak via the Western and Eastern Arthur Ranges and return via Eastern Arthur Ranges and Arthur Plains.	23:28 hrs	First & Record
1995 January	North–south traverse of Tasmania's core wilderness, including ascents of Mt Ossa, Mt Anne and Federation Peak. Penguin – Penguin Cradle Trail – Cradle Mountain-Lake	4 days	First & Record

	St Clair track (Mt Ossa climbed) – King William Range – Rasselas Track – Scotts Peak Dam (Mt Anne climbed) – Western Arthurs (Federation Peak climbed) – Old River – Melaleuca – South Coast Track – Cockle Creek.		
1998 October	Frenchmans Cap Circuit. Frenchmans Cap car park (Lyell Highway) – Loddon Plains – Summit of Frenchmans Cap – Franklin River (swim across Irenabyss) – Mary Creek Plain – Raglan Range – Nelson Falls.	6:46 hrs	First & Record
YEAR	TIGER WALKS, CROSS COUNTRY SKIING AND SNOWSHOEING – AUSTRALIAN ALPS	TIME	RECORD ACHIEVED
1985 January	Thredbo to Kiandra, NSW, including ascents of Mt Kosciuszko, Mt Jagungal, Tabletop Mountain, in summer by foot.	9:38 hrs	Record
1985 November	Perisher to Kiandra, NSW, in summer by foot.	6:10 hrs	Record (2)
1986 January	Snowy Mountains Figure of Eight, NSW. Munyang (Guthega Power Station) – Schlink Pass – Valentine Hut – Grey Mare Hut – Pretty Plain Hut – Round Mountain – Happy Jacks Plain – Brooks Hut – Table Top Mountain – Kiandra (DMR Depot) – back to Grey Mare fire road – Mt Jagungal – Mawsons Hut – The Kerries – Rolling Grounds – Mt Tate – Mt Anderson – Mt Anton – Mt Twynan – Carruthers Peak – Mt Lee – Mt Kosciuszko – Thredbo Village – Charlottes Pass – Porcupine Track – Perisher – Link Road – Munyang (Guthega Power Station).	25:14 hrs	First & Record
1986 July	Kiandra to Perisher on snowshoes, NSW.	12:30 hrs	First & Record
1989 August	Traverse of Kosciuszko National Park on snowshoes. A major traverse from Brindabella (NSW) to Suggan Buggan (Victoria), via Mt Jagungal and Mt Kosciuszko.	37:14 hrs	First & Record
1990 August	First snowshoe traverse of the Australian Alps, Canberra, ACT to Walhalla, Victoria. Included a full traverse of the Alpine track and most of the major peaks on the way. All food carried, no tent, lightweight rations.	8 days	First & Record
1993 August	Perisher to Kiandra, NSW, skiing, nude, at night.	9:15 hrs	First & Record

HIGHLIGHTS AND MILESTONES

YEAR	TIGER WALKS BLUE MOUNTAINS, NSW	TIME	RECORD ACHIEVED
1981 March	Govetts Leap Circuit, Grose Valley. Govetts Leap – Govetts Leap Road – Great Western Highway – fire road to Victoria Falls – Victoria Falls Creek – Grose River – Blue Gum Forest – Junction Rock – Govetts Leap.	3:05 hrs	First & Record
1981 April	Junction Rock to Govetts Leap, Grose Valley.	25 mins	Record
1981 October	Jenolan Caves to Katoomba. Via Jenolan River and Narrowneck.	6:05 hrs	First & Record (2)
1981 October	Katoomba return (The Hobble Walk). Narrowneck – Medlow Gap – Eastern side of Mt Warrigal – Warrigal Gap – Dingo Gap to Mobb's Soak – Knight's Deck – Carlon Head – Katoomba.	4:02 hrs	First & Record (2)
1981 December	Blackheath to Richmond via Grose Valley.	6:56 hrs	Record (2)
1983 January	Ascent of the Golden Stairs, Narrowneck.	5:25 mins	Record
1983 January	Ascent of Perrys Lookdown, Grose Valley.	20 mins	Record
1983 April	Ascent of Carlon Head, Narrowneck.	10:45 mins	Record (3)
1983 July	Southern Blue Mountains Circuit. A significant trip taking in most of the southern Blue Mountains (Katoomba to Katoomba). These included some significant mountains, such as Yerranderie Peak, Cambage Spire, Mt Cloudmaker, Mt Paralyser and Mt Guouogang.	22:43 hrs	First & Record
1983 October	Mt Solitary Circuit. Katoomba to Trespass, a pass discovered by Peter, through the northern cliffs of Mt Solitary and return via Giant Stairway.	2:45 hrs	First & Record
1983 October	Descent of Giant Stairway and return.	16:50 mins	Record
1984 August	Katoomba to Mt Guouogang return.	9:40 hrs	Record
1984 August	Katoomba to Mittagong (original route). Katoomba via Wangandery to Mittagong.	15:26 hrs	Record (2)

1984 August	Obscure Circuit. Barrymores turnoff (Megalong Valley Road) – Shattered Canyon – Mitchell's Pass – Narrowneck – Wall's Pass – Cedar Creek – Mt Solitary – Trespass (pass through northern cliffs of Mt Solitary) – Dog Face – Daylight Tunnel – Megalong Valley – Barrymores turnoff (Megalong Valley Road).	6:31 hrs	First & Record
1985 April	Blue Mountains Trilogy. Kanangra Walls (car park) – Kalang Falls – Kanangra Creek – Yellow Pup – Narrowneck – Golden Stairs – West Wall of the Three Sisters (solo, all gear carried).	10:22 hrs	Record
1985 May	Blue Gum Forest Yo-Yo, Grose Valley. A collection of ascents and descents using seven different routes.	8:06 hrs	First & Record
1985 May	Bindook to Katoomba. An unusual and hard route Peter trekked when returning from a caving trip. Batch Camp to Mt Thurat – Mt Cloudmaker – Korrowall Ridge – Mt Solitary – Katoomba (Cliff Drive).	12:31 hrs	First & Record
1985 September	Traverse of the greater Blue Mountains National Park system (Wollemi, Blue Mountains, Kanangra Boyd and Nattai National Parks). Over 330 km from Widden Cutting (Goulburn River) to Wanganderry, rising 9150 m, falling 5450 m. A tribute to Miles Dunphy.	86:00 hrs	First & Record
1986 April	Katoomba to Kanangra.	5:47 hrs	Record (6)
1986 April	The Six-Foot Track (Katoomba to Jenolan Caves).	3:22 hrs	Record
1987 February	Blue Mountains Epic Trilogy—Abseil Kanangra Falls (direct), Three Peaks, climb the West Wall of the Three Sisters.	13:05 hrs	First & Record
1987 March	Katoomba to Kanangra return.	11:45 hrs	Record (2)
1987 November	Thurat Spires by bicycle.	1 day	First
1987 October	Govetts Leap descent and ascent backwards, Grose Valley.	1:57 hrs	First & Record
1988 January	Ascent of Govetts Leap, Grose Valley, wearing flippers, snorkel and goggles. (With Neil Treseder).	1:00 hr	First

Highlights and Milestones

1988 September	First walk from Katoomba to Mittagong via Bicentennial Track. (With Tony Powell).	3 days	First
1989 March	Katoomba to Mittagong via Bicentennial Track. Run same route.	14:04 hrs	First & Record
1989 December	*The Sydney Morning Herald* trip, Blackheath to Richmond via Grose Valley. A tribute to Dot Butler.	1 day	Re-enactment
1991 April	Seven Peaks of Wollemi National Park (Mt Savage, Mt Barakee, Mt Mistake, The Maiden, Parr West, The Island, Parr South).	16:05 hrs	First & Record
1992 May	New Blue Gum Forest Yo-Yo. Another version of the previous trip, including 12 passes.	18:18 hrs	First & Record
1992 November	Traverse of the Greater Blue Mountains National Park system (Muswellbrook to Mittagong).	65:58 hrs	Record
1996 August	Ascent and descent of Yerranderie Peak.	26:45 mins	Record
1996 October	Katoomba to Black Coola and Bimlow Peak return.	16:48 hrs	Record
1998 April	Traverse of Yodellers Range, Widden Valley, NSW.	9:57 hrs	Record
1998 April	Katoomba – Mount Cloudmaker – return.	8:15 hrs	Record
1999 April	The Classic Three Peaks: Mt Cloudmaker, Mt Paralyser and Mt Guouogang (Katoomba to Katoomba).	14:19 hrs	Record (5)

IN A VOLUNTARY CAPACITY

Founder of the Three Peaks Outdoor Society, a club in which members can participate in adventure activities.

Patron and Rock Squad co-ordinator of Bushwalkers Wilderness Rescue, an organisation of volunteers that conducts bush search and rescue and cliff search and rescue operations in Australia.

Vice President of the Youth Hostels Association of NSW, which aims to help all people, especially the young, to a greater knowledge and understanding of their country and the world, by providing hostels for them in their travels and thus promote their health, education and recreation.

NSW Branch Adviser to Scout Association of Australia.

INDEX

Abbott, Tony, 259
Aboriginal people, 142, 146, 148, 163, 164–165, 167, 168–169
abseiling, 2–4, 150, 259–260
 'assist abseil', 4
 sailboard, with, 96, 270
Adventure Network International (ANI), 220, 221, 224, 227, 228, 235, 239, 261
Allen, David, 19
Allen, Pam, 247
Anderson, Rodney, 54
Anembo Canyon, NSW, 62, 269
Antarctic Traverse Expedition, 256–259, 261
Archer River, Queensland, 134, 141, 144, 270
Arthur Ranges, Tasmania, 107
Arthurs Pass Circuit, New Zealand solo traverse of, 47, 268
Ashfield
 growing up in, 11–20
Australia
 east-west drive across, 193–196, 243, 268
 run down length of (Cape to Cape run), 112–117
 west-east run across, 195–198
Australian Alps, 111
 snowshoe traverses of, 6, 103, 126–127, 274
Australian Geographic, 6, 8, 112, 116, 117, 128, 135, 152, 153, 162, 167, 183, 184, 198, 204, 223, 251, 252
Award for Citizenship 1969, 12, 18
awards and achievements, 265–277
Ayres, Alan, 73
Bain, Ike, 255
Barrington Tops, NSW
 Cape York to, 113–116, 271
 Myall Heritage Trail, to, 246–247, 273
 Walhalla, to, 109–111, 271

Bartell, Denis, 193, 196, 198, 201, 202, 203
Barton, Vicky, 27
Bass Strait
 kayaking in, 62, 117, 159–162
Bateman, Judith, 125
Batu Lawi, Borneo, 176–184
Baxter, Chris, 64
Beazley, Kim, 219
Beck, Jeff, 71
Bendeli, Nic, 78, 86
Benowie Track, NSW, 80, 271
Bicentennial medal, 118
Bicentennial Track, NSW, 119–120
bicycling
 Cameron Corner, NSW, 73–74
 New Zealand, 188, 273
 Thurat Spires, 96
Bimlow Peak, NSW, 259, 277
Bindook, NSW, 88, 276
Black Coola, NSW, 259, 277
Black Hole of Calcutta, NSW, 3
Blackheath, NSW, 81, 120, 275
Blayden, Warwick, 129–133
Bloomfield, Earle, 76
Bloomfield, Hilton, 221
Blue Gum Forest, NSW, 97, 120, 270
Blue Mountains, NSW
 canyons, 2, 56, 62, 96, 103–106
 complete traverse, 88–91
 100 classic climbs, 199–200, 268
 Seven Peaks of Wollemi, 155, 277
 3 Peaks challenge, 92–95, 259, 277
 Three Sisters climb, 86–87, 121, 122, 172, 268
 tiger walking in, 6, 80–82, 86–95, 109–111, 119–121, 155, 259, 275–277
 trilogy, 86–88

278

INDEX

Blunt, Peter, 19, 24
Bonython, Warren, 201, 202–203, 246
Booker, Emily, 98
Borneo, 174, 176–186
Bourne, Phil, 54
Branson, Dick, 161
Brown, Ian, 8, 141, 145, 146, 147-151, 160, 177–186, 199, 203, 218, 222, 223, 224, 225, 226–241, 249, 260
Buckpitt, Simon, 203
Buffett, Chris, 171
Bungonia Reserve, NSW, 63, 269
bunkers, 99–100
Bushwalkers Wilderness Rescue, 90, 110, 213
bushwalking *see* tiger walking
Butler, Dot, 120, 172, 177, 213–214, 264
Butler, Skip, 24
Butler, Wade, 213–214
Cameron Corner, NSW, 73–74
Cameron, Ross, 259
Campbell, Donald, 246
canoeing, 130–134, 135–139, 142–146, 154–155, 157–158, 188–189
  see also kayaking
  Archer River, descent of, 134, 141, 144, 270
  Coleman River, descent of, 63, 270
  Foveaux Strait, 188–189
  Macleay River, descent of, 122, 270
  Mitchell River, descent of, 141–142, 270
  Murray River to Yass, 157–158, 272
  Normanby River, descent of, 63, 270
  Nymboida River, descent of, 154, 270
  Stewart River, descent of, 144, 270
Canterbury
  growing up in, 20
canyoning, 1–5, 61, 103–106
  Anembo and Fortitude canyons, 62, 269
  Claustral Canyon, 1–5, 9, 104–106, 123, 213, 269
  Kanangra Walls, 103–104, 123–125, 269
  Wollangambe Canyon, 96
Cape York, 134, 146, 272

Barrington Tops, to, 113–116, 271
  Wilsons Promontory, to, 6, 112–117
Carlon's Head, NSW, 80
Carr, Bob, 219
Cavill, Bob, 123
caving
  Bungonia Reserve, 63, 269
Chang, Ann, 219
Chang, Dr Victor, 220
charity fundraising *see* fundraising
Charlton, Greg, 54, 65, 67
Charlton, Margaret, 54
Charnley River, WA, 163, 167–168
Chester, Quentin, 251
childhood, 11–22
Clancy, Mark, 18
Clancy, Neil, 18
Clark, Grant, 66, 76, 77
Claustral Canyon, NSW, 1–5, 9, 104–106, 123, 213, 269
climbathon, 121
Clinton, President, 220
Cocks, Helen, 203, 204, 205, 207, 208–209, 246
Cocks, Neil, 203, 204, 205, 207, 208–209, 246
Coleman River, Queensland
  canoeing, 63, 270
'cow's tail', 3
Cradle Mountain, Tasmania, 75, 82, 119, 196, 273
crocodiles, 129, 131, 132, 136, 138, 139, 142–146, 166, 167
cross-country running, 33
cross-country skiing
  Thredbo to Kiandra, 102, 274
Cubs, 18
Curlewis, Lucy, 258, 261–262
Daniels, Major Tim, 164, 179
Daniels, Warwick, 60, 93
Dare, Tracey, 196, 244
Datuk Harris bin Mohd Salleh, 185
Davies, Barry, 172

279

Davis, Steve, 105
desert traverses
  east-west drive across Australia, 193–196, 243, 268
  Gibson Desert, 1, 5, 8, 194, 195, 215–216, 267
  Greater Big Desert, 245, 246, 267
  Little Desert, 245, 267
  Simpson Desert, 194, 198, 201–210, 215, 219, 243, 267
  Strzelecki Desert, 243
  Sturt Stony Desert, 244, 267
  Tirari Desert, 244, 267
Dewhirst, Chris, 64
Dickford, Dave, 134–138
Donnelly, Alan, 226
Dorfluegger, Max, 48–49
Douglas, Malcolm, 163
draining expeditions, 98–99
Drohan, Dave, 55, 65, 76, 77, 78, 79, 80, 93, 96
Dulhunty River, Queensland, 135, 137–138, 266
Dunphy, Miles, 88
East Coast Track, Queensland, 147–149
Edwards, John, 140, 161, 217
Eichhorn, Nick, 110
Eggleston, John, 126, 156
Eliot River, Queensland, 135–136, 266
Evenden, Phil, 217–218
Everist, Hilleary De, 238
Fantini, John, 60, 93
Fardouly, Paul, 90, 99, 101, 103, 105, 122, 147, 203
Farmer, Brian, 71
Federation Peak, Tasmania, 107, 109
Ferguson, Anne, 156, 173, 246, 254
50 Peaks Challenge, NSW, 171–173, 272
Floyd, Michael, 108
Fortitude Canyon, NSW, 62, 269
Foster, Mark, 39, 40, 41, 55–57, 66, 71, 75, 77, 80, 121, 247

Foveaux Strait, New Zealand, 188–190
Fowler, Mark, 108
Franklin River, Tasmania, 247
  'No Dams' campaign, 77
  rafting, 107–109, 270
Fraser Island, Queensland
  kayak circumnavigation of, 63, 266
Frenchmans Cap, Tasmania, 64, 247, 268, 274
fundraising, 7, 9, 13, 121, 219, 223, 234, 241, 259
Gales, Stuart, 247
Gamble, Alan, 41
Gavranich, Tony, 163, 164, 165–169
Gentle, Max, 120
Gibson Desert
  crossing of, 1, 5, 8, 194, 195, 215–216
Gibson, Ian, 162
Gooch, Nick, 60
Gordon, Barbara, 13
Govett's Leap, NSW, 95, 96
Graham, Bob, 219
Great North Walk, NSW, 126, 156, 272
Greater Big Desert, SA/Victoria, 245, 246
Grey, Larry, 160
Grose Valley, NSW, 81–82, 275
group expeditions
  Charnley River, complete traverse of, 163, 167–168
  Dulhunty River, descent of, 135, 137–138, 266
  Eliot River, descent of, 135–136, 266
  Hinchinbrook Island, skyline traverse of, 141, 146, 147–152, 266
  Isdell River, complete traverse of, 163–165, 266
  Jardine River, descent of, 128–134, 266
  Manning River, complete traverse of, 163, 168
  South Pole expedition, 6, 8, 17, 198, 199, 201, 218–242, 257, 258
Hall, Lincoln, 6, 116, 252, 263
hang gliding, 67–68

Hawkins, Bill, 20
hearing disability, 11, 12
Hetherington, Marion, 224
Hickman, Belinda, 240
Hiddens, Major Les (Bush Tucker man), 164
Higgins, Barry, 92
hiking, 19, 23–25
Hill, David, 98
Hinchinbrook Island, Queensland, 141, 146, 147–152, 266
Hislop, Dave, 102
Hoare, David, 99
Hodge, Greg, 214
Howard, John, 219, 241
Hume and Hovell Walking Track, NSW, 156–157, 272
Hunter, Lois, 118
Husselbee, Mark, 23
Hyland, Grant, 72
International Trans-Antarctic Expedition 1999–2000, 256–259, 261
Irwin, Steve, 123, 129–133, 134–138, 141, 147, 172
Isdell River, WA, 163–165
James, Kerry, 219
Jamieson, Rick, 34, 37, 38, 39
Jardine, Frank, 138
Jardine River, Queensland, 128–134, 266
Jarvis, Tim, 257, 262
Jenolan Caves, NSW, 80–81, 275
Jerrems, Ray, 60, 93, 102
Kanangra Walls, NSW, 103–104, 111, 123–125, 269
  Katoomba, to, 86–87, 276
Kandelas, John, 35, 73
Katoomba, NSW
  Bindook to, 88, 276
  Black Coola and Bimlow Peak, 259, 277
  Jenolan Caves, to, 80–81, 275
  Kanangra to, 86–87
  Mittagong, to, 119–120, 277
  Mount Cloudmaker, to, 259, 277

kayaking, 6, 57, 61, 126
  see also canoeing
  Bass Strait, crossing, 62, 117, 159–162, 267
  Cairns to Lizard Island, 62–63, 266
  Fraser Island, circumnavigation of, 63, 266
  Maria Island, circumnavigation of, 74, 266
  Timor Sea, crossing, 6, 62, 160, 190–193, 267
Kelly, Jackie, 259
Kelly, Paul, 219
Kernot, Cheryl, 219
Kershaw, Anne, 235
Kiandra, NSW, 102–103, 274
Kilpinen, Robby, 102
Kimberley region, 163–169
Kinchin, David, 40, 221
Knight, Trevor, 53
Kosciuszko National Park, 126, 274
Lamble, Tim, 148, 152, 169, 248
Lattimore, Andrew ('Skin'), 43–44, 47–49
Lattimore, Margaret, 67
Lee, Gordon, 93
Leece, David, 220
Leece, John, 218, 219–221, 222–223, 224, 227, 228, 229, 236, 255, 257, 258, 261, 262
Leece, Stewart, 222, 224
Little Desert, Victoria, 245, 267
Lizard Island, Queensland, 62–63, 74
Lynn, Charlie, 259
McAuliffe, Michael, 54, 67
McCrossin, Fiona, 172
McCubbin, Charles, 201
McGarry, Janet, 171
McKenzie, Malcolm, 196, 244
Macleay River, NSW, 122, 270
McPherson, Scott, 203
McRoberts, Lieutenant Colonel J, 163–164
Madden, Linc, 25, 29, 37–38, 39, 40, 41, 56, 199
Madigan, Cecil, 207
Mallin, Bob, 18
Mallin, Greg, 18

Manning, John, 92
Manning River, WA, 163, 168
Maria Island, Tasmania
  kayak circumnavigation of, 74, 266
Marshall, Sid, 41
Martin, John, 134, 139, 217
Maxwell, Keith, 90, 92, 110
Mitchell River, Queensland, 141–142, 270
Mittagong, NSW, 90, 119–120
Moon, Dave, 128–131, 133, 194, 198
Moon, Ron, 114, 128–133, 134–139, 141, 142, 144, 193–195, 197, 203, 205, 243, 244
Moon, Viv, 114, 128, 134, 193
Mortimer, Greg, 198
Mount Anglem, New Zealand, 188
Mount Barney, Queensland, 190, 268
Mount Bowen, Queensland, 147–148
Mount Cloudmaker, NSW, 259, 277
Mount Cook, New Zealand, 47–50, 188, 268
Mount Gower, NSW, 171
Mount Kinabalu, 184–185
Mount McKenzie, NSW, 109
Mount Ruapehu, New Zealand, 187
Mount Wilson, NSW, 88
Munro, Dr Bruce, 261
Murdoch, Lachlan, 218, 219, 220, 258
Muswellbrook, NSW, 88
Mutang, James Padan, 180
Myall Heritage Trail, NSW, 246–247, 273
New Zealand, 43–51, 187–190
  bicycling, 188, 273
  rock climbing, 43, 44, 47–51, 268
  tiger walking, 44–47, 187–188, 271, 273
Newnes, NSW, 123–125, 269
Noble, Dave, 109
Norfolk Island, 170–171, 272
Norforce, 163, 164, 165
Normanby River, Queensland canoeing, 63, 270
Nymboida River, NSW, 154, 270
OAM, 8
O'Brien, Robert, 23

ocean kayaking *see* kayaking
Order of Australia Medal, 159, 162–163
orienteering, 75–76
Ortlepp, Chris, 236
Pacey, Dr Hans, 246
Paddy Pallin, 60, 61, 108, 112, 135, 152, 162, 211, 227, 241, 245, 247
Pallin, Robert, 61, 211
Paterson, Brian, 221, 223
Perisher, NSW, 103, 274
Pezzutti, Dr Brian, 220
Pigeon House Mountain, 80, 271
Pike, Glenville, 142
pirates, 190–193
Powell, Tony, 119
presentations, 9, 110, 152, 164–165, 173, 176–177, 193, 210, 222, 241–242, 245, 248, 258, 259, 261
Price, Jeremy, 24
Radcliffe, Peter, 51
rafting, 166
  Franklin River, descent of, 107–109, 270
Randell, Cathy, 90, 105, 122, 147
Randell, Greg, 141, 145, 146, 147–151
Rawson, Gilbert, 13
record breaking, 7, 60–61, 80, 83, 84, 86–87, 92, 119, 194, 195, 197, 202, 216, 249, 252, 259, 263, 265–277
rescue *see* search and rescue
Roberts, Chris, 221, 258, 262
Robertson, NSW, 170, 272
Robinson, David, 178–185
Robinson, Jack, 18
rock climbing, 26, 37–41, 55–57
  Arthurs Pass Circuit, solo traverse of, 47, 268
  Batu Lawi, 176–184
  Blue Mountains
    100 classic climbs, 199–200, 268
    Three Sisters climb, 86–87, 121, 122, 172, 268
  Borneo, in, 177–184

Frenchmans Cap, 64, 268
Mount Barney, Queensland, 190, 268
New Zealand, in, 43, 44, 47–51, 268
Three Sisters climb, 86–87, 121, 122, 172, 268
rock scrambling, 151
Rock Squad, 125, 215, 260
Rose, Fran, 101
Rover Australia, 195, 196, 198, 203, 243
Rowland, Sir James, 118
Royce, Keith, 52–53
Royal Flying Doctor Service, 201, 204
Sabah, Malaysia, 185, 272
sastrugi, 234–235, 237
Scenic Rim traverse, Queensland, 190, 273
Schofield, Peter, 55
Scotts Peak Dam, Tasmania, 107
Scouts, 18–20, 23–25, 29, 36–41, 55–56, 77, 79, 81, 221, 223, 233–234, 250–251, 260
   Trekathon, 223, 233–234
search and rescue, 1–5, 78, 89, 91, 106, 113, 121, 125, 129, 153, 154, 174, 211–215, 221, 253, 259–260
   insurance, 222, 236
self-dentistry, 17, 235
Silver Medallion, 153, 186
Simpson Desert
   crossing of, 194, 198, 201–210, 215, 219, 243
Six Foot Track, NSW, 80, 82, 276
skiing
   record, 174–175
   Thredbo to Kiandra, 102, 274
Sloss, Robert, 119, 120
Smith, Dick, 121, 153, 175–176, 214, 223
Smith, Gordon, 177, 264
snake bite, 110, 153, 214
snowshoe traverses, 6
   Australian Alps, 126–127, 274
   Kiandra to Perisher, 103, 274
   Kosciuszko National Park, 126, 274
   Perisher to Kiandra, 103, 274

Snowy Mountains Figure of Eight, 103, 274
   Thredbo to Kiandra, 103, 274
Snowy Mountains, 102–103
South Pole
   Australian expedition to, 6, 8, 17, 198, 199, 201, 218–242, 257, 258
      sponsorship, 218–219, 221–222, 223–224, 227, 228, 240
sponsorship, 112, 128, 135, 152, 163, 183, 203–204, 205, 210, 218–219, 221–222, 223–224, 227, 228, 240, 243, 253, 257, 258–259, 261
Sprent, James, 64
Stellar, Derek, 77
Stewart River, Queensland, 144, 270
Stiff, Andrew, 53, 54, 80–81, 122
Stiff, Sally, 54
Strzelecki Desert, SA/NSW, 243
Stuckey, Dave, 101
Sturt Stony Desert, Queensland, 244
swimming, 31–32
Sydney Morning Herald Trip, The, 120–121, 277
Tasmania
   tiger walking, 75, 107, 196, 247, 273–274
Taylor, Les, 224
technical mountaineering, 6
Thayer, Helen, 235
Tholstrup, Hans, 194
Thomas, Simon, 91
Thornburg, Charles, 220–221
Thorsborne, Arthur, 148–149
Thorsborne, Margaret, 148–149
3 Peaks Outdoor Society, 76–80
Thunder Canyon, NSW, 123
Thurat Spires, NSW, 96
Tickell, Rob, 37
tiger walking, 6, 7, 42, 60, 76, 79, 80–83, 177, 259
   'Australian Trilogy', 113–117, 271–272
   Barrington Tops to Myall Heritage Trail, 246–247, 273

283

Barrington Tops to Walhalla, 109–111, 271
Benowie Track, 80, 271
Bindook to Katoomba, 88, 276
Blackheath to Richmond, 81, 120, 275
Blue Mountains, 6, 80–82, 86–95, 109–111, 119–121, 155, 259, 275–277
Cape York to Barrington Tops, 113–116, 271
Cape York Peninsula, run across, 146, 272
Cradle Mountain Track, 75, 82, 119, 196, 273
criticism of, 109
definition, 263–264
50 Peaks Challenge, 171–173, 272
Frenchmans Cap circuit, 247, 274
Great North Walk, 126, 156, 272
Grose Valley, 81–82, 275
Hume and Hovell Walking Track, 156–157, 272
Jenolan Caves to Katoomba, 80–81, 275
Kanangra to Katoomba, 86–87, 276
Katoomba to Black Coola and Bimlow Peak, 259, 277
Katoomba to Mittagong, 119–120, 277
Katoomba to Mount Cloudmaker, 259, 277
Muswellbrook to Mount Wilson, 88, 276
New Zealand, in, 44–47, 187–188, 271, 273
Norfolk Island, circumnavigation of clifftops, 171, 272
Pigeon House Mountain, ascent of, 80, 271
Robertson to Warrumbungle National Park, 170, 272
Sabah, run across, 185, 272
Scenic Rim traverse, 190, 273
Scotts Peak Dam to Federation Peak, 107
Sydney Morning Herald Trip, The, 120–121, 277
Tasmania, 75, 107, 196, 247, 273–274
Walhalla to Wilsons Promontory, 117, 271
Wollemi National Park, 88–91, 155, 277
Timor Sea
  ocean kayaking in, 6, 62, 160, 190–193
Tirari Desert, SA, 244

Toomer, Philip, 125
Tremont, Steve, 59, 108, 122, 247
Treseder, Beth, 8, 28, 53–55, 83–85, 91, 98, 116, 117, 122, 155–156, 159, 170, 173–174, 179, 185, 193, 197, 198, 204, 241, 248, 254, 257–258, 261
Treseder, Dorothy, 7, 11, 13, 15, 16, 20, 26, 27, 29, 34, 40, 165, 173, 198, 252
Treseder, John, 11, 12, 13, 16, 20, 25, 27, 28, 29, 30, 36, 40, 84
Treseder, Kimberley, 8, 173–174
Treseder, Marnie, 8, 155–156, 170, 173, 253
Treseder, Neil, 15, 20, 21, 22, 23, 28, 29, 30, 33, 34, 36, 58, 68, 84, 95, 122, 241, 253–254
Treseder, Wendy, 10, 13–14, 15, 17, 20, 21, 26, 27, 28, 29, 30, 36, 53
Trihey, Lucas, 245
underground exploring, 98–102
University of New South Wales stunts, 57–59
Vertical Rescue training course, 4
Vining, Ross, 86
Volunteer Rescue Association, 125
Wagg, Geoff, 92
Walhalla, Victoria
  Barrington Tops to, 109–111, 271
  Wilsons Promontory, to, 117, 271
Ward, Morie, 178–186
Warrumbungle National Park, NSW, 170, 272
Westleigh, 18, 20, 21, 27, 29
Whelan, Howard, 162, 198
white water rafting, 154–155
wild pigs, 138, 143
Williams, Keith, 6, 77, 78, 81, 89–91, 103, 141, 145, 146, 147, 157–158, 163, 164, 165–169, 177–186, 199, 201, 203, 204–210, 218, 222, 223, 224, 225–240, 249, 260
Williams, Tom, 177–186
Wilson, Ken, 163, 165–169
Wollemi National Park, NSW, 88–91, 155, 277
Youth Hostels Association (YHA), 171–173

ABOUT THE AUTHOR

Sydney writer, Martin Long, indulges his own passion for the outdoors through his role as a Scout Leader and father of four. Family holidays are nearly always spent under canvas and weekends regularly include lightweight hikes and bushwalks. He has written advertising, direct mail and business copy for many years, articles for newspapers and professional journals and is NSW Editor for Australian Scout magazine. In his spare time he is a marketing consultant specialising in strategic marketing. He also lectures in marketing at APM Training Institute and runs marketing workshops.

Martin Long met Peter Treseder in the planning stage of the first Antarctic expedition and realised there was a rare opportunity to explore the life and pyschology of an Australian 'unsung hero'. This book is the result and he is now working on an account of the Trans-Antarctic Expedition, which set off in October 1999.